7 DAYS
A PARISIAN

7 DAYS A PARISIAN

Travel itineraries & local secrets
for the City of Lights

JIAWA LIU
@beigerenegade

murdoch books
Sydney | London

CONTENTS

Pont Alexandre III; Coulée Verte René-Dumont (opposite)

MY PARIS

A decade ago, I decided to do something completely impulsive and move to Paris.

I had visited the French capital for the first time in an attempt to 'attend' fashion week (without invitations to any shows or events). This seemed a necessary rite of passage in my fashion blogger days, and – as cliché as it sounds – I fell in love with the city. Long story short, I was back in Paris three months later, having quit my day job as a commercial lawyer in Perth, Australia, to move to the other side of the world. I have been living in Paris ever since, where I now work as a creative director and fashion editor.

Why? With its glittering Eiffel Tower rising up above the Seine, mansard rooftops peaking over the hedge maze at the Jardin des Tuileries and grand cafés with their scalloped awnings shading rows of terrace tables, Paris is one of the world's most beautiful cities.

But its irresistible appeal goes beyond its aesthetics. You see, the beauty of Paris is felt more than seen, especially when you explore the city as a *flâneur*, or 'passionate spectator', as defined by the illustrious French poet Charles Baudelaire. This quintessential French art of experiencing the city as both participant and observer is the key to revealing Paris's complex layers. From the opulent baroque courts of French kings to the bohemian movement of the Belle Époque and the dramatic infusion of modernity in the 1980s, many historic periods have shaped the face of the city. Paris's history also shaped the identity (and clichés) that we associate today with being 'Parisian' and 'French'. Parisians' love of leisurely enjoying the finer things in life – the *art de vivre* (art of living) – has its historical roots in the Renaissance, and their passion for intellectual debate is a legacy of the French Revolution.

A comprehensive understanding of French history and culture is not essential to visit Paris, nor is learning the language (though greeting locals with a simple *'bonjour'* will go a long way). But I believe your experience will be richer if you seek a deeper immersion than the typical sightseeing itinerary.

In this guide, I aim to introduce you to my Paris, a city of local secrets and hidden wonders, and a Parisian way of experiencing places – as a *flâneur*. I have not sought to cover every landmark, monument, boutique or restaurant, but instead to curate meaningful experiences offering an authentic taste of Parisian life. At the same time, I also encourage you to see the big-ticket sights, from the Musée du Louvre to the Place du Trocadéro, or your experience of Paris would not be complete.

THE PARISIAN WAY

The concept of being Parisian has fascinated people for generations. The revival of Parisian chic in the 2010s is thanks in part to two influential books exploring the subject: *Parisian Chic: A Style Guide*, by Ines de la Fressange (2011) and *How to Be Parisian Wherever You Are*, co-authored by Caroline de Maigret, Anne Berest, Audrey Diwan and Sophie

Café du Métro

Mas (2015). Ines (a French supermodel turned fashion designer) and Caroline (a Chanel muse and music producer) define Parisian chic with their own personal styles: Ines with her tomboy-chic look and Caroline with her French-girl bangs and second-day make-up. Together with other French style icons including actress Jane Birkin, singer Serge Gainsbourg and actor Jean-Paul Belmondo, their effortless-looking outfits mixing tailored and vintage pieces and denim have crystalised what is now instantly recognisable as 'Parisian'. The advent of Instagram gave birth to a whole new generation of influencers and style icons who aspire to these principles of Parisian style.

During my decade in Paris, I have discovered that many Parisian stereotypes – from walking with a baguette in hand to sipping a *café allongé* (long black) on a café terrace – ring true, and there's nothing at all wrong with that. The cinematic quality of Parisian clichés has been a huge source of inspiration for both my personal style and my work creating images and film in the fashion industry.

But being Parisian is about more than emdodying the clichés. It's about embracing the Parisian way of life. So included in this guide are seven lessons for 'being Parisian', to smooth your transition from visitor to local.

Welcome to my Paris, which, I hope, will quickly become your Paris, too.

THE PARISIAN STARTER KIT

WHAT TO WEAR

I've spent the better part of my 10 years in Paris observing Parisians, hoping their world-renowned, effortlessly chic sartorial sense will rub off on me. Their secret? Parisian style looks effortless – because it is.

Parisians have a very cavalier attitude to getting dressed. They throw on their favourite pieces without thinking too much about it; women wear minimal make-up and men let their beards grow out. Steeped in simplicity, Parisian style also speaks to the Parisian aversion to looking as though you've planned your outfit: just the right amount of effort, but almost as if it was a spur-of-the-moment – or even accidental – style choice. It's a thrown-together sweater and jeans look, topped with a bright neck scarf; or a shirt-and-pants combo layered with a cardigan and a blazer. The chosen pieces are ordinary, archetypal – a crisp white T-shirt, well-cut chinos, a relaxed coat – but carefully selected and worn for years; the Parisian is an unapologetic outfit repeater. Neutral tones and versatile styles are the foundation of the Parisian wardrobe, with eclectic accessories mixed in to mark one's identity. Often these are a vintage find or a travel souvenir: royal blue velvet slippers, cowboy boots or even a brightly coloured knitted balaclava.

If you want to dress like a Parisian, here are your wardrobe essentials.

TRENCH COAT

With the Parisian climate ranging from mild to freezing, the classic trench coat gets a workout year-round. In spring, it's worn with linen pants and sneakers. In summer, a lighter version is thrown on over dresses on cooler evenings. Longer styles are popular in autumn, and in winter a trench will be layered over knitwear, often with a hoodie nonchalantly peeking out.

SNEAKERS

Despite what the *Emily in Paris* series may have you believing, Parisians rarely, if ever, traipse around town in stiletto heels. Walking is the main form of transport in this city, and its cobblestone streets are particularly unforgiving to high heels. It may surprise some to learn that Parisians love sneakers (locals are frequently spotted in adidas Stan Smiths or Converse All Stars) and wear them frequently.

FINE LEATHER SHOES

Parisians (even the younger generations) have an enduring enthusiasm for wearing and maintaining well-made leather shoes. The *cordonnerie* (cobbler) remains a thriving trade in Paris, with the best of them capable of restoring a customer's beloved shoes to better-than-original condition. Fine leather shoes aren't reserved for formal occasions in Paris but rather worn daily, rain or shine.

BIRKENSTOCKS

The metamorphosis of the Birkenstock from orthopaedic sandal to fashion item did not pass by Paris. In fact, Paris is one of the biggest fans of the anatomically shaped cork shoe. As soon as the weather begins to warm up, two-strap Arizona sandals and half-covered Boston clogs in every colour and finish become ubiquitous across the city.

TRUE STRAIGHT JEANS

Like many people around the world, Parisians live in jeans. Parisians, however, are puritanical about 'real denim' – whether vintage or well-made modern brands (especially brands made in Japan), with more trend-driven styles such as stretch denim less commonly worn. While even Paris is susceptible to fleeting jeans trends, including flared and ultra-wide-legged styles, the timeless style is the high-waist, straight-cut jean of the 1970s (such as the Levi's 501), naturally faded from indigo to pale vintage blue after years of use. Jeans are worn casually with a white T-shirt and Birkenstock Boston clogs, or dressed up with a blazer and heels.

UNIQUE VINTAGE FINDS

With a typical Parisian wardrobe built on muted-toned basics, personal expression often comes in the form of adding a quirky vintage piece to complete a look. The emphasis is on the unexpected – a highly decorative on-the-verge-of-gaudy jacquard jacket, for example, or a *Matrix*-esque floor-sweeping leather coat. These are worn with absolute confidence and are fully intended to prompt a double-take as you walk by.

PROPER WINTER CLOTHING

Even Parisians value warmth and comfort above looking chic; when the temperature drops, out come the bulky *doudounes* (puffer jackets), high boots and balaclavas. But even these inherently unflattering layers are somehow made stylish, with oversized vintage jackets accessorised with cashmere triangle scarves tied at the neck, and Moon Boots looking not a bit out of place under ankle-length vintage fur coats. Whereas I am used to taking off my coat to reveal my 'actual' look upon arriving at an event, Parisians keep their coats on – that's the outfit.

Tradition
1,50€

HOW TO BE PARISIAN

LESSON #1

BEING PARISIAN IS FRESH DAILY BAGUETTES

For non-French people, buying fresh bread each day and walking along the street with it tucked under your arm might seem a little pretentious. But for Parisians, it's a necessity. It's unthinkable to eat day-old baguettes in France, and the qualities of an edible baguette are very strict: the crust must be so crispy that it cracks when you break it, and the inside must be soft and moist. So for the ideal baguette-eating experience, the baguette must be eaten the same day, ideally within hours of baking.

To meet this standard, bakeries produce fresh baguettes not just every day, but throughout the day, so that no matter what time you head to the bakery, you will be presented with a piping-hot, freshly baked sampling. You will even see *garçons* (waiters) running out from brasseries to collect huge bunches of fresh baguettes, to ensure the breadbasket served at each table meets the French diner's uncompromising standards, no matter the time of day.

When ordering a baguette, be sure to ask for a *tradition* (short for *baguette de tradition française*), as the word 'baguette' refers to *baguette ordinaire* or the basic version, which dries out faster.

If you look out your window onto the street at 7 pm on a weeknight, I guarantee you will see someone walking with a fresh baguette (and likely a bottle of wine, too) for their dinner. The tip of the baguette has probably already been bitten into, which isn't surprising given the irresistible impulse to savour a bite as soon as possible after purchasing it.

WHAT TO PACK

With its cobblestone streets and tiny hotel rooms, Paris is not kind to heavy, bulky suitcases. Once the reality of the inconveniences of Paris set in, you can lean into the luxury and freedom afforded by packing light.

The three most important considerations while packing for Paris are comfort, weather and propriety. Comfort comes before all else. Paris is a pedestrian-friendly city, with its abundant sidewalks and small, winding streets making it even more accessible – and enjoyable – to get around on foot than by car. So arguably the most important thing to pack is comfortable footwear: a pair of sandals or sneakers for summer, and warm boots made for walking in winter.

The next consideration is weather. Parisian summers are relatively short and mild, but the temperature can spike to 40°C (104°F) in August, so linen shirts, pants and dresses are the way to go. However, summer evenings can also be cool, so always have a light sweater or jacket on hand. The temperature drops rapidly from September, with winter setting in from November to February. The winter chill in Paris is not to be underestimated, with thermal undergarments highly recommended, along with wool or cashmere knits and an overcoat or down jacket.

Finally, it's important to ensure that your travel wardrobe is occasion appropriate. While Paris has long become accustomed to the patronage of tourists sporting too-casual attire, a smart-casual or business-casual look is viewed by the local businesses, particularly restaurants, as a sign of respect. It's always a good idea to include a lightweight blazer and black shoes in your travel wardrobe for this reason.

Read on for my essential packing list for a week in Paris.

THE — PARISIAN

SUMMER

TOPS (seven pieces from the following categories): White cotton T-shirts — Linen or cotton button-up shirts — Light wool sweater — Linen dresses

BOTTOMS: One or two pairs of jeans — One pair of linen pants or chinos, or a light skirt

OUTERWEAR: One tailored blazer — One light jacket

FOOTWEAR: One pair of sneakers — One pair of sandals — One pair of leather shoes

ACCESSORIES: Adequate underwear — Several pairs of socks — Baseball hat — Rain jacket or umbrella — Bag or backpack with a secure zip closure

STARTER KIT

WINTER

TOPS: Seven warm long-sleeved tops or shirts — Two warm wool or cashmere sweaters

BOTTOMS: Two or three pairs of thermal pants — Two pairs of jeans — One pair of smart pants

OUTERWEAR: One tailored blazer — One overcoat or down jacket

FOOTWEAR: One pair of sneakers — One pair of leather boots

ACCESSORIES: Adequate underwear — Seven pairs of warm socks — Beanie, beret, scarf or balaclava — One pair of thermal-lined gloves — Bag or backpack with a secure zip closure

LESSON #2

BEING PARISIAN IS NOT WEARING A BERET . . . OR IS IT?

For us foreigners, the soft, round, flat-crowned hat with a tiny tail on top (the tail is called a *cabillou*) is one of the most recognisable icons of Frenchness, as emblematic as the croissant and the Eiffel Tower. But the beret is not commonly worn by Parisians.

This is a shame to me because the beret is not only a cultural icon, but also an important element of French savoir-faire, with a history dating back to the Bronze Age. The modern beret took shape in nineteenth-century France and Spain, where it was worn by herders and farmers – its shape and flexible form was perfect for shading them from the sun during summer, and the felted waterproof wool protected them from rain and snow in the colder months.

The beret became synonymous with the French work ethic and camaraderie, and was even adopted as part of the military uniform. A symbol of the French Resistance during the Second World War, the beret evolved into a symbol of the bohemian lifestyle, donned by the likes of Pablo Picasso, Édith Piaf and Ernest Hemmingway.

As Hollywood embraced the beret as a symbol of Frenchness in the mid-twentieth century, however, its popularity began to wane in France. Today, berets are mostly worn by older generations of Parisians, especially in literary and artistic circles. This is slowly beginning to change as more younger Parisians incorporate the iconic hat into their winter look. I encorage you to embrace the cliché and try it yourself.

WHERE TO STAY

On my first trip to Paris, I stayed in Montmartre. Some might question this choice, given that it is some distance from the city centre, but I loved experiencing this village-like neighbourhood with its charming markets and café terraces. To this day, Montmartre remains my favourite area of Paris.

The moral of the story is that there are many compelling places to base yourself in Paris, and not just in the central and popular areas. The following hotel recommendations are based on boutique and thoughtfully designed properties – from reasonably priced to high-end – in some of Paris's most vibrant and interesting neighbourhoods.

Boudoir des Muses

BOUDOIR DES MUSES

6 Rue de Saintonge, Paris Centre

Paris, with its space limitations, has become known for transforming historic structures, including private mansions, convents, industrial halls and even a river barge, into some of the most unique boutique hotels in the world. Opened in 2024 in the Marais, the Boudoir des Muses was originally constructed in the eighteenth century to house a theatre. Shuttered in 1807 by order of Napoleon Bonaparte due to its 'immoral' performances, the theatre building has since housed businesses ranging from a brothel to a copper workshop and even the convent of the Filles du Calvaire (Daughters of Calvary) Benedictine congregation.

The 28-room boutique hotel pays homage to this rich and eclectic history, particularly the interplay between the sacred and the profane, with provocative imagery including the serpent-patterned carpet at the entrance (referencing the Garden of Eden), intimate lighting and jewel-toned colour palette creating a sense of secrecy and intrigue.

In contrast to the dark and sensual lobby area, the guestrooms (including a loft room that can sleep six) arranged around a central atrium are cosy and serene, with some rooms featuring original eighteenth-century wooden columns.

A buffet breakfast is served in the lobby area, which from 5 pm morphs into a cocktail bar with DJ sets and regular burlesque performances. The hotel also has two private spa spaces (one with a jacuzzi and sauna, the other with a hammam and pool).

C.O.Q HÔTEL PARIS

15 Rue Edouard Manet, 13th arrondissement

There's a playful nod to the *coq Gaulois* (Gallic rooster), a symbol of France, in its branding, but C.O.Q is actually an acronym for Community of Quality. Here, respected interior designers Pauline d'Hoop and Delphine Sauvaget have transformed a Haussmann building (p 67) into a homely, 50-room sanctuary blending vintage and contemporary elements. Each guestroom is unique (some have claw-foot bathtubs), and with its eclectic furniture and art pieces, plant-filled winter garden, and common lounge areas furnished with mountains of cushions, the C.O.Q Hôtel Paris feels like a cosy Parisian family home. There's even a chicken coop in the garden (fortunately for light sleepers, there are no roosters).

Breakfast including fresh eggs from the hotel's urban coop is served in the light-filled ground-floor winter garden, which transitions into a lounge and bar serving regional wines and snacks in the afternoon and evening. Located close to the historic Place D'Italie square and also Paris's Chinatown (where even McDonald's signs are written in Chinese), the hotel offers a great opportunity to explore a different side of Paris.

THE PARISIAN

GRAND PIGALLE EXPERIMENTAL

29 Rue Victor Massé, 9th arrondissement

One of the first hotels in Paris I ever stayed in, the Grand Pigalle Experimental gave me not only a great taste of the Parisian aesthetic, but also an excellent introduction to the best of the 9th arrondissement. Located in the vibrant South Pigalle area, within walking distance of Montmartre, this boutique hotel with just 37 rooms feels more like a big house.

Opened in 2015, the Grand Pigalle Experimental's interior design is the work of Dorothée Meilichzon. Her instantly recognisable style is characterised by bold colours, fluid curves and layered textures. The hotel's design and feel reflects the evolving character of the neighbourhood, blending Art Deco charm (such as its beautiful spiral staircase) and mid-century modern touches (such as bold patterns and rich textures) with playful nods to the neighbourhood's cabaret culture in the form of tassel accents and bright wallpaper.

Rooms range from standard to larger suites, some of which include intimate terraces overlooking the courtyard. My favourite thing about this hotel is the beautiful balcony rooms, where you can enjoy your morning coffee overlooking the streets of South Pigalle. Helmed by Michelin-starred chef Grégory Marchand, the ground-floor Frenchie Pigalle restaurant offers breakfast, lunch and dinner. Its bistro-style dishes are inspired by the chef's travels.

HÔTEL MADAME RÊVE

48 Rue du Louvre, Paris Centre

One of the most unique and intimate luxury hotels in the centre of Paris, the Hôtel Madame Rêve, opened in 2021, is the result of an ambitious renovation of the historic Poste du Louvre, a nineteenth-century building that once served as France's largest post office. The interior is truly sumptuous, with walnut-panelled walls from floor to ceiling, velvet drapery and approximately 800 artworks paying homage to the building's postal history. The lobby and bar are a feast for the eyes, decorated with lavish Art Deco–style furnishings.

Hôtel Madame Rêve offers 83 rooms in a number of categories, including a sprawling penthouse. Many rooms feature private terraces or balconies overlooking the hotel's signature hanging gardens, immersing you in a lush urban oasis, while others offer exceptional views of Paris including the Gothic facade of the nearby Église Saint-Eustache and even the Eiffel Tower. The design of the rooms is inspired by Parisian ateliers, blending open, workshop-style layouts with artisanal details including raw plaster walls, bronze-hued mosaic-tiled bathrooms, custom-made fabrics and parquet floors.

Hôtel Madame Rêve has two restaurants, an intimate lounge bar and an expansive rooftop bar with panoramic views. The ground-floor Kitchen by Madame Rêve serves contemporary French dishes in a grand hall with high ceilings and exposed beams, while La Plume, set on a plant-covered terrace under a vaulted glass roof on the third floor, has a seasonally changing menu blending Japanese techniques with French ingredients. Within La Plume is an elegant lounge bar, with plush armchairs and low lighting evoking the feel of a private 1970s salon. Finally, guests can reserve sun loungers on the 500-square-metre ROOF bar and terrace by day. In the evening, the space transforms into a cocktail lounge with seating for up to 150 guests in semi-private areas.

The hotel also has a wellness area including a fitness room with state-of-the-art equipment, two treatment rooms and a sunlit sauna overlooking the rooftops of Paris.

HÔTEL MONTE CRISTO

20–22 Rue Pascal, 5th arrondissement

Every detail of the Hôtel Monte Cristo reflects the colourful life and work of nineteenth-century novelist and adventurer Alexandre Dumas, including the famous book it is named for.

Located in a peaceful neighbourhood in close proximity to the buzzing commercial hub of Rue Mouffetard (p 229), the hotel occupies a Haussmann building (p 67) with an elegant stone facade and wrought-iron balconies. The interior, meanwhile, was transformed by interior design duo Pauline d'Hoop and Delphine Sauvaget with a rich mix of Orientalist influences and Gothic grandeur including dark wood panelling, richly textured wallpapers and ornate lighting.

Filled with taxidermy birds from Deyrolle (p 234), velvet armchairs, vintage rugs and shelves filled with antique books, the lobby transports you to another world. Each of the hotel's 50 rooms and suites feels like it could be in the home of a well-travelled nineteenth-century aristocrat, with tropical motifs paying homage to Dumas's mixed heritage (his grandmother was African) and his travels to the Caribbean; and vintage globes, framed maps and antique trunks referencing the spirit of exploration. Three of the four suites are themed for principal figures in *The Count of Monte Cristo* – the vengeful yet noble Edmond Dantès, his devoted former fiancée Mercédès, and the rescued Greek princess Haydée – while the fourth is inspired by the author himself.

Transitioning from breakfast buffet to formal dining area, the hotel's restaurant, Le Grand Dictionnaire, is an homage to Dumas's 1873 culinary encyclopedia, *Grand Dictionnaire de Cuisine*. It offers a seasonal menu that changes regularly. The hotel's Bar 1802 is also a destination in the Latin Quarter. A nod to Dumas's father, who was born in Saint-Domingue (now Haiti), the bar boasts France's largest rum selection, including aged rums from around the world, displayed in rows of shelving above the bar that are reminiscent of a nineteenth-century apothecary.

MOXY PARIS BASTILLE

34/36 Rue St Sabin, Paris Centre

In contrast to the classical and formal style of the typical Parisian hotel, the Moxy Paris Bastille is vibrant and social, with a focus on catering to the needs of the modern traveller in a lively and welcoming setting. The hotel has a playful and community-oriented approach, with an eclectic lobby–lounge area that feels more like an urban art installation. You are greeted upon entry by neon signage and fun pink flamingo sculptures, the furnishings mixing mid-century chairs with modern wire-frame benches and brightly coloured poufs.

Its 185 rooms are minimal, modern and comfortable, and come in an array of options, from adjoining family rooms to queen rooms with balconies and accessible rooms. Many feature floor-to-ceiling glass sliding doors that open onto a small balcony or terrace.

The Moxy's open-plan lobby doubles as a 24-hour café, bar and chill-out zone, with complimentary coffee and tea available from self-service machines. The communal area encourages socialising and is designed for lingering, with a cosy game room stocked with boardgames, toys and books; a dedicated co-working area with fast wi-fi (not always a given at Paris hotels); and the hotel's 'secret garden', a hidden retreat in the centre of Bastille. Instead of a restaurant, the hotel's 24-hour café offers a casual, self-service concept with snacks, pastries and sandwiches available around the clock. The bar serves tapas and small plates all day, including haystack fries, chickpea hummus dip with pita and mac 'n' cheese. By night, the lobby transforms into a local nightspot with DJs providing the tunes and playful cocktails served in eclectically mismatched glassware.

THE HOXTON PARIS

30–32 Rue du Sentier, Paris Centre

Known for transforming historic buildings into stylish hotels, the UK-based Hoxton hotel brand made its Paris debut in 2017. Occupying an eighteenth-century residence originally built by architect Nicolas d'Orbay for Etienne Rivié – an advisor to Louis XV – the hotel building's rich history includes a period in the nineteenth century when it functioned as a textile factory. Original features such as iron columns, spiral staircases and mosaic marble floors have been meticulously restored, while its 172 guestrooms in an array of configurations have high ceilings, decorative cornices and reclaimed oak chevron flooring, complemented by contemporary furnishings inspired by twentieth-century French designers like Jean Prouvé and Mathieu Matégot. Some rooms have private sun terraces furnished with loungers and outdoor dining areas overlooking the central courtyard, while light-filled communal areas with large couches encourage guests to mingle.

Rivié is the Hoxton's all-day brasserie specialising in traditional French cuisine with a modern twist, while the casual wine bar, Planche, serves exclusively biodynamic and organic wine. Located above the gorgeous spiral staircases, Jacques' Bar specialises in cocktails. With fast wi-fi, plentiful communal working nooks and a welcoming laptop policy, the Hoxton is also a popular place for digital nomads and local freelancers to work.

Hôtel Madame Rêve

WHEN TO VISIT

With packed café terraces spilling out onto the streets in summer and extravagant Christmas decorations decorating arcades in winter, Paris changes dramatically throughout the seasons.

The fashions change in tandem with the deciduous trees, and even the light transforms from month to month. There's no bad time to visit Paris, and each season has its unique draws.

SPRING

MARCH TO MAY

After Paris's long, cold winter, the city slowly begins to warm up in March and there is an ambiance of renewal and optimism across the city. Flowers burst into bloom, enhancing parks and public spaces such as Rue Saint Antoine near the Saint-Paul métro station in the Marais, the Père Lachaise Cemetery in the 20th arrondissement and Notre-Dame de Paris with its blossoming cherry trees.

The weather is still crisp, so you will need a coat most days, but when the sun is out you can shed some layers and soak it up on a park bench or sunny café terrace. April and May are known for light, misty rain called *bruine* – it's not heavy enough to necessitate umbrellas or raincoats, but it can still make some outdoor activities impractical.

Square Samuel Paty

Chanel runway show in the Grand Palais during Paris Fashion Week

STARTER — KIT

KEY EVENTS AND HOLIDAYS

—— **Paris Fashion Week Womenswear Autumn/Winter:** With so many fashion weeks held in Paris throughout the year, it seems that it's always fashion week. But the autumn/winter womenswear showcase held in early March is one of the most important events on the global fashion calendar. Though the shows and events are industry and A-list access only, non-invitees can still immerse themselves in the transformation of the city as the international fashion crowd descends, particularly in the Marais area. Many of the city's shopping streets are taken over by pop-up showrooms where brands show their new collections, and venues that hold the biggest fashion shows (including the Grand Palais for the Chanel show, Musée Rodin for the Dior show and the Musée du Louvre – known simply as the Louvre – for the Louis Vuitton show) become hotspots for celebrity spotting.

—— **Easter:** Called Pâques in France (after the Latin word *pascua*, which means 'food'), Easter is one of the nation's major Christian holidays. Parisian churches including Notre-Dame de Paris, Basilique du Sacré-Coeur and Saint-Sulpice hold special masses throughout the Holy Week leading up to Easter, which usually falls in April. Easter egg hunts (*chasses aux oeufs*) are organised in parks, châteaux and gardens, and Paris's chocolatiers display extravagant chocolate sculptures.

—— **Paris Marathon:** Attended by some 55,000 runners from over 100 nations, the Paris Marathon is held on the first or second Sunday of April. The scenic 42.2-kilometre (26-mile) route changes slightly from year to year, typically commencing on the Avenue des Champs-Élysées de Paris (near the iconic Arc de Triomphe de l'Étoile, known simply as the Arc de Triomphe) and heading along Rue de Rivoli, through the courtyard of the Louvre and onto the Place de la Bastille. It then loops through the Bois de Vincennes park and heads back through the city along the Seine towards the Bois de Boulogne park before ending near the Arc de Triomphe. Registrations fill up fast, but you don't need any qualifications or training to participate – many ordinary Parisians enter to challenge themselves.

The most exciting vantage points along the route include the starting line, the 2-kilometre (1.2-mile) mark on Place de la Concorde and the finish line on Avenue Foch where you can partake in post-race festivities, with live music and DJs on a central stage, and food and drink stalls.

—— **Nuit des Musées:** Held on the Saturday closest to 18 May, La Nuit des Musées (Night of the Museums) is a cultural event observed not only in France but across Europe, which sees museums and other cultural institutions open late into the night with free access.

—— **French Open:** Tennis lovers converge at the clay courts of Roland Garros from the last week of May to early June for the Grand Slam tournament.

Le Hibou

Place Dauphine

SUMMER

JUNE TO AUGUST

The flowers of spring give way to a lush green city in June. Paris warms up to T-shirt and dress weather, summer-only venues open their doors and year-round cafés pull their terrace tables and chairs out of storage. These tables immediately fill with locals eager to enjoy the social pastime of *apéro* (p 43), which really comes into its own during the warmer months.

The temperature heats up dramatically in July, and indoor spaces that aren't fitted with climate control (and even some that are) feel clammy. Many Parisians abandon chic-ness in pursuit of staying physically cool, and libraries and museums fill with Parisians in search of effective air-conditioning.

Paris experiences a great exodus in August as the residents of northern France (including the region's restaurant, shop and hotel owners) migrate south for the entire month. Paris becomes a virtual ghost town, with only the most touristic areas remaining in operation. While many unwitting visitors are disappointed to find shops and venues they had come to visit closed for the summer, August is a fascinating time to visit Paris – the streets are uncharacteristically calm, the métro is crowd-free and even the city's notorious traffic jams ease.

KEY EVENTS AND HOLIDAYS

—— **Nuit Blanche:** Held on the first Saturday of June, Nuit Blanche (White Night) is an annual all-night arts festival when museums, galleries and cultural institutions open their doors until the wee hours for free, showcasing contemporary art installations, performances and exhibitions throughout the city.

—— **Fête de la Musique:** On the evening of 21 June, Paris comes alive with music and street parties as part of the Fête de la Musique (Festival of Music). Take care on the streets after dark.

—— **Men's and Haute Couture Fashion Weeks:** The fashion shows held from late June to early July are dedicated to men's ready-to-wear and haute couture. While the two womenswear fashion weeks are the major events of the fashion calendar, the menswear and haute couture showcase is shorter (running for six days) and has a more laid-back atmosphere, but it still has its fair share of important shows held by major fashion houses.

—— **Summer Sales:** Paris's highly anticipated *les soldes* (the sales) occur twice a year. The summer sales generally begin on the last Wednesday of June, and continue for four weeks. Big shops, department stores and many independent shops participate in the sales season, with reductions between 30 and 70 per cent, increasing as the sales period progresses.

—— **Bastille Day:** Commemorating the 1789 storming of the Bastille prison – a pivotal event in the French Revolution – France's national day (known in France as La Fête Nationale, or the National Holiday) is observed on 14 July. There's a military parade on the Avenue des Champs-Élysées, with solders marching from the Arc de Triomphe to the Place de la Concorde. On Bastille Day, all museums, including the Louvre, offer free entry and extended hours. The day concludes with France's most spectacular fireworks at 11 pm.

—— **Tour de France:** Traditionally, the famous cycling race concludes in Paris on the last Sunday of July with a grand finale on the Avenue des Champs-Élysées, where spectators can watch the final few laps of the race.

—— **Paris Plages:** Parisians flock to *la plage* (the beach) in July and August, when temporary, free-access artificial beaches are created on the banks of the Seine, complete with real potted palm trees and deckchairs. In recent years, sections of the Canal Saint-Martin have also been transformed into summer beaches.

Forma gallery

AUTUMN

SEPTEMBER TO NOVEMBER

I first experienced Paris in September and it remains one of my favourite months of the year in the city. The September weather is warm enough that you don't feel cold, but cool enough to layer up, and with minimal rain.

As Parisians return to the city en masse from their summer holidays to slowly ease back into their work routines, the city feels the most local and intimate. Seemingly overnight, the trees turn golden brown and then go completely bare, blanketing the streets with their leaves. While spring paints the city in vibrant colours, autumn washes the city in a cinematic sepia.

With lots of art and design events in autumn, it's the best season for art buffs to visit.

Cité Charles Godon

Chez Marianne

KEY EVENTS AND HOLIDAYS

—— **Paris Design Week:** Held twice a year, in early September and mid-January, Paris Design Week is a major contemporary design event with both industry-focused and public events. Throughout the week the city is taken over by exhibitions and installations. The prominent Maison & Objet fair is held at the Parc des Expositions de Villepinte, with over 3000 exhibitors presenting the latest trends in furniture, lighting and decor.

—— **Paris Fashion Week Womenswear Spring/Summer:** Held from late September to early October, the womenswear spring/summer showcase is the biggest and busiest Paris fashion week of all, setting the direction for the next year in fashion. Major brands pull out all the stops for these shows.

—— **Art Basel Paris:** One of the city's most significant art events, Art Basel is hosted under the magnificent glass roof of the Grand Palais in mid-October and sees top galleries around the world present works to international art collectors.

Halloween: Halloween doesn't generate the same level of excitement in France as it does in other countries, but there are a lot of themed activities you mightn't expect. Chocolatiers like À la Mère de Famille (p 268) often release a fun Halloween chocolate collection and several haunted house experiences pop up in the lead-up to 31 October, including Le Parc de L'étrange (Park of the Strange), which transforms a Parisian park into a haunted forest. Paris's theme parks including Disneyland Paris, Jardin d'Acclimatation and Parc Asterix also embrace the spooky season.

Armistice Day: Commemorated on 11 November by nations involved in the First World War, Armistice Day is marked in Paris with a military parade and ceremony, culminating in the symbolic placing of a wreath by the French president at the Tombe du Soldat Inconnu (Tomb of the Unknown Soldier) beneath the Arc de Triomphe and the rekindling of the eternal flame (which is lit daily throughout the year at a 6.30 pm ceremony).

FAB Paris: FAB Paris is a major art fair that emerged from the 2022 merger of two notable French art events: Fine Arts Paris and La Biennale des Antiquaires. Held at the Grand Palais in mid-to-late November, the fair hosts approximately 100 exhibitors showcasing art from antiquity to the present day, including old masters, modern and contemporary art, sculpture, jewellery and books and manuscripts.

Beaujolais Nouveau: Beaujolais nouveau is a young red wine made from gamay grapes grown in the Beaujolais region, north of Lyon. It is traditionally released on the third Thursday of November, kicking off the nationwide celebration of Beaujolais Nouveau. In Paris, the annual release of Beaujolais nouveau is marked by tastings and wine-paired menus offered by many restaurants, bars and bistros.

THE PARISIAN

WINTER

DECEMBER TO FEBRUARY

Winter in Paris is cold – sometimes literally freezing with occassional snowfalls in January or February. The winter weather can also be unpredictable, with sunny mornings often followed by rainy afternoons. Many Parisians go into hibernation to wait out the cold grey days, but there are actually many benefits for wintertime visitors. Apart from the few days around Christmas and New Year's Eve, this is Paris's low season, so it's a good time to experience the city without the crowds and score good deals on accommodation.

While it may be too cold to spend a lot of time outdoors, it's a great time to experience the city's consistently well-heated indoor spaces. Grab a table at a lively brasserie and tuck into a decadent Parisian-style hot chocolate or French comfort foods like creamy *tartiflette* (a gratin of potatoes, cheese, onion and bacon pieces) and raclette, which is more of a social activity than a dish, with wheels of cheese melted over fire, then scraped onto plates and eaten with boiled potatoes and charcuterie.

KEY EVENTS AND HOLIDAYS

——— **Le Grand Palais des Glaces:** There are a surprising number of public events and activities in Paris during the winter months. One of the most beloved traditions is Le Grand Palais des Glaces, held from mid-December to early January, when a giant 2700-square-metre indoor ice rink is installed under the great glass roof of the Le Grand Palais (p 112). The late-night session runs until 2 am, with DJs and light shows.

——— **Christmas:** Charming Christmas markets pop up all over popular Parisian neighbourhoods like the Jardin des Tuileries, Montmartre and Saint-Michel as early as mid-November and operate through early January. These Alsatian-inspired markets are characterised by rows of stalls resembling timber houses. They sell arts and crafts and Christmas decorations, and serve hot mulled wine, pretzels, comforting street-food dishes and a wide array of sausages (from German bratwurst to African spicy sausages) with sauerkraut.

Another beloved Christmas tradition is the extravagant decorations adorning Paris's big department stores, including whimsical window displays that change every year. The Galeries Lafayette (p 261) erects its monumental Christmas tree in the centre of the department store that reaches all the way to its great dome and Le Bon Marché (p 232) always creates a window display that is a sophisticated modern interpretation of holiday themes.

——— **New Year's Eve:** Paris puts on a suitably spectacular show for New Year's Eve with a light show, an eight-minute fireworks display and a concert on the Avenue des Champs-Élysées. There are no fireworks displays on the Eiffel Tower, however, with these reserved for Bastille Day.

——— **Epiphany:** Celebrated on or around 6 January, L'Épiphanie (Epiphany) or La Fête des Rois (The Festival of Kings) is a Christian feast day commemorating the visit of the Magi (Three Wise Men or Three Kings) to the infant Jesus. An occasion for families and friends to come together, the key tradition that marks this event is the *galette des rois* (king's cake). This pastry is typically a flaky, round cake filled with *frangipane* (almond cream). Hidden within the galette is a small trinket called a *fève* (originally a bean, now often a porcelain figurine). Whoever finds the *fève* in their slice is crowned king or queen for the day and dons a paper crown that comes with the cake. During the Festival of Kings, the *galette des rois* is sold in every bakery and patisserie in Paris.

——— **Winter Sales:** The second big sales season in Paris begins on the second Wednesday of January and lasts for four weeks.

——— **Men's and Haute Couture Fashion Weeks:** The autumn/winter edition of the men's ready-to-wear fashion week and haute couture week are held in late January. This is the most relaxed edition of the fashion weeks with the cold weather deterring strong international attendance.

——— **Paris Design Week:** The second edition of Paris Design Week is held in mid-January.

——— **Chinese New Year:** Occurring sometime between 21 January and 20 February each year, Chinese New Year or Lunar New Year celebrations are centred in Paris's Chinatown, the 13th arrondissement and the Belleville area, with red lanterns strung up and lively parades held with traditional lion and dragon dances. The city's larger department stores also participate with special decorations and installations. For me, the best thing about Chinese New Year is the food, with a number of Asian street food festivals popping up across town.

——— **Valentine's Day:** As you can imagine, Valentine's Day is rather a big deal in the City of Love with many romance-adjacent businesses and brands like restaurants, hotels, florists, perfumeries, chocolate makers, pâtissiers and even river cruise companies taking full advantage by offering special products and services on 14 February. The city comes alive with romantic events such as concerts by candlelight, love-themed exhibitions and themed parties. Love is in the air everywhere you look around.

Cour du Commerce Saint-André

HOW TO BE PARISIAN

LESSON #3

BEING PARISIAN IS EMBRACING *APÉRO*

Apéro (pre-dinner drinks) is of paramount importance to French and Parisian society, akin to a national sport. Not just a social gathering to mark the end of the workday, it's also essential for building relationships with friends and colleagues. In France, it's often said that it's impossible to form a close personal relationship with someone until you have had *apéro* with them.

While *apéro* is technically a pre-dinner drink, sometimes it can displace dinner altogether. Enter the *apéro dînatoire*, which sees drinks served with small plates and finger foods such as cheese, charcuterie, bread and dips. For most expats, this does not a dinner make and may leave you frantically searching the city for a fast-food fix when you finally leave *apéro*.

The *apéro* hour (or hours) is also an ideal stage for observing the drinking habits of Parisian society, from young students and professionals knocking back cheap beers to elegantly dressed ladies of leisure, Hermès Birkin bags on their elbows, whose drink of choice is rosé with a glass of ice on the side and the quintessential complimentary peanuts. Aspiring gourmands are partial to white wine, while red wine is typically consumed at informal business gatherings. Champagne is usually ordered later in the evening, often by self-made mature women, for whom only the finest will do.

Given the cultural importance of *apéro*, you would think that Paris would be full of bars and nightclubs. While the city has its fair share of both, most of the drinking happens at its countless cafés and brasseries. Come *apéro* hour, these establishments transform as their terrace tables swell with Parisians ordering pre-dinner drinks with cheese and charcuterie boards.

MONEY & COSTS

Paris has an international reputation for being an expensive city, but the reality is more nuanced. While some things in Paris are extremely expensive, others are surprisingly good value.

Parisians spend approximately 7 per cent more to live than the rest of France. Costs also change dramatically from neighbourhood to neighbourhood, even at chains like McDonald's, where prices are higher in city-centre outlets. Eating out and accommodation are typically the biggest expenses for visitors. While an espresso or black coffee is only about €2, a coffee with milk or cream costs between €5–10. I once paid 15€ for coffee on the Avenue des Champs-Élysées! A sit-down lunch under €15 is difficult to find, and dinner typically starts from €25 per person.

Hotel rates in Paris are as high or sometimes higher than in other major European cities. Hotel costs can also greatly fluctuate between the seasons and during major events and festivals.

Many Parisian pleasures, however, are surprisingly good value. Gourmet food items such as wine, Champagne, foie gras and cheese are all affordable; it's not unusual to pick up a good bottle of wine at the supermarket for €8, a quality foie gras for €13 or a wheel of good quality Camembert or a wedge of 24-month-aged Comté (Alpine-style cheese from Franche-Comté) for €5–10.

French designer clothing and beauty products from the likes of Chanel and Louis Vuitton are cheaper in France, sometimes vastly, as prices in other countries include importation costs. On top of that, travellers benefit from a tax refund (known in France as TVA) of up to 12 per cent (p 46).

Despite the popularity of living in Paris, rental costs are low compared with other major global cities including New York City and London. Among the cheapest accommodations are one-room studios on the top floor of Haussmann apartment buildings (p 67) known as *chambres de bonne*. These have as little as 9 square metres (30 square feet) of floor space and maybe a shared bathroom, and can cost €600–700 per month. Airbnb and other sharing economy platforms tend to offer lower rates than hotels, with rates decreasing in recent years.

Getting around Paris is also relatively inexpensive. A métro ticket costs €2.50 no matter how far you go and taxis are more affordable than in other major cities.

STARTER KIT

Odéon métro station

Carette, Place des Vosges

AVERAGE COSTS IN PARIS

Hotels	€150+ per night
Airbnb	€120+ per night
Cup of coffee	€2–8
Fast food meal or takeaway sandwich	€6–15
Sit-down lunch	€15–25 per person
Glass of wine at a restaurant	€5–15
Dinner	€25–40 per person
Fine dining meal	€60–80 per person
Métro	€2.50 per ticket
Paris Visite travel pass (for unlimited public transport)	€29.90 for a one-day pass
Taxi from Charles de Gaulle Airport to city centre	Right Bank (Rive Droite): €56 Left Bank (Rive Gauche): €65
Taxi from Paris Orly Airport to city centre	Right Bank: €44 Left Bank: €36
Taxi	€15 for a 15-minute ride
Uber	€10 for a 15-minute ride
Vélib' public bike-sharing service	€5 for a one-day pass (including 30 minutes of rides)
Lime electric bike hire	€3.99 for a one-day pass (including 30 minutes of rides)

BUDGET TIPS

—— **Base yourself in an up-and-coming neighbourhood:** Generally, neighbourhoods in the centre of Paris and close to big monuments like the Eiffel Tower and Arc de Triomphe are the most expensive to stay and eat in. Instead, choose to stay in gentrifying neighbourhoods such as the 13th and 18th arrondissements; they have some of the city's best-value and most interesting culinary offerings.

—— **Make sure it's an official taxi:** Always be sure to take an official 'Taxi Parisien' from Charles de Gaulle or Orly airports, which adhere to regulated, metered fares. Clearly marked official taxis line up just outside the baggage claim areas; decline offers from individuals inside the arrivals halls. Taxi fares from airports to central Paris are fixed based on whether you are going to the Left Bank or Right Bank, and official drivers are prohibited from charging more than these rates, such as extra luggage surcharges.

—— **Rent a bike:** If you're able to, utilising the city's bike-hire schemes can be very cost-effective for travelling short distances. At €21.99, a seven-day Lime pass is more economical than a one-day Paris Visite travel pass (€29.90).

—— **Dine at restaurants offering 'la formule':** Many Parisian restaurants offer good value two-course set menus at lunchtime known as *la formule*, costing around €18–25.

—— **Hit bakeries and delicatessens for lunch:** Another good-value lunch option is the city's amazing bakeries and delis, which typically serve quiches, sandwiches and salads for under €10. Famous sandwich shops such as Bagels & Brownies (p 236) offer gourmet bagels from €9.

—— **Don't overlook *traiteurs*:** You can also find good-value meals at *traiteurs*, the French version of the takeaway shop. Chinese, Japanese, Lebanese and other Mediterranean *traiteurs* can be found around the city. They generally serve generous meals for less than €15.

—— **Claim your tax deduction:** Non-EU residents can reclaim the French VAT (TVA) on purchases totalling at least €100 in a single shop by requesting a tax-free form from the retailer at the time of purchase. Not all retailers in Paris offer this service, especially small independent boutiques, but you will find *détaxe* desks in all major department stores. You'll need to show your passport, so it's a good idea to keep it on you if you are planning to shop.

When you depart France, you will need to have this form validated at a self-service kiosk or manual customs booth for the refund process to be completed. You can find these in most terminals at Charles de Gaulle and Orly airports, and Gare du Nord – be sure to check if there is a kiosk in the terminal you are flying from before you go through security. You should bring the products you purchased with you just in case you are requested to present them.

—— **Use a digital bank:** Digital banks with competitive conversion rates and low fees like Wise and Revolut can help you save on international transaction fees.

—— **Time museum visits wisely:** Most major museums in Paris offer free admission on the first Sunday of each month, offering a great way to save money if you don't mind the crowds.

DO I NEED TO HAVE CASH ON ME?

Generally, you will be fine with a credit card or contactless payment, but there are exceptions to keep in mind. First, it is a courtesy to pay for small purchases such as coffees in cash – while all businesses in Paris are expected to provide you with a way to pay by card, it comes at a cost to the business. It's also a good idea to bring cash to flea markets, where vendors may not have card facilities.

Winona

PARLEZ-VOUS FRANÇAIS?

You don't need to be able to speak French to visit Paris as most Parisians speak a basic level of English. Learning at least a few French pleasantries and phrases, however, can go a long way. Walking into a shop and immediately speaking to staff in English, for example, will not be well received. It's more appropriate to ask politely if they speak English (ideally in French, with a simple '*parlez-vous Anglais?*'). Also, saying '*bonjour*' (hello) to waitstaff, hotel receptionists and shopkeepers before you ask them for assistance is a must. If you forget to do so, you will likely be greeted with a pointed '*bonjour!*', to make it known that your omission has been noticed. A simple '*merci*' (thank you) at the conclusion of your interaction is also expected and appreciated.

That said, addressing staff in French in the city centre and touristy areas might result in waitstaff rolling their eyes and replying in English, as if to say, 'Why are you trying to speak French to me, as you see I speak English perfectly well!' Some shopkeepers may also be so used to receiving tourists that they reply to you in English. Just go with it and if all else fails, use a translation app.

NAVIGATING PARIS

Paris may look easy to get around due to its relatively compact size, but sometimes travelling even short distances can be a trek. Choosing the right method of transportation at the right time is key. In general, it's best to walk during rush hour (8–10 am and 5–8 pm) when services are crowded, traffic is slow and tensions run high. Keep in mind that getting to the airport (Charles de Gaulle or Orly) by taxi can take an hour or longer from the city during rush hour.

TAXI AND UBER

There is a good reason why many Parisians are reluctant to travel out of their own neighbourhoods: the old city planning can make travelling between arrondissements a tedious and time-consuming task. Most locals consider taxis, Ubers and buses last-resort transport options and use them only when other methods are not practical. Paris's notoriously bad traffic means travelling by vehicle is usually the slowest, even when compared with walking.

MÉTRO

The Paris Métro, built in 1900, is one of the oldest in the world, so it's not surprising that it's not the best adapted for the modern layout of the city and the movements of its people. Generally, the métro works very well if you are going just a few stations and especially in straight lines around the centre. Trips involving multiple line changes, however, can make a geographically short journey complex. As a general rule, allow 30–45 minutes to travel between non-adjacent arrondissements. If you're planning to use the métro a lot, consider purchasing a Paris Visite travel pass (p 45), which allows unlimited travel across various public transport networks for up to five consecutive days.

WALKING

The best and often fastest way to explore Paris is on foot, taking in the architecture as you stroll, popping into small shops along the way and turning down sidestreets to discover their secrets. If it will take you 20 minutes or less to walk to your destination, I always recommend going on foot.

BIKE-SHARING SERVICES

With electric scooter hire banned in 2023, hiring a bike is the fastest and usually the most convenient way to move around Paris, with bikes generally permitted to travel in both directions on roads otherwise limited to one-way traffic (check signs carefully). Cycling in Paris, however, can be dangerous. Bike paths are often shared with bus lanes or leave very little space for bikes to pass next to cars. Paris's bike-sharing services do not provide helmets but I strongly recommend buying and wearing one.

— **Vélib' Métropol:** The city has its own bike-sharing system called Vélib' Métropol, offering both mechanical and electric bikes at docking stations throughout the city. Users can purchase single trips as well as short-term passes using the Vélib' app or at machines found at Vélib' docking stations.

— **Private electric bike-sharing services:** Privately owned electric bike-sharing services are ubiquitous in Paris, the major brands being Lime, Dott and more recently, Voi. Rather than having docking stations, these bikes can be found at bike parking spaces around the city. You can book them by signing up on their respective apps. At a glance, it seems expensive: the rental fee is around €0.25 per minute, and depending on the service, a €1 unlocking fee may also be charged, so a 15-minute ride costs about €5, which is more expensive than the métro. Passes are more economical, offering significant savings on the per-minute rate.

I often choose Lime because its bikes are everywhere, but it's not a bad idea to sign up to all of the services, so you will always find a bike when you need one.

Place du Trocadéro

Abbesses métro station

SAFETY

As much as I love Paris, it is not the world's safest city. Petty crime is the biggest issue for visitors – pickpocketing is so prolific that I don't know a single person (myself included) who has not had a wallet or phone stolen at least once. Parisians have built up such vigilance against pickpocketing that few locals risk walking out the door (and especially using the métro) with a handbag lacking a zip closure and we keep one hand on our bag at all times. Keeping your phone or wallet in your pocket is a complete no-no.

As a general rule, avoid streets near RER stations, big crowds and streets where people loiter, and be wary of strangers who engage you in conversation (usually to sell you something or ask you to fill in a survey for charity) in tourist hotspots. This is a famous strategy used by pickpocketing gangs: while one member distracts the well-meaning tourist with conversation, another member will liberate them of their valuables. Unfortunately, women and tourists of Asian appearance are prime targets.

THE PARISIAN ETIQUETTE

Paris has a cultural identity that values artistic freedom, intellectualism and meritocracy, which means it is generally more casual compared with some other countries, but there are still some social conventions to observe.

DRESS CODE

When you arrive in Paris, you will notice that Parisians generally dress with a certain polish, and while they prefer relaxed looks, it is rare to find them in sweatpants, shorts or flip-flops. A degree of formality is also expected at most restaurants – while Parisians are understanding towards tourists who are not familiar with the unsaid dress code, wearing activewear and sneakers is frowned upon. You may even be unceremoniously turned away by some venues.

RESTAURANTS AND RESERVATIONS

There is no hard rule about restaurant reservations in Paris. Many Parisian bistros are tiny and have limited capacity, making it a good idea to call ahead, especially to dine on the weekend or during peak seasons or holidays. However, it's very common in Paris to just walk in. If you haven't made a reservation, it doesn't hurt to simply ask at the door of any restaurant whether you can have a table. Most of the time, even if the restaurant is currently full, they will be happy to let you wait for the next available table. With a lot of capacity and *service continu* (all-day service) late into the night, traditional brasseries offer an easy solution if you're in a bind.

For dress codes, prices ranges and tipping etiquette for every type of Parisian restaurant, see the Cheat Sheet at the back of the book (p 338).

DO I NEED TO TIP?

In Paris a 15 per cent service charge is included by law on menu prices, so there is no obligation to tip and it's not necessarily expected. However, if you are happy with the food and service, it's a nice gesture to tip. Most Parisians leave a few euros to round up the bill. You can give this tip by card (some venues offer the option on the card machine; if not, just tell them how much you want to pay) or leave some euros on the table when you leave. If you are on a budget or if your experience was not exceptional, it is absolutely normal to not leave a tip.

PARISIAN FAUX PAS TO AVOID

——— **Not greeting hospitality staff:** A simple '*bonjour*' (good morning) or '*bonsoir*' (good evening) is expected and appreciated.

——— **Asking for special changes or substitutions to menu items:** While allergies are an exception, Parisians don't traditionally take vegetarianism or veganism very seriously, and traditional brasseries and bistros don't usually offer vegetarian options. You may be met with an abrupt '*C'est pas possible*' (it's not possible), if you ask for a vegetarian version of a dish – chefs are proud of their dishes and take alternation requests as a slight. However, Paris has many plant-based eateries.

——— **Speaking loudly in public:** Parisians value discretion and personal space. You will stand out in the wrong way for talking and laughing loudly on public transport and in restaurants and museums.

——— **Putting bread on your plate:** It's considered unrefined in France to rest your bread on your plate. You should put it directly on the table instead.

——— **Going against the flow in the métro:** Two things you should do to avoid annoying Parisians are to stand on the right of escalators to leave enough room for people to pass on the left, and to always wait for everyone to finish getting off the métro before trying to get on.

View from Le Cabanon de la Butte restaurant

HOW TO BE PARISIAN

LESSON #4

BEING PARISIAN IS DOING *LA BISE*

La bise means 'the kiss', but the French greeting is not really a kiss; it's more of a touching of the cheek on both sides while making a kissing sound. There are specific and equally important rules around *la bise*, which every Parisian knows: when it should be done, how it should be done and to whom it should be done.

The first rule is that for most introductions *la bise* is the only acceptable greeting. Extending a hand for a handshake outside a professional environment is considered cold and rude, and can thus begin a relationship on a bad footing. While some foreigners may consider kissing too intimate, in France a hug is considered to be far more intimate or too forward (hint: don't offer a hug).

The second rule is that, while shaking hands is acceptable between males in non-professional introductions, *la bise* should still be done if one of the greeters is female. So, men may find themselves in a situation where their female friend receives *la bise*, while they receive a handshake.

The requirement to always greet with *la bise* can pose logistical issues when dining in a large group. Each person must exchange *bises* with each other, so you can imagine how long this might take! And it gets more awkward when a late arrival turns up. Each time, everyone must stand up from their seats and reach over candlesticks and flower arrangements to achieve this feat.

If you want to know for sure whether you should do *la bise* or not, just wait for the other person to take the initiative. If they do, it would be considered very rude not to reciprocate.

PETS

Parisians love pets. Almost all cafés are pet friendly, with many owners putting out bowls of water for their patrons' dogs. Most shops, department stores and restaurants are pet friendly, too. If you're not sure, call ahead or ask before entering. Many hotels and Airbnbs also allow pets; sometimes a small additional fee or security deposit is required.

Dogs are allowed on public transport, but a recent rule change means only dogs small enough to fit in a bag are allowed. Many indignant Parisians have rebelled against the rule by placing their large dogs in large bags to circumvent it. In practice, large dogs are generally still tolerated if well behaved.

Unfortunately, pets are generally not allowed in many of the city's parks. There are some designated dog parks, however, like Square Nadar (p 159) in Montmartre.

Rue des Eaux

PARIS JE T'AIME

The city's official tourist office, Paris je t'aime (Paris, I love you), is an excellent resource for visitors. Its website (parisjetaime.com) is very comprehensive and it facilitates ticket purchases for museums, monuments, cruises and other activities. There is also the Paris je t'aime app, which you can filter to discover attractions, restaurants and more, and even an official concierge service operating daily between 10 am and 5 pm. Call +33 (0)1 49 52 42 81 or email your questions to concierge@parisjetaime.com.

In a departure from the traditional tourism office format, Paris je t'aime recently set up a network of more than 30 tourist information points within the city's dark-green Haussmann-style newspaper kiosks. Located everywhere from Gare du Nord to Place du Trocadéro, the kiosks have traditionally been hubs for local information and now the newspaper vendors have become official ambassadors for the city.

View from Maison de Balzac

HOTE

Plaque in honour of the late fashion designer Sonia Rykiel at her former home, 60 Rue des Saints-Pères

Rue des Francs-Bourgeois

Rue de Turbigo

HOW TO BE PARISIAN

LESSON #5

BEING PARISIAN IS COMPLAINING ABOUT PARISIANS

In this compact city where space, including personal space, is difficult to come by, it's not surprising that Parisians are often in conflict with each other, bickering over everything from noisy neighbours to the correct time and method of disposing of Christmas trees. A perfect example is the great electric scooter controversy of the early 2020s. What seemed like a perfect solution to ease Paris's traffic woes polarised Parisian society. Non-scooter-riding Parisians complained about the scooter-riding Parisians driving too fast on pavements and bringing their scooters into métros and supermarkets, and scooter riders complained about non-riders being bigoted and intolerant. In the end, riding bikes became more popular and the war raged on between cyclists and non-cyclists. Most pedestrians dislike cyclists, who do not always respect pedestrian crossings, while cyclists dislike pedestrians for getting in their way. Drivers, especially taxi drivers, typically dislike both for all the same reasons.

With a large proportion of the city's residents originally hailing from beyond Paris, it's popular to blame perceived transgressions on 'Parisians'. A taxi driver, for example, might roll her eyes at a cyclist riding close to her on the road and say: 'I hate Parisians!' despite being a local resident herself.

ABOUT PARIS

Place du Calvaire

ABOUT PARIS

To fully appreciate the beauty and depth of Paris today is to acknowledge its rich and complex history, woven over more than two millennia.

Paris was born on a small island in the middle of the Seine, now called Île de la Cité. Occupied from about 250 BC by the Gauls, a Gallic tribe that inspired the Asterix comics, it was conquered in 52 BC by the Romans, who named it Lutetia; this is why there are so many references to Lutetia in the central neighbourhoods of Paris. By the late Roman Empire the city was known as Parisius, and finally Paris.

Until the 1800s the city was contained within the Wall of the Ferme Générale (Farmers-General), which roughly followed the routes now traced by Line 2 and Line 6 of the Paris Métro. These days, many street names contain the old French word *faubourg*, which means 'outside of town'.

The medieval period introduced Gothic architecture to Paris, with the pointed arches, flying buttresses and gargoyles of Notre-Dame de Paris, built between the twelfth and fourteenth centuries, typical of the period. Then came the Renaissance, marking a profound transformation of Paris's architecture, art and cultural life that was heavily influenced by Italian art and antiquity. The subsequent Baroque period added further grandeur and ornamentation, seen in many of King Henry II's urban developments such as the Place des Vosges and Place Vendôme.

However, the most significant developments that define the modern face of Paris came in the mid-nineteenth century. The first was the 1860 expansion of the city, which saw outlying neighbourhoods such as Montmartre officially become part of Paris. The second was the massive urban renewal project led by Georges-Eugène (Baron) Haussmann. The project necessitated the razing of many of Paris's narrow and labyrinthine medieval streets and buildings to make room for wide, tree-lined boulevards, spacious public parks and uniform buildings characterised by the cream-coloured stone facades and mansard roofs we associate with Paris today. Coveted by Parisians and expats, Haussmann-style apartments are beloved for their parquet floors, large French windows and balconies with wrought-iron railings. Top-floor apartments commanding views over the city's rooftops are particularly sought-after.

The early twentieth century saw the emergence of the Art Nouveau and Art Deco movements characterised by intricate ironwork and the incorporation of organic forms, as seen in French architect Hector Guimard's alien-esque Paris Métro entrances (including Abbesses and Saint-Michel–Notre-Dame). Geometric shapes and streamlined forms were also incorporated into the designs of buildings such as the Palais de Chaillot.

The 1980s saw a new cultural revolution in Paris, led by then-President François Mitterrand. Modern buildings and monuments like the Pyramide du Louvre (Louvre Pyramid), the Opéra Bastille and the Grande Arche de la Défense were erected to juxtapose ornate historical monuments.

While other cities have grown taller and taller with skyscrapers towering over their historic districts, Paris's skyline has been preserved largely as it was in the nineteenth century, thanks to the city's heritage protection zones and building height regulations. With only a small handful of exceptions made for buildings such as the 210-metre-high (689-feet-high) Tour Montparnasse (Montparnasse Tower), Paris's new buildings are capped at 37 metres (121 feet) or approximately 12 storeys. This preserved historical skyline stands in stark contrast to the modern commercial district of La Défense, west of Paris, which looks like a glittering futuristic city by comparison.

NEIGHBOURHOODS

Despite the relatively small size of Paris – stretching 12 kilometres (7.5 miles) from east to west and less than 10 kilometres (6 miles) north to south – there is so much diversity from neighbourhood to neighbourhood, even from one street to another.

The village-like charm of Montmartre transforms abruptly into the energetic nightlife of Pigalle; the Marais, with its high concentration of fashion boutiques and art galleries, leads into the grittier, multicultural Belleville. The street that I lived on for many years in the 18th arrondissement, Avenue de Saint-Ouen, is a bustling main road lined with fast-food and phone shops, and it's just steps from the upscale residential 17th arrondissement with its independent interior design stores and quaint restaurants.

Paris is made up of 20 numbered *arrondissements* (districts) and 80 named *quartiers* (neighbourhoods). Arrondissements are arranged in a clockwise spiral starting from the 1st arrondissement at the centre, which contains Paris's most important landmarks including the Musée du Louvre (Louvre Museum, or simply the Louvre) and the Jardin des Tuileries (Tuileries Garden). As the arrondissements spiral outwards like an *escargot* (snail) shell, they no longer have chronological relationships, which can be confusing for visitors. It also means that the arrondissements become progressively larger with the northern 18th arrondissement, for example, being the same size as the 9th and 10th arrondissements combined.

To further confuse things, Parisians prefer to call districts and neighbourhoods by popular names based on history and local identity, which often date back centuries, rather than by the actual arrondissement or *quartier* name. There have also been recent administrative changes including the combining of the central arrondissements.

Discover your new favourite corner of Paris with this guide to the city's arrondissements and key neighbourhoods.

Rue du Chevalier de la Barre

NEIGHBOURHOODS

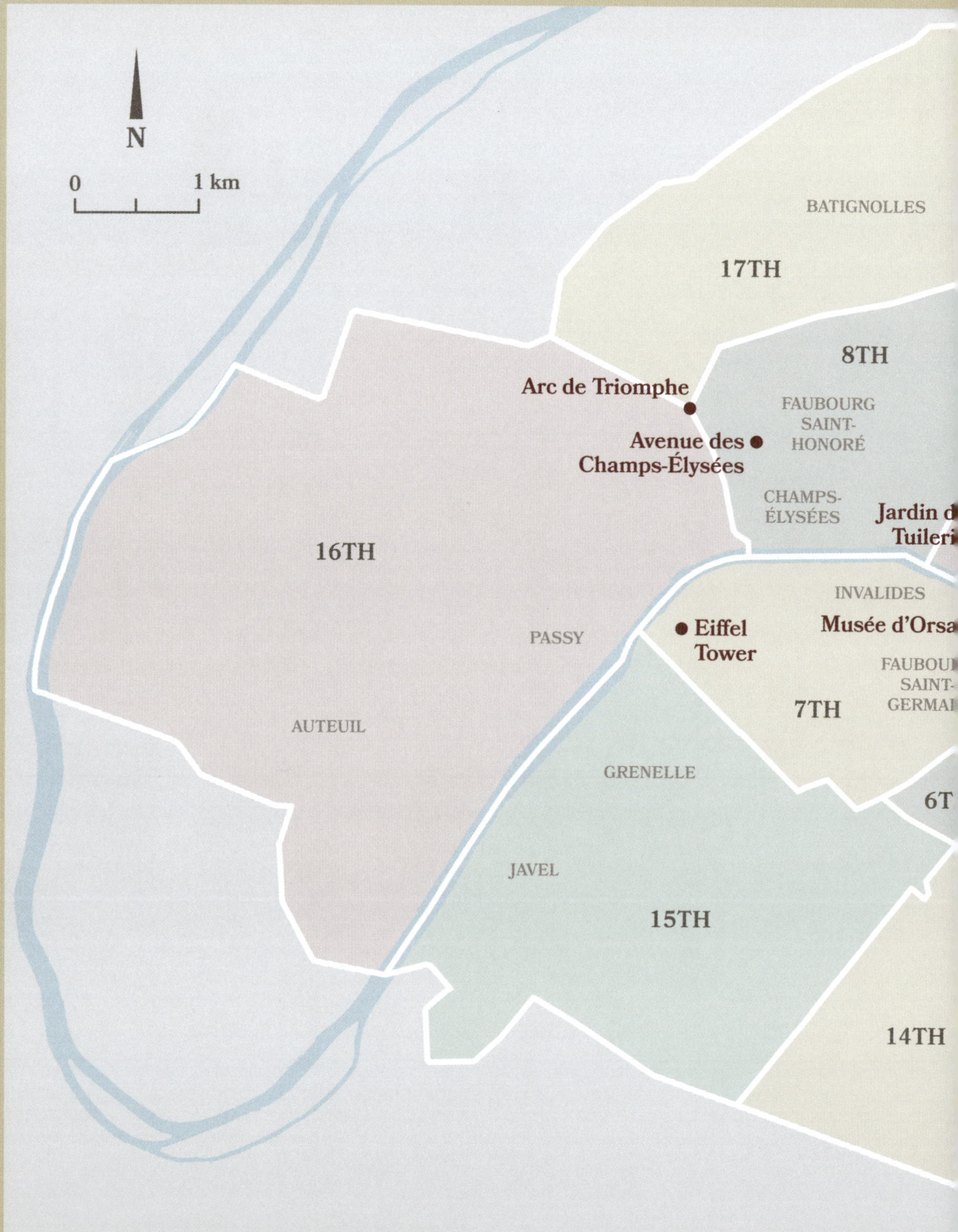

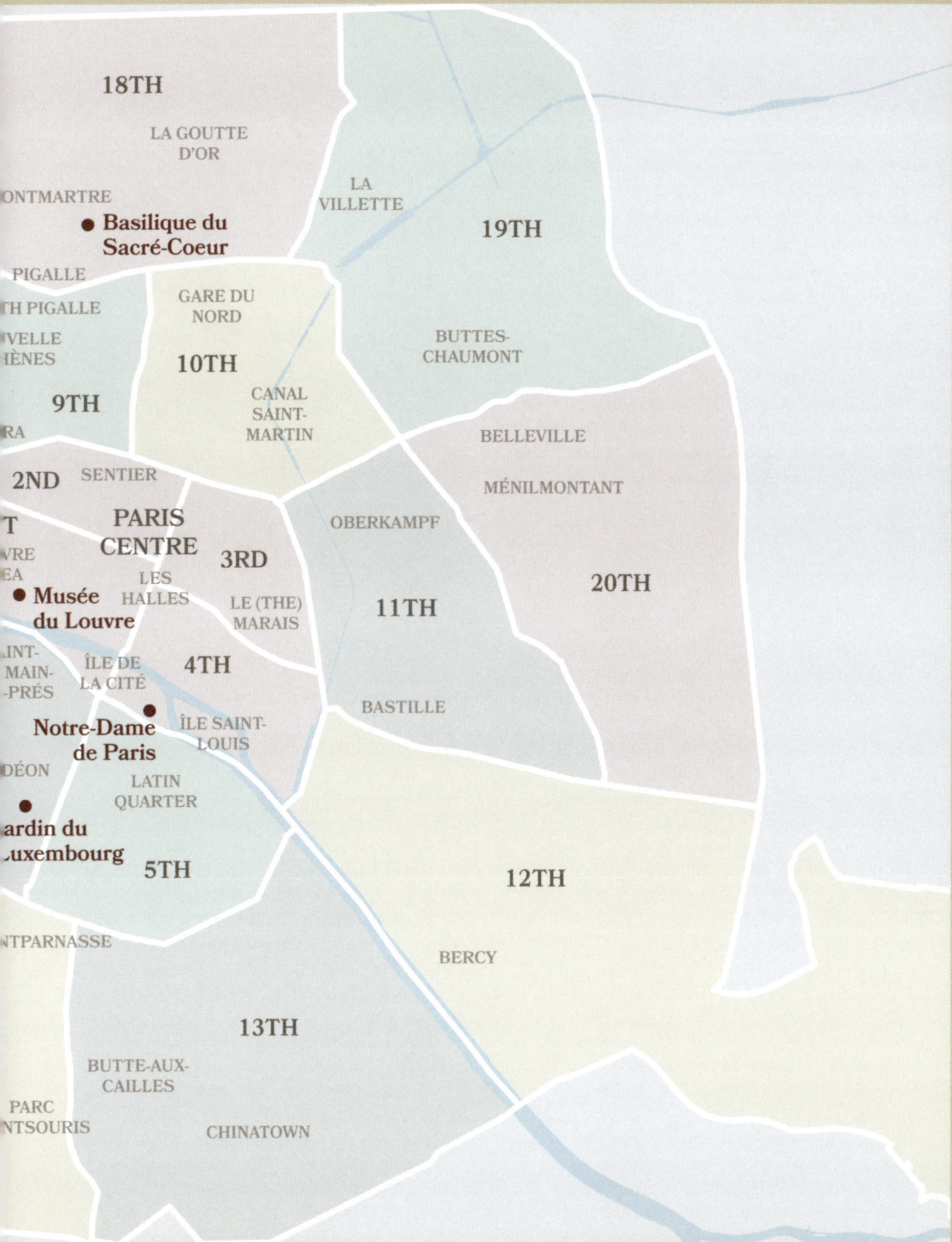
18TH
LA GOUTTE D'OR
ONTMARTRE
Basilique du Sacré-Coeur
PIGALLE
TH PIGALLE
VELLE
HÈNES
9TH
RA
LA VILLETTE
19TH
GARE DU NORD
10TH
CANAL SAINT-MARTIN
BUTTES-CHAUMONT
BELLEVILLE
MÉNILMONTANT
2ND
SENTIER
PARIS CENTRE
3RD
OBERKAMPF
20TH
LES HALLES
Musée du Louvre
LE (THE) MARAIS
11TH
ÎLE DE LA CITÉ
4TH
-PRÉS
Notre-Dame de Paris
ÎLE SAINT-LOUIS
BASTILLE
DÉON
LATIN QUARTER
ardin du
uxembourg
5TH
12TH
TPARNASSE
BERCY
13TH
BUTTE-AUX-CAILLES
PARC
NTSOURIS
CHINATOWN

NEIGHBOURHOODS

Paris Centre

Louvre area, Le (the) Marais, Les Halles, Île de la Cité, Île Saint-Louis, Sentier

HISTORICAL IDENTITY: Heart of ancient Paris, medieval district with aristocratic roots, historic Jewish quarter

PERSONALITY: Trendy, historic, vibrant, artsy, LGBTQIA+ community

KEY SIGHTS: Avenue des Champs-Élysées, Centre Pompidou, Hôtel de Ville, Jardin des Tuileries, Musée du Louvre, Notre-Dame de Paris, Palais-Royal, Place des Vosges

In 2020, the 1st through 4th arrondissements were officially combined and named Paris Centre. Located on the Right Bank of the Seine, this is the historical and cultural heart of Paris. It's where Paris originated on Île de la Cité (one of the area's two islands, along with Île Saint-Louis) and expanded over centuries to encompass nearby villages until it became the Paris we know today. This area houses the city's most cherished monuments including the Louvre, Jardin des Tuileries and the Notre-Dame cathedral, as well as Paris's oldest neighbourhoods dating back to medieval times including the Marais, Sentier and Les Halles. It also contains the neo-Renaissance Hôtel de Ville (the city hall of Paris) and the Avenue des Champs-Élysées, where you will find the flagship stores of some of the world's most renowned luxury brands.

At the crossroads of the Halles and Marais districts, the striking metal-and-glass Centre Pompidou art centre is expected to reopen in 2030 following a major renovation.

LOUVRE AREA

Parisians don't commonly refer to this area as a neighbourhood, but it's a useful way to describe this part of Paris Centre encompassing major attractions including the Louvre, the Jardin des Tuileries and the Palais-Royal.

The beating heart of historic and cultural Paris, the Louvre requires little introduction. Visited by up to 30,000 people per day, its vast repository of art is incomparable. Directly west of the Louvre, the Arc de Triomphe du Carrousel

spectacularly marks the entrance to the elegant Jardin des Tuileries. If you look directly through the Arc de Triomphe du Carrousel towards the Louvre, you will see the symmetry of the Axe Historique (Historical Axis). This is an astonishing alignment of monuments, buildings and thoroughfares extending west from the centre of Paris to La Défense and including the Place de la Concorde, Avenue des Champs-Élysées and the Arc de Triomphe de l'Étoile. It was not only designed for visual effect, but to symbolise the advances of France throughout its history, with La Grande Arche de la Défense designed as a symbol of modernism.

The Louvre historically served as a royal residence and the Tuileries Palace (destroyed in 1871) was used as the main residence for several French monarchs. Opposite the Louvre, the Palais-Royal also functioned as a royal residence.

Rue de Rivoli is a significant thoroughfare in the Louve district. Commissioned by Napoleon Bonaparte in the early nineteenth century and defined by its neoclassical architecture, the street was named to commemorate the 1797 Battle of Rivoli when French forces triumphed over the Austrian Army. Rue de Rivoli was expanded in the mid-eighteenth century to become a major east–west axis of the city. A more recent move to pedestrianise the centre of Paris has seen sections of the street designated for foot and bike traffic only. While this has made the area pleasant to visit and linger in, it has put more pressure on cross-city traffic – travelling by taxi or Uber through the centre of Paris is not advised!

THE MARAIS

Home to Paris's oldest planned square – Place des Vosges – the Marais is a popular hub for the millions who travel to Paris each year for fashion weeks and art fairs. It's difficult today to imagine the marshland this neighbourhood was built upon (*marais* means 'marshes'). By the fourteenth century the Marais had become affluent and many of Paris's grand *hôtels particuliers* (urban mansions) were built here by the aristocracy. In the nineteenth and early twentieth centuries the Marais became known as the city's Jewish quarter. An influx of Chinese immigrants settled around the Rue au Maire and Rue du Temple areas in the mid-twentieth century. Many have since moved on, but you can still find plenty of Chinese grocers and restaurants on Rue au Maire and Rue Volta.

The Marais is informally split into Haut Marais (Upper Marais) in the northern part of the former 3rd arrondissement and Bas Marais (Lower Marais), which covers much of the former 4th arrondissement. Haute Marais is known for its trendy boutiques, contemporary art galleries, vintage shopping and lively food scene.

Bas Marais is rich in history, featuring small medieval cobblestone streets, historic buildings and a vibrant LGBTQIA+ scene. It's also home to a Jewish community around Rue des Rosiers, where there are many kosher eateries.

LES HALLES

Les Halles has served as Paris's primary fresh food marketplace since the twelfth century, earning it the nickname 'the Belly of Paris'.

The golden wave-like Canopy of Les Halles is unmistakable, as is the Église Saint-Eustache towering over the plaza. The canopy and the Forum des Halles – an expansive underground shopping and transport hub built in 2010 – that it shades is the centre of the Les Halles neighbourhood, surrounded by the Jardin Nelson Mandela. As you approach the canopy, an underground world is dramatically revealed with many levels housing shops and the Châtelet–Les Halles métro station, the biggest métro station in Paris, with Réseau Express Régional (RER) stations serving destinations beyond the city.

SENTIER

Between Rue Montmartre to the west and Boulevard de Sébastopol to the east is the Sentier district, the historical centre of Paris's textiles and garments industries. From the early twentieth century, Jewish immigrants, especially from North Africa, settled in this district and established businesses. Jewish merchants played a significant role in making Sentier a central point for Paris's textile trade, as humorously portrayed in the cult French film *La Vérité Si Je Mens! (Would I Lie to You?)* and its sequels.

Palais Royal

Rue de l'Échaudé

5th arrondissement

Latin Quarter

HISTORICAL IDENTITY: Centre of university life since medieval times, intellectual hub

PERSONALITY: Lively, academic, bohemian

KEY SIGHTS: Jardin des Plantes, Musée National d'Histoire Naturelle, Panthéon, Sorbonne

On the Left Bank, the 5th arrondissement is one of the city's oldest districts. It is also home to the Latin Quarter, the heart of student life in Paris.

This area's roots date back to the Roman era when the city was known as Lutetia. The Romans built the Cardo Maximus (a main north–south road), thermal baths and an amphitheatre, parts of which survive as the Arènes de Lutèce ruins and gardens. The University of Paris (predecessor to the Sorbonne) was established here in the Middle Ages, attracting scholars, writers and revolutionaries to the neighbourhood over the centuries. The area's historic bookshops are remnants of this history.

The French Revolution had a profound impact on the 5th arrondissement. The Panthéon, originally a church, was repurposed as a mausoleum for national heroes. then from the nineteenth century it became the final resting place of France's greatest figures including French writers and thinkers Victor Hugo, Voltaire and Jean-Jacques Rousseau, Polish-French physicist and chemist Marie Curie and French novelist Émile Zola.

Today, the winding medieval streets near the Seine are packed with restaurants geared towards tourists. Other major sights in the 5th include the Jardin des Plantes (Paris's botanical gardens) and the Musée National d'Histoire Naturelle (Natural History Museum).

6th arrondissement

Saint-Germain-des-Prés, Odéon

HISTORICAL IDENTITY: Historic café culture, post–Second World War intellectualism

PERSONALITY: Chic, literary, artistic

KEY SIGHTS: Café de Flore, Église Saint-Germain-des-Prés, Jardin du Luxembourg, Les Deux Magots

Also known as Saint-Germain-des-Prés (or just Saint-Germain), the 6th arrondissement is one of the city's most prestigious and culturally rich districts, long associated with intellectual life, artistic movements and literary history. Its name comes from the sixth-century Abbaye de Saint-Germain-des-Prés (only the church still stands today), while the wide boulevards and elegant mansard-roofed buildings that define the 6th today are thanks to Baron Haussmann's nineteenth-century renovation of Paris (p 67).

During the Enlightenment movement that took place from the late seventeenth to the early nineteenth centuries, Saint-Germain attracted renowned philosophers and writers who would meet for lively debate at the Café Procope, the oldest café in Paris, which is still operating today. After the Second World War, Saint-Germain again became an epicentre of intellectuals during the existentialist movement, which emphasised individual freedom, authenticity and the search for meaning.

Today the 6th arrondissement remains one of the most expensive and sought-after areas to live in Paris, with the city's cleanest and best-maintained streets and public areas, including the Jardin du Luxembourg.

Maison Fleuret

HOW TO BE PARISIAN

LESSON #6

BEING PARISIAN IS NOT HAVING A DRIVER'S LICENCE OR A TV

While many people couldn't imagine life without a car, only a small percentage of Parisians own one. Some Parisians don't even bother getting their driver's licence. With more than 300 métro stations and 16 métro lines criss-crossing the city, and taxis and bicycles to fill in the gaps, why bother? But the main reason many Parisians don't own a car is because most apartments don't come with garages or even street parking. Space (of any kind) is a luxury afforded to a rare few Parisians, with a severe shortage of residential rental properties forcing most renters – especially young first-time renters – to live in apartments the size of a typical suburban bathroom; your Parisian apartment might not even have a private bathroom.

But Parisians aren't fazed by this living space issue, because Parisian life is lived outside. Parisians are incredibly social creatures and often stay out late after work to have *apéro* (p 43) with friends and colleagues. With many Parisians utilising their apartments for little more than sleeping or hosting at-home *apéro*, home furnishings like televisions are almost irrelevant.

NEIGHBOURHOODS

7th arrondissement

Invalides, Faubourg Saint-Germain

HISTORICAL IDENTITY: Aristocratic residences, military history

PERSONALITY: Elegant, affluent, institutional

KEY SIGHTS: Eiffel Tower, Les Invalides, Musée d'Orsay, Musée Rodin

Renowned for its historical significance, cultural institutions and architectural landmarks including the Eiffel Tower, the 7th arrondissement is a blend of political, cultural and residential spaces.

Originally an agricultural suburb, the area began to urbanise in the seventeenth century with the construction of the Hôtel des Invalides (commonly called Les Invalides), a hospital and retirement home for veterans that still functions today. The complex also houses military history museums, the national cathedral of the French military and Napoleon's tomb. In the eighteenth century the Faubourg Saint-Germain neighbourhood within the arrondissement became a favoured residential area for French nobility, leading to the construction of numerous aristocratic mansions. After the French Revolution many of these mansions were repurposed into government institutions including the Assemblée Nationale. The arrondissement is also home to some of the city's most important museums including the Musée d'Orsay and Musée Rodin.

Musée Rodin

8th arrondissement

Avenue des Champs-Élysées, Faubourg Saint-Honoré

HISTORICAL IDENTITY: Prestigious avenues, centre of luxury and politics

PERSONALITY: Parisian elegance and grandeur

KEY SIGHTS: Arc de Triomphe de l'Étoile, Avenue des Champs-Élysées, Palais de l'Élysée, Place de la Concorde

The prestigious 8th arrondissement is defined by grandeur, from the Arc de Triomphe de l'Étoile, to the expansive Avenue des Champs-Élysées, which leads to the extravagant Place de la Concorde. It's also the seat of the Palais de l'Élysée (Élysée Palace), the official residence of the French President since the nineteenth century. The area formed by Avenue des Champs-Élysées, Avenue Montaigne and Avenue George V is known as the 'Golden Triangle'. Home to Paris's most luxurious hotels and the opulent boutiques of major luxury brands, it's the most elegant of all Parisian neighbourhoods.

9th arrondissement

Opéra, South Pigalle, Nouvelle Athènes

HISTORICAL IDENTITY: Birthplace of Romanticism and nineteenth-century artistic movements

PERSONALITY: Trendy, local, cultural, historic

KEY SIGHTS: Musée de la Vie Romantique, Musée National Gustave Moreau, Palais Garnier

The 9th arrondissement is one of Paris's most multifaceted neighbourhoods, with the elegant Opéra district defined by the opulent Palais Garnier opera house and the Galeries Lafayette and Printemps department stores contrasting with the lively former red-light district of South Pigalle. Established in the nineteenth century, the 9th arrondissement rapidly became a hub for entertainment and commerce, its importance solidified by the 1875 construction of the Palais Garnier – a masterpiece of baroque architecture – and the development of the Grands Boulevards shopping and theatre district during the Belle Époque era.

Passage Verdeau

OPÉRA

The Opéra district is grand and elegant with the Avenue de l'Opéra leading from the Louvre to the Palais Garnier opera house. Lacking the trees that normally line Haussmann-designed avenues, it offers an unobstructed view of the Palais Garnier's grand facade, with its ornate blue dome and golden statues. The streets radiating from the Palais Garnier are filled with shops, the Galeries Lafayette department store and the historic Café de la Paix.

SOUTH PIGALLE

Located at the foot of the Butte Montmartre (Montmartre Hill), South Pigalle has evolved from a red-light district into one of Paris's trendiest neighbourhoods with many cafés, bars and boutiques. It's an increasingly popular residential area for young professionals, boasting a lively and authentic local neighbourhood vibe just streets away from touristy Montmartre.

NOUVELLE ATHÈNES

Built in the aftermath of the French Revolution and Napoleonic Wars, the Nouvelle Athènes (New Athens) district is known for its Greek Revival architecture inspired by the Romantic movement of the late eighteenth to the mid-nineteenth century. Notable figures who lived and worked here at the time include painter Eugène Delacroix, composer Frédéric Chopin and writer Alexandre Dumas. The circular Place Saint-Georges is the district's centrepiece. It's a peaceful place to sip a coffee at À La Place Saint-Georges and visit museums including the Musée de la Vie Romantique (Museum of Romantic Life) and Musée National Gustave Moreau (Gustave Moreau National Museum).

NEIGHBOURHOODS

10th arrondissement

Canal Saint-Martin, Gare du Nord

HISTORICAL IDENTITY: Industrial era developments, transportation hubs

PERSONALITY: Bohemian, diverse, bustling

KEY SIGHTS: Canal Saint-Martin, Gare de l'Est, Gare du Nord

The identity of the 10th arrondissement could not be more different from that of its neighbour the 9th. The nineteenth-century construction of the Canal Saint-Martin, an artificial canal made for moving goods between Paris's neighbourhoods and the establishment of major railway stations including the Gare du Nord and Gare de l'Est transformed this neighbourhood into a transit and logistics hub.

This is one of Paris's most multicultural neighbourhoods with Rue du Faubourg-Saint-Denis known for its Turkish delicatessens, the Porte Saint-Denis for its Kurdish bakeries and Passage Brady for its many Indian and Pakistani eateries. The Rue du Château-d'Eau, meanwhile, is known for its Afro-Caribbean hair salons.

The 10th also has its own bohemian identity with the Canal Saint-Martin area drawing artists and creatives to its cultural scene.

Canal Saint-Martin

11th arrondissement

Bastille, Oberkampf

HISTORICAL IDENTITY: Revolutionary history, working-class roots

PERSONALITY: Energetic, youthful, vibrant nightlife

KEY SIGHTS: Cirque d'Hiver, Opéra Bastille, Place de la Bastille, Rue Oberkampf

Historically a hub of artisans and craftspeople, the 11th arrondissement set the scene for some of the key events of the French Revolution. Place de la Bastille was the site of the 14 July 1789 storming of the Bastille (now commemorated as Bastille Day, France's national day), which led to the overthrow of King Charles X. The Place de la Bastille and its 47-metre-tall (154-feet-tall) July Column supporting the gilded 'Spirit of Freedom' figure commemorates the Revolution and the lives lost during it.

The 11th has more recently attracted a cohort of young Parisian creatives, professionals and expats. Key areas include Rue Oberkampf and Rue de Charonne, both dotted with boutiques, cafés, bars, live music venues and restaurants. Boulevard Voltaire is also a major thoroughfare connecting Place de la République to Place de la Nation and is lined with shops, cafés and theatres including the renowned Bataclan Theatre. Rue Amelot is home to Cirque d'Hiver, the world's oldest covered circus, and Rue du Faubourg Saint-Antoine reflects its artisanal heritage with its concentration of fashion boutiques and home decor stores. It also has a variety of dining options.

On the eastern edge of Place de la Bastille, the Opéra Bastille is one of Paris's two principal opera and ballet performance venues. The other one is Palais Garnier in the 9th arrondissement.

12th arrondissement

Bercy

HISTORICAL IDENTITY: Former wine warehouses, artisanal heritage

PERSONALITY: Modern, cultural, residential

KEY SIGHTS: Parc de Bercy, Bercy Village, Accor Arena, Viaduc des Arts

The Seine forms a natural border on the southern edge of the 12th, Paris's easternmost arrondissement. Historically a hub for trades such as carpentry and joinery, this arrondissement underwent significant urban renewal in the 1980s under then-President François Mitterrand.

'Bercy' is used to describe two local attractions: the 140-hectare Parc de Bercy, home to the Accor Arena concert venue; and the adjacent Bercy Village, a rare modern commercial centre in Paris located in renovated nineteenth-century wine storehouses. The 'village' is home to numerous big-brand shops spanning beauty to footwear, small boutiques, restaurants and cafés, and a cinema. Other local attractions include the Viaduc des Arts, a unique linear park and artisan hub adapted from an old railway viaduct. The 12th arrondissement also incorporates the Bois de Vincennes, a vast public park housing a zoo and the former royal residence Château de Vincennes.

13th arrondissement

Butte-aux-Cailles, Chinatown

HISTORICAL IDENTITY: Industrial past, immigrant communities

PERSONALITY: Village-like, multicultural, artistic

KEY SIGHTS: Bibliothèque Nationale de France, Les Olympiades, Place d'Italie

Originally an industrial suburb, the 13th arrondissement's proximity to the Bièvre river facilitated the operation of tanneries, mills and dyeing workshops. Since the 1970s and '80s, the 13th has emerged as an enclave of the Asian community. Also called the *Quartier Asiatique* (Asian Quarter), it's known for its Chinese, Vietnamese, Laotian and Cambodian communities.

The 13th is home to the François Mitterrand site of the Bibliothèque Nationale de France (National Library of France). Other places of interest include the Place d'Italie, a large circular plaza where eight major thoroughfares of the 13th arrondissement meet; and Les Olympiades, a modern residential district built in the 1960s and '70s that feels like it could be in Hong Kong.

The neighbourhood also hides a lesser-known village-like neighbourhood called Butte-aux-Cailles, which evokes Montmartre with its narrow cobblestone streets.

CAFE
coffee
et
couleurs
toute la
Journée
tabac
NEXT DOOR
TABAC

METRO

LESSON #7

BEING PARISIAN IS 'NOT BAD'

Complaining is a beloved pastime in Paris, but that's not to say that Parisians are negative or pessimistic – it's simply a different form of expression entwined with the French language. For example, on a sunny day a Parisian is more likely to say, 'Wow, for once it's not raining!' rather than, 'It's such a nice day.'

When something is just okay, they say '*c'est bien*' ('it's good'), but when something is great, they say '*pas mal*' ('not bad') – a sincere compliment. If something is really bad but not a complete disaster, they say '*pas terrible*' ('not terrible'). The quality of something in French, therefore, is based on the level of how 'not bad' it is.

This goes hand-in-hand with the brand of nonchalance Parisians are renowned for. In Australia, where I grew up, there is a cultural obligation to express warmth and enthusiasm towards each other, even if you don't mean it. Parisians, on the other hand, aren't big on small talk and pleasantries, so don't be surprised if your comment about, say, the cold weather, is met with a straight-faced: 'Yes, it's winter. What do you expect?' This lack of social obligation to be agreeable can also be seen in a Parisian's eagerness to engage in heated intellectual conversation in a way that might seem intense for foreigners. Launching into a discussion with a stranger on the street about the state of the French economy or the politics of dog-owner behaviour is not unusual in Paris. When they do not agree with another person's opinions, they are certainly not afraid to say so.

It is this approach to life that probably gave Parisians a reputation for being rude, but I see it as refreshing honesty. With the French saying exactly what they think and saving compliments for when they are really deserved, you could argue that a compliment from a French person is the most authentic compliment of all.

14th arrondissement

Montparnasse, Parc Montsouris

HISTORICAL IDENTITY: Early twentieth-century artistic hub, intellectual gatherings

PERSONALITY: Residential, serene

KEY SIGHTS: Cimetière du Montparnasse, Les Catacombs de Paris, Parc Montsouris, Tour Montparnasse

In the south of Paris, the 14th arrondissement is best known for the Tour Montparnasse, one of the only high-rise buildings outside of the La Défense business district. Upon its 1973 completion, it was the tallest building in Paris. Building height restrictions that preserve Paris's skyline mean the tower stands out dramatically and offers a unique panoramic view of the city from its 56th-floor observation deck.

While the 14th is known predominantly as a residential neighbourhood, there are several sights here. The Cimetière du Montparnasse houses the graves of many historical figures including existentialist philosophers Jean-Paul Sartre and Simone de Beauvoir, and nineteenth-century poet Charles Baudelaire; and the Parc Montsouris is one of the city's largest green spaces. Le Catacombs de Paris – the extensive network of underground tunnels constructed in the seventeenth century that hold the remains of over six million Parisians – is also found here.

15th arrondissement

Grenelle, Javel

HISTORICAL IDENTITY: Industrial history, post-war urban development

PERSONALITY: Spacious, residential

KEY SIGHTS: Île aux Cygnes, Parc André Citroën, Parc des Expositions

Incorporating the former villages of Vaugirard – known for its vineyards and stone quarries – and Grenelle and Javel, the 15th arrondissement in the southwest of Paris is still known colloquially by its old village names.

Today, the 15th is predominantly residential, but it also contains a number of sights including Parc des Expositions, a major exhibition centre that regularly hosts trade fairs; the Parc André-Citroën, a vast contemporary park located on the former Citroën car factory site with a tethered helium balloon you can take a ride in; and the Musée Bourdelle sculpture museum. There is also the Centre Commercial Beaugrenelle, a large modern retail complex on the Seine; and Île aux Cygnes, a narrow artificial island park.

Musée Bourdelle

Place du Trocadéro (left);
Palais de Tokyo (right)

16th arrondissement

Passy, Auteuil, Chaillot

HISTORICAL IDENTITY: Upper-class residential areas, architectural heritage

PERSONALITY: Quiet, affluent, traditional

KEY SIGHTS: Bois de Boulogne, Maison de Balzac, Musée Marmottan Monet, Place du Trocadéro, Pont de Bir-Hakeim

The 16th arrondissement was created during the 1860 expansion of Paris. Incorporating the former villages of Passy, Auteuil and Chaillot, it became an affluent and stately neighbourhood over time, comparable to New York's Upper East Side or London's Kensington. It's home to the Place du Trocadéro, the world-famous square facing the Eiffel Tower across the Seine.

Beyond the Place du Trocadéro the 16th has a number of notable sights including the Musée Marmottan Monet, dedicated to the works of Claude Monet; the Maison de Balzac, the former home of novelist Honoré de Balzac; and one of Paris's largest parks, the Bois de Boulogne. The 16th is connected to the 15th by a unique two-level bridge, the Pont de Bir-Hakeim.

17th arrondissement

Batignolles

HISTORICAL IDENTITY: Village origins, nineteenth-century urbanisation

PERSONALITY: Trendy, artistic, local

KEY SIGHTS: Marché des Batignolles, Parc Clichy-Batignolles – Martin Luther King

On the northwestern edge of Paris, the 17th arrondissement is a large, mainly residential neighbourhood historically defined by the contrasting affluent Ternes and Monceau districts around the Parc Monceau and the working-class area of Batignolles.

The arrondissement has undergone major urban development, with rapidly gentrifying Batignolles now a lively neighbourhood of village-like cobblestone streets filled with trendy cafés, restaurants and independent boutiques. The Parc Clichy-Batignolles – Martin Luther King, completed in 2021, saw old railway yards transformed into a 10-hectare (24.7-acre) modern park and residential district with commercial spaces including the Marché des Batignolles (Batignolles Market).

NEIGHBOURHOODS

18th arrondissement

Montmartre, Pigalle, La Goutte d'Or

HISTORICAL IDENTITY: Bohemian enclave, historic arts community

PERSONALITY: Artistic, multicultural, village-like, lively

KEY SIGHTS: Basilique du Sacré-Coeur, Marché Dejean, Moulin Rouge, Place du Tertre

On the northern fringe of the city, the 18th arrondissement is one of Paris's most culturally and historically rich neighbourhoods, intimately linked with the bohemian movement of the Belle Époque era. One of the largest arrondissements, the 18th is also diverse with the quaint historical buildings of Montmartre contrasting with the flamboyant cabaret theatres of Pigalle and the grittier, more multicultural neighbourhoods of La Goutte d'Or (home to the West African–focused market, Marché Dejean) and La Chapelle.

Though not technically in the 18th, the Marché aux Puces de Saint-Ouen – one of the world's biggest flea markets – is also associated with this arrondissement.

NEIGHBOURHOODS

MONTMARTRE

Perched atop Butte Montmartre, a 130-metre (426.5-foot) hill at the highest point of Paris, Montmartre has played a key role in shaping Paris's identity over centuries. Formerly a rural village known for its vineyards and windmills (only two of which remain), Montmartre means 'mount of martyrs', a reference to the execution of Saint Denis, the first bishop of Paris, who was beheaded by the Romans on this hill in the third century. This established Montmartre as a sacred site, leading to the twelfth-century Saint-Pierre de Montmartre church and the Abbaye de Montmartre (Montmartre Abbey), which was destroyed during the French Revolution (its church still stands).

In the late nineteenth century, attracted by its affordable living conditions and liberal atmosphere, Montmartre became a magnet for artists including Pablo Picasso and Vincent van Gogh.

The bohemian spirit they cultivated here lives on in areas like the Place du Tertre, which is always filled with street artists; the Bateau-Lavoir, a historic artist's residence; and Le Chat Noir, a popular gathering spot for artists. The streets are filled with former art studios, characterised by their large glass windows.

Montmartre is especially crowded on weekends with both international and French tourists. But it's easy enough to escape the crowds in the village-like neighbourhood's labyrinthine streets. At the centre of Montmartre is the Basilique du Sacré-Coeur, whose terrace offers spectacular views of Paris.

PIGALLE

South of Montmartre and bordering the 9th arrondissement, Pigalle is best known as Paris's red-light district. Its development as the entertainment hub of Paris began in the late nineteenth century, when Paris experienced a cultural and social transformation that embraced more liberal attitudes toward sexuality. Racy cabaret theatres like the infamous Moulin Rouge were established, which over time were followed by the sex shops and strip clubs found here today.

These venues now coexist with Pigalle's modern personality as a hub of the Parisian music scene, with live music venues including La Cigale, Le Trianon and La Machine du Moulin Rouge. There is also a high concentration of music shops, particularly along Rue de Douai, focusing mostly on guitars, digital pianos and DJ equipment.

Rue du Mont-Cenis

Hotel Amour

19th arrondissement

La Villette, Buttes-Chaumont

HISTORICAL IDENTITY: Industrial past, nineteenth-century park developments

PERSONALITY: Cultural institutions, green spaces

KEY SIGHTS: Cité des Sciences et de l'Industrie, Parc des Buttes-Chaumont, Parc de la Villette

Occupying the northeastern corner of Paris, the 19th arrondissement's main sights include the rolling hills of Parc des Buttes-Chaumont and Parc de la Villette, Paris's largest park. Located in the latter is Cité des Sciences et de l'Industrie, Europe's largest science museum; and the Philharmonie de Paris concert hall complex. Picturesque promenades follow the banks of the arrondissement's canals – Canal de l'Ourcq and Canal Saint-Denis – which converge at Bassin de la Villette, a popular spot for boating and leisure.

20th arrondissement

Belleville, Ménilmontant

HISTORICAL IDENTITY: Working-class neighbourhoods, waves of foreign immigration

PERSONALITY: Bohemian, multicultural

KEY SIGHTS: Cimetière du Père Lachaise, Parc de Belleville, Rue de Ménilmontant

Located on the city's eastern edge, the 20th arrondissement was annexed to Paris in 1860 by combining outlying villages including Belleville and Ménilmontant. These areas were known for their working-class populations and artisanal industries.

The most famous landmark in the 20th is Cimetière du Père-Lachaise (Père-Lachaise Cemetery), the largest cemetery in Paris and the final resting place of numerous notable Parisian residents including Irish writer Oscar Wilde and French singer Édith Piaf.

Over time, the 20th arrondissement has attracted immigrants from many countries, and since the 1980s the Belleville area has become known as Paris's Chinatown, with many renowned Chinese restaurants and grocery shops.

MICHEL
96
SOLDES
-50%
LE SAINT GERVAIS
RESTAURANT
SAUF

André R. CHOUKROUN

ITINERARIES

Pont Saint-Michel

INTRODUCTION

Revealing local secrets and immersing you in beautiful spaces and artisan communities, the itineraries that follow are designed to distil the essence of Paris in one week, with each single-day itinerary focusing on a specific theme. Rather than packing in too much, each itinerary encourages you to embrace the city's *flâneur* identity – to take time to savour and observe. Before you hit the streets of Paris, here are a few tips.

——— These seven itineraries can be enjoyed in any order, but consider your timing. It's a peculiarity of Paris that many businesses close on Mondays and Sundays, and most museums close on Tuesdays. (For the opening days of Paris's best-known museums, see pp 334–7).

——— For each day, I've included several additional venues in the area that you can mix and match to personalise your experience. Venues with no entry fee are also noted.

——— Be prepared to spend a fair bit of time exploring on foot. In other words, choose your footwear carefully. I recommend comfortable thick-soled sandals or sneakers, unless my tip for the day suggests otherwise.

——— Bring a chic jacket to throw on over summer clothes as evenings can be cool, and layer up in winter. It's easier, and usually cheaper, to bring your own rain gear and a reusable water bottle to refill at your hotel before you head out for the day, as drinking fountains aren't always easy to find.

——— Most itineraries are contained within one neighbourhood for ease of exploring on foot, but some days will see you cross two or three neighbourhoods, which may require a taxi, Uber, métro or bicycle journey (p 49).

——— Be mindful that pickpockets and unscrupulous vendors operate across the city. Keep a close eye on your possessions, especially your mobile phone, and politely but firmly turn away any strangers who approach you to fill in a survey or to offer 'free' products as you explore Paris.

Bonnes découvertes!

Le Dilettante bookshop

DAY 1

KEY NEIGHBOURHOODS

CONCORDE

LOUVRE AREA

SAINT-HONORÉ–PLACE VENDÔME

This itinerary invites you to experience the heart of Paris like a *flâneur*, taking you on a leisurely discovery of some of the city's most famous parks, museums and monuments. From the symmetrical gardens of the Jardin des Tuileries to the grand courtyards of the Louvre and the gilded Pont Alexandre III bridge, this is Paris at its most iconic. Savour the sights, as well as the many opportunities to recharge at cafés along your route.

THE BIG SIGHTS

The Eiffel Tower from Pont Alexandre III

ITINERARY

This itinerary is recommended on

MONDAY
WEDNESDAY
THURSDAY
FRIDAY
SATURDAY

TIPS

Some locations, including museums and upscale shops, expect a degree of formality, so **AVOID WEARING VERY CASUAL CLOTHING OR SPORTSWEAR.**

BOOK TICKETS to major attractions including the Musée du Louvre (p 115) **IN ADVANCE TO GET IN FASTER.**

AVOID CROWDS at the Musée du Louvre by planning to visit on a Friday evening, when it's open until 9.45 pm. Mondays and Wednesdays are typically the busiest.

Be particularly wary of **PICKPOCKETS** at major attractions.

You can usually get a table at **BOFINGER** (p 135) without a reservation, but to be sure, **BOOK AHEAD.**

DAY 1

RUE TRONCHET
9TH
RUE SCRIBE
BOULEVARD HAUSSMANN
Richelieu-Drouot
BOULEVARD MONTMARTRE
RUE
Grands Boulevards
BOULEVARD DES ITALIENS
Opéra
BOULEVARD DES CAPUCINES
Madeleine
2ND
RICHELIEU
VIVIENNE
RUE DU QUATRE SEPTEMBRE
Quatre Septembre
BOULEVARD DE LA MADELEINE
RUE DES CAPUCINES
RUE DE LA PAIX
Ultramod
MONTMARTRE
GAILLON
AVENUE
RUE DANIELLE CASANOVA
PLACE-VENDÔME
Bourse
RUE RÉAUMUR
Bibliothèque Nationale de France Richelieu
Librairie Jousseaume
3
Rue Saint-Honoré
15
17
Place Vendôme
RUE DES PETITS CHAMPS
DE
2
Le Valentin Vivienne
18
Ex Nihilo
1
RUE DE RIVOLI
L'Ingénieur Chevallier
Pyramides
Galerie Vivienne
RUE ÉTIENNE MARCEL
19
16
Angelina
Santa Maria Novella
L'OPÉRA
RUE
PALAIS-ROYAL
Tuileries
RUE DES PYRAMIDES
Merci #2
LOUVRE
Musée National Picasso
8
7
4
Palais-Royal
PARIS CENTRE
Jardin des Tuileries
Café Kitsuné – Louvre
RUE SAINT-HONORÉ
DU
HALLES
AVENUE DU GÉNÉRAL LEMONNIER
1ST
Palais Royal–Musée du Louvre
QUAI AIMÉ CÉSAIRE
RUE DE
La Distillerie de l'Arbre Sec
PLACE DU CARROUSEL
5
Musée du Louvre
QUAI VALÉRY GISCARD D'ESTAING
QUAI FRANÇOIS MITTERRAND
RUE DE L'AMIRAL DE COLIGNY
Louvre-Rivoli
RIVOLI
Pont Royal
Musée d'Orsay
Pont du Carrousel
Samaritaine
QUAI VOLTAIRE
La Seine
6
Pont Neuf
RUE DU BAC
Bouquinistes de Paris
QUAI DE LA MÉGISSERIE
RUE DE LILLE
QUAI DE CONTI
Neuf
RUE DE L'UNIVERSITÉ
RUE DES SAINTS-PÈRES
RUE BONAPARTE
6TH
Pont
20
Bofinger
SAINT-GERMAIN-DES-PRÉS
MONNAIE
1ST

ITINERARY

④ Palais-Royal

MORNING

—— Make your way to Bourse métro station and begin your day nearby at ① **Galerie Vivienne** (p 111), one of Paris's oldest and most beautiful covered malls. Have breakfast at ② **Le Valentin Vivienne** (p 137), a tearoom known for its homemade sweet treats and savoury dishes, then explore the Galerie, making sure to stop by historical bookshop ③ **Librairie Jousseaume** (p 127).

① Galerie Vivienne

—— Exit Galerie Vivienne onto Rue des Petits Champs and enter the gardens of the ④ **Palais-Royal** (p 119) via its colonnaded rear entrance on Rue de Beaujolais. Stroll through the gardens, observing local life, en route to the Cour d'Honneur where you will find the striking *Les Deux Plateaux,* better known as the *Colonnes de Buren* (*Buren Columns*), a modern art installation by the French artist Daniel Buren.

—— Leave the Palais-Royal through its south entrance beside the Comédie-Française, cross Rue Saint-Honoré and Rue de Rivoli and enter the Louvre courtyard through Passage de Richelieu. As your eyes adjust to the light, take in the modern glass Pyramide du Louvre, contrasted against the ornate twelfth-century architecture.

⑤ Musée du Louvre (opposite)

ITINERARY

AFTERNOON

——— Spend the afternoon exploring the immense ⑤ **Musée du Louvre** (p 115) and then skip ahead to the evening itinerary, or save the museum for another day and continue east through the Louvre courtyard to the Cour Carrée (Square Court). Marvel at the extravagant architecture then exit the museum grounds onto Rue de l'Amiral de Coligny. Turn right and head south toward the Right Bank of the Seine. Then turn left along the Quai du Louvre and you will be in the midst of the ⑥ ***Bouquinistes*** (booksellers) **de Paris** (p 110), which stretch along both banks of the Seine.

——— Retrace your steps to the courtyard of the Louvre. From the Place du Carrousel, head north and stop for lunch at ⑦ **Café Kitsuné – Louvre** (p 135), which serves classic French café dishes with a Japanese twist. Grab a seat on the second floor overlooking the picturesque Place André Malraux and watch life go by below.

⑧ Jardin des Tuileries

⑥ Bouquinistes de Paris

—— After lunch, return to Place du Carrousel and head west through the Arc de Triomphe du Carrousel, the neoclassical arch that marks the entrance to the ⑧ **Jardin des Tuileries** (Tuileries Garden, p 113). Take a leisurely stroll through the expansive garden, admiring its symmetrical tree-lined walks and large fountains, and maybe take a seat on the iconic park chairs and blend in with the locals.

—— Continue through the garden to the ⑨ **Musée de l'Orangerie** (p 117) to marvel at Claude Monet's magnificent *Nymphéas* (*Water Lilies*) series.

—— Exit the museum via its west entrance and make your way to ⑩ **Place de la Concorde** (p 120). Admire the immense square's 3000-year-old Luxor Obelisk and the views of the Eiffel Tower to the southwest. Then head south toward the Seine, and before the Pont de la Concorde (Concorde Bridge) turn right onto Quai des Tuileries and follow this road as it slopes down to meet the riverside Port de la Concorde. Stroll west along this picturesque path to ⑪ **Pont Alexandre III** (p 122). Linger for a while to admire the gilded lampposts and statues of the famous bridge, and the Eiffel Tower across the river.

—— Head north on Avenue Winston Churchill to visit the iconic ⑫ **Grand Palais** (p 112) and the ⑬ **Petit Palais** (p 119) opposite. Along with the Eiffel Tower, these venues were built for the 1900 Exposition Universelle (also known as the world's fair) and continue to hosts events and exhibitions today.

—— Take a taxi (or rent a bike and cycle) to the ⑭ **Laulhère** boutique (p 126) on Rue du Faubourg Saint-Honoré to browse its selection of authentic French berets made via traditional techniques. Indulge in some retail therapy as you wander east along the luxury boutique-lined streets of Rue du Faubourg Saint-Honoré and ⑮ **Rue Saint-Honoré** (p 123).

Concorde métro station

EVENING

——— After all that shopping, take a break at ⑯ **Angelina** (p 134), an historic café on Rue de Rivoli, and taste its famous thick and rich hot chocolate, as well as its signature Mont Blanc (chestnut dessert) if you fancy a sweet treat. There's often a queue to enter Angelina – afternoons are generally quieter.

——— Explore the extravagant octagonal square of ⑰ **Place Vendôme** (p 121) during the golden hour (the soft light before sunset), admiring the light play on its gilded classical symmetry and the monumental Colonne Vendôme (Vendôme Column). Then step back onto Rue Saint-Honoré to visit the stores of two of my favourite perfume brands: ⑱ **Ex Nihilo** (p 124), an innovative independent Parisian perfumery combining traditional techniques with new technology to create customised scents; and ⑲ **Santa Maria Novella** (p 132), one of the world's oldest pharmacies.

——— For a dinner befitting your visits to some of the city's most iconic sights, head to ⑳ **Bofinger** (p 135), the epitome of the great Parisian brasserie of la Belle Époque (the Beautiful Era). Typical of Parisian brasseries, the menu is traditional Alsatian cuisine, which gained popularity in nineteenth-century Paris.

⑰ Place Vendôme

⑱ Ex Nihilo

⑳ Bofinger

This is FREE | Additional VENUE

Bibliothèque Nationale de France Richelieu
—— LIBRARY

The Richelieu branch of the National Library dates back to 1721, when Abbé Bignon, librarian to King Louis XV, initiated the relocation of the royal library from the Louvre to its current location. It officially became the Bibliothèque Nationale during the French Revolution, when its collections expanded with confiscated works from aristocratic estates and religious institutions.

The highlight of the library is the magnificent Oval Reading Room, which features nine interconnected domes, each supported by slender cast-iron columns. The library is open to the public free of charge and is a favourite haunt of students who come here to study.

ADDRESS: *58 Rue de Richelieu*

ARRONDISSEMENT: *Paris Centre*

CLOSEST MÉTRO STATION: *Bourse*

Bouquinistes de Paris

—— BOOKSTALLS

The rows of forest-green bookstalls lining the stone walls along the banks of the Siene are one of the most emblematic images of Paris. You may recall the scene in Woody Allen's *Midnight in Paris* (2011) where Gil browses the stalls while reflecting on his longing for the city's 'golden age'. These unique stalls are collectively known as the *bouquinistes* (booksellers) de Paris.

The tradition of selling books on the banks of the Seine began in the sixteenth century with itinerant peddlers known as *colporteurs*, who sold books and pamphlets from portable stalls. The practice became so commonplace that in 1859 city authorities granted *bouquinistes* the right to establish fixed stalls along the riverbanks. Each was allocated 10 metres (33 feet) of railing, and by 1891 they were permitted to leave their boxes attached to the railings permanently. In 1930 the dimensions of the boxes were standardised, resulting in the uniform look of the stalls.

Today the stalls occupy 3 kilometres (1.8 miles) along the Seine: between Pont Marie to the Quai du Louvre on the Right Bank and from the Quai de la Tournelle to the Quai Voltaire on the Left Bank. It's a quintessential Parisian experience to browse the stalls on a sunny day.

The 240 approved stalls have remained rent free and are often passed down through familial generations. *Bouquinistes* must adhere to strict rules such as maintaining a specific ratio of books to other items, keeping their stalls in good condition and respecting the heritage of the trade.

During preparations for the Paris 2024 Summer Olympics, a proposal to temporarily remove many of the *bouquinistes'* stalls for safety reasons caused such an outcry that President Emmanuel Macron intervened to halt the plan. This icon of Paris also inspired Chanel's 2018 autumn/winter haute couture show, which featured a realistic replica of the *bouquinistes* on the Grand Palais (p 112) runway.

ADDRESS: *Banks of the Seine in Paris Centre*

ARRONDISSEMENT: *Paris Centre*

CLOSEST MÉTRO STATION: *Pont Neuf or Saint-Michel Notre-Dame*

Galerie Vivienne

—— ARCADE

I've always loved the beautifully decorated *passages couverts* (covered arcades) of Paris, most of which have glass roofs that let natural light beam down onto their mosaic floors. Built in 1826, Galerie Vivienne is one of Paris's most beautiful *passages couverts*. Designed by architect François-Jean Delannoy in the neoclassical Pompeian style and characterised by its harmonious proportions and elegant decorative elements, the arcade showcases motifs symbolising success and prosperity. A spectacular glass canopy extends over the entire length of the gallery, culminating in a rotunda with a hemispherical glass dome, and the floors are adorned with intricate mosaics crafted by Italian mosaicist Giandomenico Facchina.

Galerie Vivienne historically housed a variety of high-end shops including tailors, bootmakers, wine merchants and booksellers. The rise of the great department stores such as Galeries Lafayette (p 261) and Le Bon Marche (p 232) triggered the decline of the *passages couverts* as commercial centres, but these days they are enjoying a revival as shopping destinations. Plus, Galerie Vivienne still houses historic and rare shops including the Librairie Jousseaume (p 127) bookshop.

ADDRESS: *4 Rue des Petits Champs*

ARRONDISSEMENT: *Paris Centre*

CLOSEST MÉTRO STATION: *Bourse*

Grand Palais

Jardin des Tuileries

Grand Palais

—— EXHIBITION HALL

With its glass barrel-vaulted roof dominating the skyline along the Seine, the Grand Palais exhibition hall – built for the 1900 world's fair – is one of the city's most recognisable landmarks.

Its immense glass dome was the largest in Europe upon its opening, the steel framework rivalling the complexity of the Eiffel Tower. The grandeur of this enormous structure (it has 72,000 square metres (236,220 square feet) of floor space) is elevated when sunlight floods into the expansive space, making you feel small amidst its extravagant proportions.

The Grand Palais has hosted some of the most significant events of Paris over the years, including fencing and taekwondo events during the Paris 2024 Summer Olympics. In winter it transforms into one of the world's largest indoor ice rinks. The Grand Palais is also indelibly linked with French fashion culture; since 2006 it has been the official venue of the Chanel runway shows. During the late Karl Lagerfeld's tenure at the brand's helm, the venue was transformed by fantastical sets including a life-sized cruise ship, a beach with sand and undulating waves, and even a fully stocked supermarket complete with Chanel-branded goods.

ADDRESS: *3 Avenue du Général Eisenhower*

ARRONDISSEMENT: *8th*

CLOSEST MÉTRO STATION: *Champs-Élysées–Clemenceau*

Jardin des Tuileries

—— GARDEN

The Jardin du Tuileries (Tuileries Garden) is an expansive and picturesque garden connecting the Louvre (p 115) and the Place de la Concorde (p 120). Lined with chestnut trees, it was originally created in 1594 at the behest of Catherine de' Medici as the garden of the Palais des Tuileries (Tuileries Palace) and was opened to the public in 1667. Named after the *tuileries* (tile factories) that once stood on the site, the garden was originally designed in the Italian Renaissance style and was later remodelled in the style of the gardens of Versailles, featuring meticulously symmetrical pathways, geometrically arranged flower beds and manicured lawns.

The garden is beloved for its wealth of public art. Classic works include *Mercury Riding Pegasus* by Antoine Coysevox, *Nymph with a Shell* by Louis Auguste Lévêque and *Theseus and the Minotaur* by Étienne-Jules Ramey, while contemporary highlights include various works by Aristide Maillol. There are more sculptures hidden in the Hedge Garden, where art students can often be seen practicing their sketching.

During summer and winter the Fête de Tuileries Paris (Tuileries Funfair) sets up next to the Rue de Rivoli with a ferris wheel offering a unique view of the city over the Place de la Concorde. The garden also hosts other events and art fairs throughout the year, notably the Dior ready-to-wear runway show that transforms the garden during fashion week. While professional photography is prohibited in the Jardin des Tuileries, it's allowed in the Hedge Garden.

ADDRESS: *Place de la Concorde*

ARRONDISSEMENT: *Paris Centre*

CLOSEST MÉTRO STATION: *Tuileries*

Musée du Louvre

—— ART MUSEUM

The world's most famous museum was originally built as a twelfth-century fortress intended to protect Paris from Viking invasion. The building now known simply as the Louvre was also a royal palace until King Louis XIV moved his court to the Palace of Versailles. It finally became a public museum in 1793 during the French Revolution. Its collection of over 500,000 pieces spanning 9000 years of history includes some of the world's most iconic masterpieces, chief among them are Leonardo da Vinci's *Mona Lisa* and the ancient Greek *Venus de Milo* sculpture, whose captivating mystery is in her broken arms, which have never been definitively reconstructed to show how the figure originally appeared.

Designed by Chinese-American architect I. M. Pei, the Louvre Pyramid rising above the museum courtyard was mercilessly criticised for destroying the historical aesthetics of the museum when it was unveiled in 1989. But it's now an iconic feature that never fails to captivate me when I come here for photoshoots or pass through the museum courtyard on my way between the Left Bank and Right Bank.

Get ahead of the crowds and plan your visit in advance – the official website has a downloadable map and an interactive floor plan. If time is tight, you might want to beeline for the Denon wing housing the aforementioned masterpieces alongside similary iconic works such as Eugène Delacroix's *Liberty Leading the People*. My favourite part of the Louvre is the Court Marly in the Richelieu wing, known for its seventeenth-century classical French baroque sculptures that once adorned the royal gardens of the Palace of Versailles. Arranged on stepped terraces in dramatic groupings, the figures depict mythological gods, heroes and equestrian statues of famous military leaders. Intended to celebrate the grandeur of the French monarchy, these statues now stand as models for the young modern bohemians of Paris – art and design students – who gather in the Court Marly to sketch.

One of the Louvre's best kept secrets is its École du Louvre (Louvre School), which holds regular public lectures and seminars (in French) on art and history.

ADDRESS: *Rue de Rivoli*

ARRONDISSEMENT: *Paris Centre*

CLOSEST MÉTRO STATION: *Palais Royal–Musée du Louvre or Louvre–Rivoli*

Additional VENUE

Musée National Picasso

—— ART MUSEUM

Many influential figures who helped create our modern notion of French-ness were not French at all. Take Italian noblewoman Catherine de' Medici, whose patronage of architecture in the sixteenth century shaped the face of today's Paris; and German-born Karl Lagerfeld, who, in his 36 years as creative director at Chanel, defined Parisian chic. And there's Spaniard Pablo Picasso, whose artistic legacy is firmly rooted in France. His life and works are celebrated in a number of museums in Paris, but fans shouldn't miss the Musée National Picasso. Established in 1985, the museum is housed in the Hôtel Salé, a grand seventeenth-century mansion that at one point was a school attended by celebrated novelist Honoré de Balzac.

The museum's 5000-strong collection of paintings, sculptures, drawings and prints spreads over five levels. A grand staircase on the ground floor – based on Michelangelo's design for the Laurentian Library in Florence – sweeps up to the first floor, which is dedicated to Picasso's early works and his Blue Period. The second floor focuses on his Cubist works and sculptures, while the third floor contains Picasso's personal archives of photographs, sketches and letters. Featuring a spectacular glass ceiling, the top floor hosts temporary exhibitions.

Additionally, the museum houses Picasso's personal collection of works by other artists such as Renoir, Cézanne and Matisse.

ADDRESS: *5 Rue de Thorigny*

ARRONDISSEMENT: *Paris Centre*

CLOSEST MÉTRO STATION: *Saint-Sébastien–Froissart*

Musée de l'Orangerie

ART MUSEUM

With its long, cold and sunless winters, Paris is generally not conducive to growing orange trees, yet they were all the rage in the seventeenth century and onwards, with many orangeries constructed to shelter them. Built by Napoleon III in the southwest corner of the Jardin des Tuileries (p 113) in 1852 to store the garden's citrus trees in winter, the *orangerie* was transformed in the 1920s to house impressionist Claude Monet's *Nymphéas* (Water Lilies) series – painted when he was going blind due to cataracts. Eight large-scale paintings from the *Nymphéas* series are displayed in two oval-shaped rooms, creating an immersive panoramic effect.

With large windows designed to allow optimal light for the orange trees that used to be housed inside, the museum also showcases the Walter-Guillaume Collection featuring artworks by Paul Cézanne, Henri Matisse, Amedeo Modigliani, Pablo Picasso, Pierre-Auguste Renoir and others.

ADDRESS: *Jardin des Tuileries*

ARRONDISSEMENT: *Paris Centre*

CLOSEST MÉTRO STATION: *Concorde*

Additional VENUE

Musée d'Orsay

—— ART MUSEUM

Home to the world's largest collection of Impressionist and Postimpressionist art, the Musée d'Orsay is exalted ground for nineteenth-century art lovers. Its establishment was instrumental to cementing the place in the art world of artists such as Claude Monet and Pierre-Auguste Renoir.

Before the museum was established in 1986, nineteenth-century art was scattered across the museums of Paris with no single institution dedicated to this important period. An initiative to highlight the artists and works of this era saw the disused Gare d'Orsay train station, originally built for the 1900 word's fair, transformed into a museum. The station's iconic architecture was largely preserved including its curved glass roof and airy open spaces, where modern concrete structures juxtapose with the building's decorative Beaux-Arts design.

The museum now holds France's most treasured collection of masterpieces from 1848 to 1914 with highlights including Claude Monet's *Impression, Sunrise*, Édouard Manet's *Olympia* and Edgar Degas's *The Ballet Class*. Other notable works include Vincent Van Gogh's *Starry Night Over the Rhône* and *Self-Portrait*, and a bronze cast of Auguste Rodin's *The Thinker* (the original is housed at the Musée Rodin, p 195).

Dramatically located behind the museum's iconic clock, the Café Campana is a great spot for a break.

ADDRESS: *Esplanade Valéry Giscard d'Estaing*

ARRONDISSEMENT: *Paris Centre*

CLOSEST MÉTRO STATION: *Assemblée Nationale*

This is FREE

Palais-Royal

—— PALACE

Originally built in 1639 as the personal residence of King Louis XIII's chief minister, Cardinal Richelieu, this opulent palace became royal property upon his death just three years later and remained a royal residence for nearly 140 years. In 1780 it came into the possession of Louis Philippe II, who turned it into a commercial enterprise by building apartments and commercial spaces, and opening the gardens and arcades to the public. The Palais-Royal soon became the entertainment centre of Paris, its popularity among gamblers richly described by Honoré de Balzac in his story of a young Parisian aristocratic wannabe in *Le Père Goriot* (1835). Today the Palais-Royal houses several major institutions including the Ministry of Culture.

Many tourists don't make it past French artist Daniel Buren's sculptural artwork, *Colonnes de Buren,* in the Cour d'Honneur – the formal approach to the Palais-Royal. But it's worth continuing into the garden, where tree-lined paths lead the eye toward the magnificent former palace, Grecian statues peak out among rose bushes and manicured hedges demarcate mini-gardens furnished with park chairs and benches. It's an unexpected place to observe well-dressed Parisians in their natural habitat. Yes, it's the same park from the first season of *Emily in Paris* (2020) where the title character first meets her friend, Mindy Chen.

ADDRESS: *Rue Saint-Honoré*

ARRONDISSEMENT: *Paris Centre*

CLOSEST MÉTRO STATION: *Palais Royal–Musée du Louvre*

This is FREE

Petit Palais

—— ART MUSEUM

Opposite the Grand Palais (p 112), the Petit Palais was also constructed for the 1900 world's fair. A masterpiece in its own right, its grand staircase leads visitors through the entrance with its decorated arch and gilded wrought-iron gate, while the interior is intricately decorated with mosaics, murals and sculptures. There's also a charming semicircular inner garden bordered by a richly decorated peristyle (row of columns that forms a continuous porch).

The Petit Palais now houses the Musée des Beaux-Arts de la Ville de Paris (City of Paris Museum of Fine Arts). The museum's collection spans works from antiquity to 1914 and includes a magnificent collection of eighteenth- and nineteenth-century paintings by the likes of Paul Cézanne, Claude Monet and Camille Pissarro. The permanent collections are free to visit.

ADDRESS: *5 Avenue Dutuit*

ARRONDISSEMENT: *8th*

CLOSEST MÉTRO STATION: *Champs-Élysées–Clemenceau*

Place de la Concorde

—— SQUARE

In the very centre of Paris, Place de la Concorde is the city's largest and one of its most historically significant squares. Among the many historic events that took place here, the most notable are the executions of King Louis XVI and Marie Antoinette. Renamed Place de la Révolution during the French Revolution, the original name was restored in 1795 as a reconciliatory gesture – *concorde* means harmony or agreement.

The eighteenth-century square features an octagonal layout bordered by moats (now filled in) and stone balustrades, forming a grand esplanade connecting the Avenue des Champs-Élysées to the Jardin des Tuileries (p 113). The entrance to the Jardin des Tuileries to the east is marked by an ornate gilded wrought-iron gate flanked by two equestrian sculptures: *Fame Riding Pegasus* and *Mercury Riding Pegasus* by Antoine Coysevox. (Like many outdoor sculptures in Paris, these are replicas with the originals housed in the Louvre.) Connected to the southern side of the square is the Pont de la Concorde, which bridges the Seine.

Dominating the centre of Place de la Concorde is the 23-metre-high (76-foot-high) Luxor Obelisk, a 3000-year-old monument gifted by Egypt in the 1830s. German-born French architect Jacques-Ignace Hittorff designed the two gorgeous fountains that flank the obelisk: the Fontaine des Mers to the south, celebrating maritime navigation; and the Fontaine des Fleuves to the north, symbolising river navigation. These fountains are adorned with intricate sculptures of deities and aquatic motifs, taking inspiration from the fountains of St Peter's Square in Rome.

On the east side of the square stands the Hôtel de la Marine, originally the royal Garde-Meuble (storage depot) and later the French Navy Ministry. Opposite is the glamorous Hôtel de Crillon, a visiting celebrity favourite that has made cameos in countless books and films.

In recent years Place de la Concorde has been the focus of urban redevelopment aimed at expanding its pedestrian appeal. Following the transformation of the square into an urban sports arena during the Paris 2024 Summer Olympics, Place de la Concorde now features expansive walkways connecting pedestrians to the Jardin du Tuileries and the Avenue des Champs-Élysées. There are plans to continue transforming it into a *place-jardin* (garden square), complete with expansive lawns and restored historical features. This initiative is part of a broader effort by the city to make Paris Europe's first 'garden capital'.

ADDRESS: *Place de la Concorde*

ARRONDISSEMENT: *Paris Centre*

CLOSEST MÉTRO STATION: *Concorde*

Place Vendôme

—— SQUARE

One of Paris's most spectacular squares, the Place Vendôme was built in the baroque-classical style, marked by the monumental Colonne Vendôme (Vendôme Column) commissioned by Napoleon Bonaparte to commemorate the Battle of Austerlitz. Now pale green from oxidisation, the 44-metre-high (144-foot-high) column was constructed using bronze from captured enemy cannons and features a spiralling bas-relief depicting Napoleon's victories.

Place Vendôme evolved from a military symbol to a centre of luxury fashion and jewellery; it is now home to the flagship stores of high-end jewellers including Boucheron, Chaumet, Van Cleef & Arpels and Cartier, as well as luxury fashion house Louis Vuitton. It's also the home of the iconic Hôtel Ritz Paris. Notable former residents of Place Vendôme include Coco Chanel, who made the Hôtel Ritz her home for 30 years until her 1971 death; and celebrated composer and pianist Frédéric Chopin, whose last apartment was on the square.

ADDRESS: *Place Vendôme*

ARRONDISSEMENT: *Paris Centre*

CLOSEST MÉTRO STATION: *Concorde or Opéra*

Pont Alexandre III

—— BRIDGE

Named for Tsar Alexander III of Russia to honour his role in forging the 1892 Franco-Russian Alliance, this magnificent bridge straddling the Seine was unveiled at the 1900 world's fair. The design is an Art Nouveau masterpiece, characterised by the fantastical gilded bronze statues atop 17-metre-tall (56-foot-tall) columns at each end of the bridge and its rich decoration including floral garlands. The bridge's beauty also lies in its engineering – it's a single-span arch bridge with no central struts.

The Pont Alexandre III is an unforgettable place to watch the sunset on the Seine, as well as the lights of the Eiffel Tower glittering after dark. It's directly south of the glass-domed Grand Palais (p 112) and the Petit Palais (p 119), also built for the world's fair and designed to be viewed together in a harmonious triptych (a trio of artworks displayed side by side).

ADDRESS: *Pont Alexandre III*

ARRONDISSEMENT: *Paris Centre*

CLOSEST MÉTRO STATION: *Invalides*

Rue Saint-Honoré

—— STREET

Rue Saint-Honoré has become synonymous with luxury. The 1.9-kilometre (1.2-mile) street traces its origins to the Middle Ages, evolving from a modest path to a major link between the Place Vendôme (p 121) and the vibrant Les Halles district. It is the home of countless luxury boutiques, designer shops and concept stores. In recent years it has also become an enclave of luxury perfume houses including Diptych, Byredo, Acqua di Parma, Ex Nihilo (p 124) and Santa Maria Novella (p 132).

ADDRESS: *Rue Saint-Honoré*

ARRONDISSEMENT: *Paris Centre*

CLOSEST MÉTRO STATION: *Louvre–Rivoli, Palais-Royal–Musée du Louvre, Tuileries or Concorde*

Ex Nihilo

—— PERFUME

Paris has been at the heart of the perfume world for centuries and is home to many revered 'noses', or master perfumers. Among the city's newer cult perfumeries, Ex Nihilo (named for the Latin phrase meaning 'out of nothing') has a novel approach to luxury perfumery, emphasising personalised experiences. One of their most popular fragrances is Fleur Narcotique, characterised by a combination of floral, fruity and musky notes.

The flagship boutique distinguishes itself from other perfume houses by its modern design, featuring an electric-blue awning and marble signage. Only available in the boutique is the 'Osmologue', a pioneering device enabling customers to add raw ingredients including iris pallida, vanilla bourbon and rose centifolia to base scents to create a personalised fragrance. There are two to three combinations to choose from for each base scent, all approved by the in-house nose. Your perfume is then blended before you by the Osmologue, which precisely measures and combines the new composition. The bottle can also be personalised with a selection of luxe engraved bottlecaps inlaid with the likes of mother-of-pearl and buffalo horn, and a customised label.

ADDRESS: *352 Rue Saint-Honoré*

ARRONDISSEMENT: *Paris Centre*

CLOSEST MÉTRO STATION: *Tuileries*

EX NIHILO
EX NIHILO
EX NIHILO
SPIKY MUSE
eau de parfum
EX NIHILO
SPIKY MUSE
eau de parfum

Laulhère

BERETS

You can find berets everywhere in Paris, but if it carries the 'Laulhère' tag, you can be sure it's a quality product. France's oldest beret maker, Laulhère was founded in 1830 in Oloron-Sainte-Marie, at the foothills of the Pyrenees, and has been synonymous with the beret for nearly two centuries. Even today, each Laulhère beret is meticulously handcrafted by skilled artisans. At their flagship store you can choose from a huge range of colours and styles including limited-edition berets, and be personally fitted by the knowledgeable staff. Berets are generally made in one size, but as it is a felted fabric it can be stretched by a traditional machine in-store to fit you perfectly.

ADDRESS: *14 Rue du Faubourg Saint-Honoré*

ARRONDISSEMENT: *8th*

CLOSEST MÉTRO STATION: *Concorde*

Librairie Jousseaume

—— BOOKS

Established in 1826, Librairie Jousseaume's twin set of bookshops face each other in the heart of Galerie Vivienne (p 111). Works from the nineteenth and twentieth centuries occupy every available space inside the main shop, rendering it a mini maze. In the premises opposite, more bookcases surround a wooden winding staircase and chandelier.

A favourite among intellectuals and avid readers due to its extensive collection (including titles in English) and prime location near the Palais-Royal (p 119), the bookshop gained its current name when the Jousseaume family took over in 1890. The business has stayed in the family with François Jousseaume currently at the helm. François takes pride in displaying the shop's books the same way it has been done for generations, offering a window into nineteenth-century Paris.

ADDRESS: *45-46-47 Galerie Vivienne*

ARRONDISSEMENT: *Paris Centre*

CLOSEST MÉTRO STATION: *Bourse*

SHOPPING

Additional VENUE

L'Ingénieur Chevallier

——— EYEWEAR

Few artisan eyewear brands can match the illustrious history of L'Ingénieur Chevallier, which has created optical instruments for the French Navy and eyewear for French royalty since the eighteenth century.

After inheriting his grandfather's spectacles shop in 1796, Jean Gabriel Augustin Chevallier rose to become the city's preeminent optician, credited with inventions including the optical microscope and achromatic lenses. Louis Daguerre – one of the inventors of photography – used Chevallier's lenses to create *Boulevard du Temple*, the first photograph featuring people (a shoeshiner and his client) in 1838. The brand expanded into luxury eyewear in the nineteenth century, transforming the monocle into ornate opera glasses decorated with embellishments including mother-of-pearl, ivory and tortoiseshell, which became highly sought after by the theatre-going elite.

The company was passed down through generations before being acquired by the Bonnet family, owners of prestigious eyewear house Maison Bonnet, in 2021. While Maison Bonnet continues to specialise in bespoke eyewear, L'Ingénieur Chevallier bridges the gap between bespoke and ready-to-wear. Only available in-store, all frames by L'Ingénieur Chevallier are meticulously handcrafted and produced in extremely limited quantities. Each pair is adjusted to the client for a personal fit.

ADDRESS: *17 Rue des Pyramides*

ARRONDISSEMENT: *Paris Centre*

CLOSEST MÉTRO STATION: *Pyramides*

Additional VENUE

Merci #2

—— FASHION AND HOMEWARES

Parisian concept store Merci is a Marais institution, revered for its expertly curated selection of fashion and homewares. This second store occupies a former 1950s post office that has been transformed into a 600-square-metre (1969-square-foot) industrial-style loft. The renovation unveiled a stunning glass roof, allowing natural light to flood the space, with notable interior design features including the copper checkout counter by sustainable furniture designer Piet Hein Eek, an *urushi* (Japanese lacquerware) table by artist Jo Nagasaka and dressing rooms finished with curtains embroidered by Marseille-based artist Sarah Espeute. An homage to the original Merci is the red Fiat presiding above the fashion section, recalling the famous red car parked in the Merci Marais courtyard.

Like the Merci flagship, Merci #2 offers a broad range of products that cater to every aspect of Parisian life including homewares, clothing for men, women and children from both emerging and established brands (as well as its own), stationery, beauty products and toys. Merci's own label has produced seasonal collaborations with the likes of cult Californian supermarket Erewhon and urban clothing brand Carhartt.

The name 'Merci' comes from the store's original incarnation as a philanthropic venture. Its current owner continues to give back by donating a portion of profits to non-governmental organisations.

ADDRESS: *19 Rue de Richelieu*

ARRONDISSEMENT: *Paris Centre*

CLOSEST MÉTRO STATION: *Pyramides*

Additional VENUE

Samaritaine

—— DEPARTMENT STORE

Glamorous *grands magasins* (department stores) transformed urban life in late nineteenth-century Paris. Recently restored to its former glory, Samaritaine offers an evocative glimpse into the city's golden age of department store shopping.

Named for the biblical Samaritan woman depicted on a hydraulic pump near Pont Neuf (p 323), the lavish Art Nouveau department store first opened in 1870. In the early twentieth century it became renowned as a place where you could find everything and expanded, but by the 1970s its profits had begun to decline and in 2005 it closed.

After acquiring Samaritaine in 2010, French luxury goods conglomerate LVMH embarked on an ambitious (and controversial) restoration of the building involving hundreds of artisans. The restoration of the intricate frescos decorating the fifth floor alone (including a 115-metre/377-foot peacock fresco beneath the glass atrium) took five years. Also meticulously restored was the grand staircase, with gold leaf applied by hand to the railings; and the 600-square-metre (1969-square-foot) glass floor of the fifth floor, involving the production and installation of thousands of glass tiles.

Finally reopened in 2021, Samaritaine offers an opulent and intimate experience, as the smallest of Paris's major department stores. It houses around 700 luxury brands focusing on beauty, fashion and accessories from iconic labels like Louis Vuitton, Dior and Cartier to contemporary and emerging brands such as Ganni and By Far. My favourite part of Samaritaine is its beauty floor, which stocks over 200 brands.

ADDRESS: *9 Rue de la Monnaie*

ARRONDISSEMENT: *Paris Centre*

CLOSEST MÉTRO STATION: *Pont Neuf*

Santa Maria Novella

—— PERFUME

Cult Italian luxury fragrance brand Santa Maria Novella dates back to 1221 when Dominican friars used medicinal herbs from the gardens of Florence's Basilica of Santa Maria Novella to prepare remedies for the infirmary. Their expertise became renowned over the years; in 1533 they created a special fragrance for the young Catherine de' Medici in honour of her marriage to Henry II of France. In 1612 they officially opened their pharmacy, which also offered fragrances.

Today, signature fragrances include the timeless L'Iris Eau de Parfum, a powdery scent that symbolises Florence; Melograno, a scent inspired by pomegranate; and Pot Pourri, a warm blend of Italian herbs, grasses, fruits and resins created in 1928.

The next best thing to visiting the brand's historic store in Florence is visiting its flagship Paris boutique with its dark wood cabinets and marble floors that pay homage to the original Italian pharmacy.

ADDRESS: *318 Rue Saint-Honoré*

ARRONDISSEMENT: *Paris Centre*

CLOSEST MÉTRO STATION: *Tuileries*

Additional VENUE

Ultramod

—— HABERDASHERY

When I was looking for some worthy buttons to repair a thrifted cardigan, a trendy Parisian friend brought me to Ultramod. With such a non-historical-sounding name, I was surprised to discover that this is the oldest *mercerie* (haberdashery shop) in Paris.

Originally opened in 1832, Ultramod's original décor and rich stock of rare vintage trimmings have been preserved by its current owners. The shop is packed with all manner of pom-poms, fringing, lace and ribbons; some decoratively draped over lampshades. And as for buttons, there are walls of them, many of them handmade and antique. Even if you're not into handicrafts, some antique pearl buttons or a length of vintage silk velvet ribbon make for a whimsical souvenir.

ADDRESS: *4 Rue de Choiseul*

ARRONDISSEMENT: *Paris Centre*

CLOSEST MÉTRO STATION: *Quatre-Septembre*

Angelina

—— CAFÉ

Paris is renowned for its hot chocolate, and while it can be found in almost every café, quality and style can vary. For me the perfect hot chocolate is the thick and creamy style served at historic teahouse Angelina. There are several locations in Paris (and beyond), each offering a different ambiance, but it's worth queuing for a table at the original – founded in 1903 – where past patrons include Coco Chanel and French novelist Marcel Proust.

The lush interior was designed in typical Belle Époque style with decadent murals interspersed by large mirrors. Brunch-style dishes are available, but most people come for Angelina's signature *chocolate chaud* (hot chocolate) and a Mont Blanc (chestnut dessert). For a more relaxed hot chocolate experience, visit the laid-back Mademoiselle Angelina outpost in the Jardin du Luxembourg (p 223).

ADDRESS: *226 Rue de Rivoli*

ARRONDISSEMENT: *Paris Centre*

CLOSEST MÉTRO STATION: *Tuileries*

Bofinger

—— BRASSERIE

Named for its founder, Frédéric Bofinger, and pronounced 'bo-fan-jay', Bofinger is a faithful remnant of the great nineteenth-century Parisian restaurants. From its glamorous Art Noveau design (note the winding staircase and magnificent glass dome) to its traditional menu, everything about it is as you would imagine in a classic Parisian brasserie. And no wonder – established in 1864, it is one of the city's oldest.

Bofinger specialises in traditional Alsatian cuisine from the Alsace region of eastern France, with Alsatian beers among the options on tap. Influenced by the culinary traditions of its German and Swiss neighbours, Alsatian cuisine is rustic and hearty, centred on earthy ingredients like potatoes, cabbage and pork. Expect many iterations of sauerkraut paired with sausages, bacon and salted pork. There's even a 'sea sauerkraut' served with fish or langoustines (a type of small lobster) and boiled potatoes.

ADDRESS: *5-7 Rue de la Bastille*

ARRONDISSEMENT: *Paris Centre*

CLOSEST MÉTRO STATION: *Bréguet–Sabin*

Café Kitsuné – Louvre

—— CAFÉ

Maison Kitsuné is a French-Japanese brand founded in 2002 by Gildas Loaëc (former manager of legendary French electro duo Daft Punk) and Japanese architect Masaya Kuroki. Originally a record label before expanding into fashion and hospitality, it's instantly recognisable by its orange fox iconography – *kitsune* means 'fox' in Japanese. The brand opened its first Café Kitsuné in Tokyo in 2013 and its second in Paris near the Louvre, in 2019. Now with five locations in the city, the café is as well known (if not more so) as the brand itself. The second floor of its flagship café looks over the picturesque Place André Malraux square and its twin fountains, the Fontaines du Théâtre-Français. It's a great vantage point for people-watching.

Coffee (served in distinctive branded takeaway cups) and delectable pastries and cookies are available all day. A savoury international brunch menu (spanning Turkish eggs to a smoked salmon bagel) is also available until 3 pm.

ADDRESS: *2 Place André Malraux*

ARRONDISSEMENT: *Paris Centre*

CLOSEST MÉTRO STATION: *Palais-Royal–Musée du Louvre or Pyramides*

EAT & DRINK

Additional VENUE

La Distillerie de l'Arbre Sec

DISTILLERY

Apéro (pre-dinner drinks) is such a revered French tradition (p 43) that the suggestion of skipping straight to dinner may be met with looks of horror. It's not only wine that is enjoyed during *apéro*, but also artisanal spirits such as gin produced by this independent micro-distillery, whose name means The Dry Tree Distillery.

Combining traditional craftsmanship with modern innovation, the distillery creates small-batch gins infused with French-grown botanicals including juniper, citrus and herbs. These unique blends can be tasted as part of the distillery's tours and tastings, where visitors can see the distilling process firsthand. There are also create-your-own gin workshops in which you can select botanicals and aromatics to craft a unique recipe, distill it on a mini copper still and leave with a personalised 70cl bottle of your creation.

ADDRESS: *52 Rue de l'Arbre Sec*

ARRONDISSEMENT: *Paris Centre*

CLOSEST MÉTRO STATION: *Pont Neuf*

La Distillerie de l'Arbre Sec

Le Valentin Vivienne

—— CAFÉ

In the Galerie Vivienne (p 111), this tearoom, patisserie and restaurant is known for its decadent baked goods. Extravagant displays of Mont Blanc (chestnut cream) pastries, pistachio tartlets and *baba au rhum* (rum-infused cake) are visible through the window, and the seating spills onto the mosaic floor of the covered passage under the glass ceiling. The tearoom also serves savoury dishes including quiches and *croque monsieurs* (French toasted cheese sandwiches). There's also another outpost of Le Valentin Vivienne in the Passage Jouffroy, near Grands Boulevards métro station.

ADDRESS: *35 Galerie Vivienne, 4 Rue des Petits Champs*

ARRONDISSEMENT: *Paris Centre*

CLOSEST MÉTRO STATION: *Bourse*

DAY 2

KEY NEIGHBOURHOODS

MONTMARTRE
BATIGNOLLES
PIGALLE

Introducing Paris at its most cinematic, this itinerary is designed for first-timers as well as visitors rediscovering the city. As you explore the winding cobblestone streets and secret passages of Montmartre and surrounding neighbourhoods, embrace the opportunity to be a tourist and soak up Paris in its picture-postcard glory.

CINEMATIC PARIS

ITINERARY

This itinerary is recommended on

WEDNESDAY
THURSDAY
FRIDAY
SATURDAY

TIPS

Montmartre's hilly topography calls for **COMFORTABLE SHOES.**

AIM FOR A CLEAR DAY to capture the panoramic views from the top of Montmartre.

THERE ARE OFTEN LONG LINES TO ENTER THE BASILIQUE DU SACRÉ-COEUR (p 149) so it's a good idea to go early (the basilica opens at 6.30 am and the dome at 10 am), or later in the day to avoid crowds.

You'll find plenty of charming cafés and restaurants around Place du Tertre (p 156) for a quick bite, but I suggest seeking out **OFF-THE-BEATEN-TRACK SPOTS** for more memorable dining experiences, including the ones you'll find in this itinerary.

Reserve ahead for dinner at **CAFÉ DE LA BUTTE** (p 168).

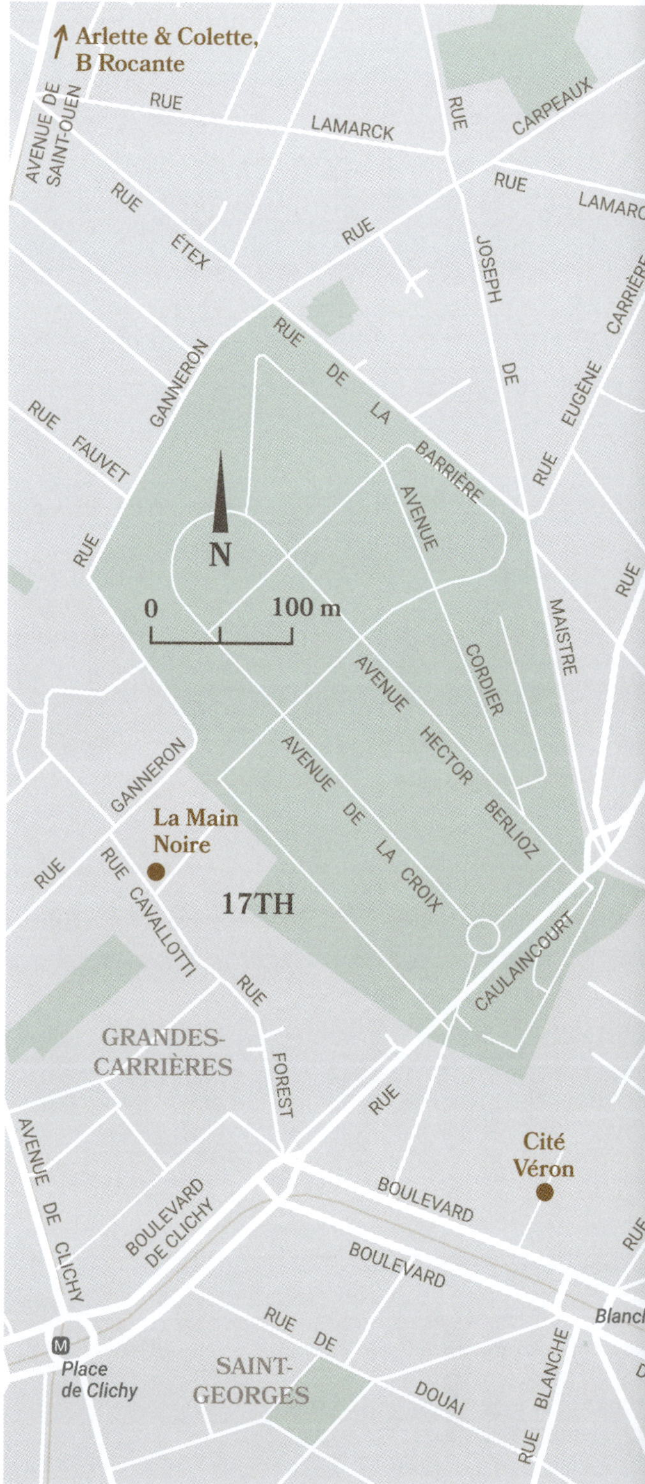

DAY 2

Marché aux Puces
CLIGNANCOURT
18TH
Fromagerie Chez Virginie
Café Dose 3
Lamarck–Caulaincourt 2
Café de la Butte 21
Boris Lumé 1
Allée des Brouillards 5
Place Dalida 4
Marcelle 6
Villa Léandre 7
Rue de l'Abreuvoir 8
Les Cinq Marches
MONTMARTRE
Moulin de la Galette 15
Rue Lepic 18
Armande 17
Atelier Tholozé 16
Place Émile Goudeau 14
Dalí Paris
Place du Tertre 9
Basilique du Sacré-Coeur 10
Square Nadar 11
Halle Saint-Pierre 12
Rue des Abbesses 19
Curiositas
Fotoautomat 13
La Cave des Abbesses 20
Abbesses
Anvers
Les Crèmes, La Blouse de Lyon
RUE MARCADET
RUE DU RUISSEAU
RUE DUHESME
RUE LAMARCK
RUE CAULAINCOURT
AVENUE JUNOT
RUE SAINT-VINCENT
RUE DES SAULES
RUE CORTOT
RUE NORVINS
RUE LEPIC
RUE THOLOZÉ
RUE DURANTIN
RUE GABRIELLE
RUE AZAÏS
RUE BERTHE
RUE DES TROIS FRÈRES
RUE VÉRON
RUE GERMAIN PILON
RUE HOUDON
RUE DES MARTYRS
RUE D'ORSEL
PLACE SAINT-PIERRE
RUE RONSARD
RUE DE LA BONNE
RUE DU MONT CENIS
RUE FRANCŒUR
RUE DU BAIGNEUR
RUE CUSTINE
BOULEVARD MARGUERITE DE ROCHECHOUART
BOULEVARD DE CLICHY

ITINERARY

MORNING

The best way to begin a day in Paris is with a Parisian croissant. Grab one to go at the ① **Boris Lumé** boulangerie (p 168) on Rue Caulaincourt in Montmartre, a short walk east from the Lamarck–Caulaincourt métro station. Lumé trained under prominent French bakers including Joël Robuchon and Cyril Lignac, and his pastries are delicate and rich, while the croissants are crispy and flaky on the outside and buttery and soft on the inside, just as they should be. Like many bakeries in Paris, Boris Lumé is closed on Mondays and Tuesdays; you can also get a Parisian croissant fix at nearby Maison Lardeux, another beloved traditional Parisian bakery.

② Lamarck–Caulaincourt

① Boris Lumé

Walk to ② **Lamarck–Caulaincourt** métro station (p 152), which you may recognise from the 2001 film *Amélie*. Linking Rue Lamarck and Rue Caulaincourt, this unique train station is built over two levels. From Rue Caulaincourt you can admire the picturesque Art Nouveau métro sign and curved stairs leading down to a little square, which descends again down the long staircase of Rue de la Fontaine-du-But. Here you will find ③ **Café Dose** (p 169), a cosy micro-roastery that makes an ideal coffee stop.

Head south from Lamarck–Caulaincourt station and climb the stairs of Rue Girardon to find yourself at ④ **Place Dalida** (p 154), dedicated to the celebrated Italian-French singer and actress Dalida. A bust of Dalida sits in the centre of the square, reflecting her importance to the neighborhood; she lived in Montmartre for 25 years.

DAY 2

⑧ Rue de l'Abreuvoir

—— Turn right to enter one of Paris's fascinating – yet often overlooked – secret passages, the ⑤ **Allée des Brouillards** (Alley of Mists, p 148). Taking this route, you are rewarded on the other side with Place Casadesus, a peaceful escape from the crowds of Montmartre. It's also a clever shortcut to your next destination.

—— You've earned a leisurely brunch at the Villa Léandre branch of ⑥ **Marcelle** (p 173). This restaurant offers an all-day brunch menu including a decadent French toast with salted butter caramel toffee sauce and bananas. Before moving on, you might want to stroll along nearby ⑦ **Villa Léandre** (p 159), a pretty street known for its pastel-hued English-style houses.

—— Backtrack through Allée des Brouillards and continue south to explore ⑧ **Rue de l'Abreuvoir** (p 157), admiring the highly Instagrammable La Maison Rose restaurant with its pastel-pink facade on the way. Arrive at ⑨ **Place du Tertre** (p 156), the historical heart of bohemian Montmartre, usually teeming with street artists and tourists.

⑨ Place du Tertre (top); Moulin Rouge (bottom)

ITINERARY

AFTERNOON

—— Head toward the Basilique du Sacré-Coeur via Rue Saint-Éleuthère. The road will soon curve around to your first view of the Tour Eiffel (Eiffel Tower) rising up above a sea of rooftops in the distance. After admiring the view, continue along Rue Saint-Éleuthère, which becomes Rue du Cardinal Dubois, until you reach the terrace of the ⑩ **Basilique du Sacré-Coeur** (p 149). You are now standing atop the Butte Montmartre (Montmartre Hill), the highest natural point in Paris, famed for its panoramic views. The grand steps leading to the basilica are an informal community meeting place filled with locals, tourists and street performers. Stay for a while and enjoy the lively atmosphere – but be wary of pickpockets.

Street performer at the terrace of the Basilique du Sacré-Coeur

⑩ Basilique du Sacré-Coeur

—— Before making your way down from the top of Montmartre, stop by ⑪ **Square Nadar** (p 159), a dog park in an unexpected location. You don't need a furry friend to visit; take a seat on one of the benches in the centre of the park and look through the gaps in the trees for another secret Eiffel Tower view.

—— Descend the 222 winding, terraced stairs of Square Louise Michel to reach the base of the Basilique du Sacré-Coeur. This picturesque walk takes you through hidden grottos and past the beautiful fountain adorned with marine gods and goddesses created by French sculptor Paul Gasq in 1932.

—— At the base, head right to visit the ⑫ **Halle Saint-Pierre** museum (p 152). Stop for a coffee break in its café, bathed in light from the round building's large glass windows. Check out the musem's thought-provoking 'outsider art' exhibitions and visit the bookshop.

⑲ Rue des Abbesses

—— Walk the small cobblestone streets of Montmartre taking in the village ambience and pop into little shops that catch your eye. Snap a photo to remember the day at the ⑬ **Fotoautomat** (p 151) vintage photo booth. The analogue photo development process means your black-and-white photo should last over 100 years!

⑭ Place Émile Goudeau

—— Continue to ⑭ **Place Émile Goudeau** (p 155), home to the infamous former artist residence Bateau-Lavoir. Imagine Pablo Picasso (who once lived there) sitting on the benches and having intellectual debates with his contemporaries. Head up Rue d'Orchampt to the north and turn left onto Rue Lepic, admiring one of Montmartre's two surviving windmills, ⑮ **Moulin de la Galette** (p 154), as you pass, then walk down the stairs onto Rue Tholozé. Here you will find ceramics workshop and boutique ⑯ **Atelier Tholoze** (p 160). You are sure to be greeted by its resident cat, Elfo.

—— Have a late lunch at ⑰ **Armande** (p 167), which offers a rotating selection of fresh, homemade dishes. I highly recommend the crab rolls.

—— Head back up Rue Tholozé and explore ⑱ **Rue Lepic** (p 157), a historic street that wraps around the Butte Montmartre and is home to a number of small boutiques and cafés. Follow this until it meets picturesque ⑲ **Rue des Abbesses** (p 156) with its quaint shopfronts and eclectic boutiques. Also stop by Place des Abbesses where you can admire the iconic Art Nouveau Abbesses métro station entrance designed by French architect Hector Guimard, and also Le Mur des Je t'aime (Love Wall) where 'I love you' is written 311 times in 250 different languages and dialects.

ITINERARY

EVENING

——— Enjoy *apéro* (p 43) with a charcuterie platter at ⑳ **La Cave des Abbesses** (p 170). Ask the sommelier to suggest an ideal wine from their extensive list.

——— For one last foray before dinner, double back to the north and explore streets you haven't yet seen including the charming Rue Saint-Vincent and its ivy-covered wall (between street numbers 32 and 42, bordering the Cimetière de Saint-Vincent), which is especially beautiful in autumn when the ivy leaves turn a fiery red.

Rue Saint-Vincent (above and opposite)

⑳ La Cave des Abbesses

——— Take a short walk to dinner at ㉑ **Café de la Butte** (p 168), a classic French bistro serving comforting dishes such as *magret de canard* (duck breast) with a flavourful Tunisian twist.

㉑ Café de la Butte

ATTRACTIONS

Allée des Brouillards

—— STREET

Allée des Brouillards is a small lane and somewhat of a secret passage in Montmartre, connecting Place Dalida (p 154) and Place Casadesus. The mysterious name (meaning 'Alley of Mists') may have come from the mist that rose up from the natural springs that used to exist in this area. It runs alongside the eighteenth-century *folie* (country retreat) Château des Brouillards (Castle of Mists), the former home of many iconic artists including the family of Impressionist painter Pierre-Auguste Renoir. Secluded and hidden, especially in summer, by the lush greenery of Place Dalida on one side and an enigmatic staircase on Place Casadesus on the other side, it's often overlooked by tourists.

ADDRESS: *Between Rue Giardon and Rue Simon Dereure*

ARRONDISSEMENT: *18th*

CLOSEST MÉTRO STATION: *Lamarck–Caulaincourt*

This is FREE

Basilique du Sacré-Coeur

—— BASILICA

Like the Eiffel Tower, the basilica atop the Butte Montmartre is visible from all over Paris. If the Romanesque-Byzantine architecture seems out of place among Paris's other predominantly Gothic-style churches, it's because the basilica is relatively modern. Built between 1875 and 1914, its construction was mired in controversy due to political, social and cultural tensions at the time. Not only did many Parisians object to the construction of a religious institution in a neighbourhood known for bohemianism and secular free-thinking, but also to its appearance. Many called it an eyesore, but the landmark has now become part of Montmartre's identity.

Designed in a Greek-cross layout, the basilica's soaring arches and multiple domes are reminiscent of Istanbul's Hagia Sophia mosque and Venice's Basilica San Marco. As you enter, you're greeted by the grandeur of the *La Mosaïque du Coeur* – one of the largest mosaics in the world – depicting Jesus Christ with arms outstretched to reveal a golden heart. Stained glass windows bathe the interior in glittering colours and you can pay €7 to climb the 300 steps up to the large central dome for panoramic views of Paris.

The basilica's terrace offers the highest natural viewpoint in Paris with breathtaking views of the city and the Eiffel Tower. Among the excellent street performers you can see here is Iya Traoré, who performs impressive soccer freestyle acts, notably while hanging off the top of the lamppost on the terrace with the rooftops of Paris serving as a striking backdrop to his feats of agility and strength. On your way up or down the steps of the basilica, pause at the elbow of Rue Saint-Éleuthère, east of the terrace, where across the wrought-iron fence you can see the Eiffel Tower rising up above the rooftops.

ADDRESS: *35 Rue du Chevalier de la Barre*

ARRONDISSEMENT: *18th*

CLOSEST MÉTRO STATION: *Abbesses*

Additional VENUE

Cité Véron

—— STREET

Next to the iconic Moulin Rouge – known for its extravagant but touristy cabaret shows – is a little alley with an old steel sign saying 'Cité Véron'. A *cité* usually refers to a small, enclosed street or alley, of which Cité Véron is a famous example. Only 2.5 metres (8 feet) wide and extending for 80 metres (262 feet), this little passageway was home to the writer Boris Vian in the 1950s, who lived at 6 Bis Cité Véron. Lined by charming houses with pretty gardens, it's an unexpected oasis in the Pigalle nightlife district.

ADDRESS: *Off Place Blanche*

ARRONDISSEMENT: *18th*

CLOSEST MÉTRO STATION: *Blanche*

Additional VENUE

Dalí Paris

—— ART MUSEUM

Spanish-born surrealist painter Salvador Dalí is one of the big influences in my work as a creative director. For many editorials and campaigns I relish the opportunity to create impossible scenes with something that tricks the eye. One image I created for Valentino a few years ago was loosely inspired by *Dalí at the Age of Six*, in which it looks like the sea is being lifted like a sheet by a young boy. While many of Dalí's most iconic works are housed in other museums around the world, Dalí Paris will introduce you to Dalí's unique style of dream-like scenes and often grotesque figures.

Founded by Italian collector Beniamino Levi in 1991, the museum houses over 300 original Dalí works including sculptures, engravings, lithographs and a selection of paintings. Accessed from the ground floor on Rue Poulbot, the first level offers thematic exhibitions and showcases his 'metamorphosis of matter' themes. Descending to the lower space, you find yourself in a maze-like gallery that showcases Dalí's most iconic three-dimensional works such as *Space Elephant* and *Alice in Wonderland*.

ADDRESS: *11 Rue Poulbot*

ARRONDISSEMENT: *18th*

CLOSEST MÉTRO STATION: *Abbesses*

Fotoautomat

—— PHOTO BOOTH

There are countless modern photo booths found in métro stations and supermarkets across Paris, but there are only a few vintage *fotoautomats* popping out nostalgic strips of black-and-white photos.

Dating from the 1960s, the Montmartre Fotoautomat is one of many old photo booths lovingly restored to its original condition. Unlike modern photo booths, *fotoautomats* maintain analogue silver nitrate development, a vintage development method that creates photos that last over a century without fading.

Other restored fotoautomats found around Paris include a beautiful model at the Palais de Tokyo (p 197), but the Montmartre Fotoautomat is the best known, thanks in large part to its conspicuous streetside location. These days it has become a destination for influencers, many of whom queue on weekends to take their photos in – and with – the booth.

ADDRESS: *53 Rue des Trois Frères*

ARRONDISSEMENT: *18th*

CLOSEST MÉTRO STATION: *Abbesses*

ATTRACTIONS

Halle Saint-Pierre

—— MUSEUM

Originally a covered market, then repurposed in 1986 as a museum and gallery, this distinctive rounded building sits at the foot of the Basilique du Sacré-Coeur. The cast iron structure, triangular roof and large semicircular windows are inspired by buildings designed by legendary nineteenth-century French architect Victoe Baltard, such as Les Halles market. The interior is luminous and expansive thanks to the high ceilings and large arched windows. In winter it's a comforting sanctuary from the cold. The winding staircase takes you to the second-floor museum showcasing temporary exhibitions focusing on *art brut* ('outsider' art). It's a great place to immerse yourself in the bohemian culture of Butte Montmartre, which lives on today in the young artists and creatives who still gather in this neighbourhood.

The ground floor has a lively café and bookshop that serve as a vibrant local meeting spot, and the basement houses a vintage *fotoautomat* (p 151).

ADDRESS: *2 Rue Ronsard*

ARRONDISSEMENT: *18th*

CLOSEST MÉTRO STATION: *Anvers*

Lamarck–Caulaincourt

—— TRAIN STATION

Fans of *Amélie* will recognise this métro station (serving Line 12) from the 2001 film. The distinct double-level station designed specifically for Montmartre's hilly topography features elegant Art Nouveau wrought-iron details and floral motifs. Its double staircase links Rue Lamarck and Rue Caulaincourt, and the entrance is located in between. Admire the views from the top of the stairs, elevated above the streets of Paris.

ADDRESS: *Enter via Rue Lamarck or Rue de la Fontaine-du-But*

ARRONDISSEMENT: *18th*

CLOSEST MÉTRO STATION: *Lamarck–Caulaincourt*

Halle Saint-Pierre (opposite)

Moulin de la Galette

—— WINDMILL

Owned by the Debray family for generations (several members were killed defending it during the Napoleonic and Franco-Prussian wars), this seventeenth-century windmill is one of only two historic Montmartre windmills surviving today. Originally called Moulin Radet, it was converted into a popular dance hall and café in the nineteenth century. Its name comes from the flat cakes known as *galettes* (a small round brown bread), which were baked at the mill and served to patrons with local wine – a scene famously depicted in Renoir's 1875 masterpiece *Bal du moulin de la Galette* (*Under the Arbour at the Moulin de la Galette*). A café-restaurant still operates here, but see pp 166–73 for my local dining picks.

ADDRESS: *83 Rue Lepic*

ARRONDISSEMENT: *18th*

CLOSEST MÉTRO STATION: *Lamarck–Caulaincourt*

Place Dalida

—— SQUARE

This calm square is dedicated to celebrated former resident Dalida, best known for songs such as 'Je suis malade' ('I'm sick'). A bronze bust in Dalida's image – sculpted by a contemporary French artist known by the pseudonym Aslan – was installed in the centre of the square in 1997 to commemorate the tenth anniversary of her death. You will notice that the bronze part of her chest is very polished as it has become tradition for visitors to touch the bust for luck.

It's difficult to understate Dalida's superstardom in France. She recorded diverse styles of pop, disco, Arabic melodies and world music in more than 10 languages and was a pioneer of the disco movement in France, popularising the genre in the 1970s with hits like 'J'attendrai' and 'Gigi in Paradiso'. I've always felt that the serenity of the square is incongruous with Dalida's larger-than-life persona. She is often remembered for performing in flowing, shimmering gowns and dramatic costumes, and her rich, warm and emotional vocal deliveries are instantly recognisable. Even now, most French people of every generation know her songs by heart and her music regularly features on party playlists.

ADDRESS: *Intersection of Rue de l'Abreuvoir and Rue Girardon*

ARRONDISSEMENT: *18th*

CLOSEST MÉTRO STATION: *Lamarck–Caulaincourt*

Place Émile Goudeau

—— SQUARE

A hotel I booked during my early days in Paris overlooked this charming square lined by horse-chestnut trees and gently sloping down to meet a café terrace. Place Émile Goudeau was named for the French poet, novelist and founder of the literary group Les Hydropathes (which banned drinking water at their wine-fuelled meetings). It is best known for housing the Bateau-Lavoir, a piano factory converted into artists' studios in the late 1800s; its nickname (Laundry Boat) is thought to refer to the way the rickety building swayed in the wind like the laundry boats on the Seine. Despite the primitive conditions of the dormitory-like building, the Bateau-Lavoir was a hub for early twentieth-century artists including former resident Pablo Picasso, who painted *Les Demoiselles d'Avignon* (*The Young Ladies of Avignon*) here. This revolutionary work laid the foundation for the cubist movement.

Destroyed by a fire in 1970, the Bateau-Lavoir was rebuilt in 1978 and continues to function as artists' studios; its distinctive dark green facade is found in the northwestern corner of the square.

ADDRESS: *Rue Ravignan*

ARRONDISSEMENT: *18th*

CLOSEST MÉTRO STATION: *Abbesses*

Place du Tertre

—— SQUARE

When I first stumbled onto this bustling square filled with painters and portrait artists with their portable easels, paints and brushes, I felt like I'd travelled back in time.

Place du Tertre (Square of the Hill) was originally part of the Benedictine Abbaye de Montmartre Abbey (Montmartre Abbey), established in 1133 by King Louis VI. It was opened to the public and became the village square of Montmartre in 1635. The late nineteenth and early twentieth centuries saw old windmills and disused industrial buildings converted into art studios (most still remain today), attracting an influx of artists, writers and intellectuals including Pablo Picasso, Vincent van Gogh and Pierre-Auguste Renoir. The neighbourhood became a haven for free-thinkers and nonconformists, giving birth to the bohemian movement. The street-artist tradition also began during this time, when the literally starving artists of Montmartre would sell their art in the streets. Today street artists are regulated by the city – artists must apply for permits and only a certain number are allowed to work there at any given time.

Some artists here are known for demanding exorbitant prices after the work has been completed. If you're looking to have your portrait painted, avoid an uncomfortable situation and deal only with artists displaying official permits and agree on the price beforehand.

ADDRESS: *Place du Tertre*

ARRONDISSEMENT: *18th*

CLOSEST MÉTRO STATION: *Abbesses*

Rue des Abbesses

—— STREET

With its picturesque cobblestones, quaint shopfronts and eclectic boutiques, Rue des Abbesses is one of the most charming streets in Paris. Every so often the street is taken over by a *vide-grenier* (garage sale, p 327), with countless stalls selling second-hand goods. In winter Rue des Abbesses hosts one of Paris's best Christmas markets with the aroma of toasted chestnuts and mulled wine filling the street.

The Abbesses métro station has one of the city's most beautiful Art Nouveau entrances, designed by French architect Hector Guimard. If the lifts are out of service, you will see how deep the station lies as you head down the 181 steps of the incredible spiral staircase, descending 36 metres (118 feet) to the platform. It's worth taking the stairs anyway to admire the murals depicting historical scenes of Montmartre.

ADDRESS: *Rue des Abbesses*

ARRONDISSEMENT: *18th*

CLOSEST MÉTRO STATION: *Abbesses*

Rue de l'Abreuvoir

—— STREET

In the heart of Montmartre, Rue de l'Abreuvoir is one of the most picturesque streets of Paris and makes you feel like you've been spirited away to an old country village. *Abreuvoir* means 'watering place' or 'trough', reflecting Montmartre's origins as a rural village. In the late nineteenth century Montmartre transformed into an artistic and bohemian enclave and Rue de l'Abreuvoir became a popular destination for painters, writers and poets.

The narrow, winding cobblestone street is lined by townhouses and villas with ivy-covered walls and colourful shutters – a rarity in Paris. Rue de l'Abreuvoir is also home to La Maison Rose, one of Paris's most photographed cafés, on the corner of Rue de l'Abreuvoir and Rue des Saules.

ADDRESS: *Rue de l'Abreuvoir*

ARRONDISSEMENT: *18th*

CLOSEST MÉTRO STATION: *Lamarck–Caulaincourt*

Rue Lepic

—— STREET

Rue Lepic is a charming historic street ascending the Butte Montmartre, culminating at Place Jean-Baptiste Clément. Characterised by its serpentine route, the 755-metre-long (2477-foot-long) street was home to notable figures such as Vincent van Gogh and his brother Theo, who resided at number 54 from 1886 to 1888. In 1898 Louis Renault famously drove the Voiturette – his first produced automobile – up the steep incline of Rue Lepic, demonstrating its capabilities and securing initial orders.

Today Rue Lepic is a quiet street slightly removed from Montmartre's touristic centre, lined with cafés, shops and historical sites such as the Moulin de la Galette (p 154).

ADDRESS: *Rue Lepic*

ARRONDISSEMENT: *18th*

CLOSEST MÉTRO STATION: *Blanche or Abbesses*

Villa Léandre

—— STREET

It might feel counterintuitive to visit a street known for its English-style houses in Paris, but hear me out. Located between Montmartre and Batignolles, quaint Villa Léandre is lined by pastel-coloured houses with pitched roofs and brick facades covered in cascades of ivy. Inspired by English cottages, the houses on this charming street were built in response to the industrial urbanisation that was occurring all over Paris in the early 1900s. Montmartre is one of the only neighbourhoods in Paris where this architectural style can be found.

ADDRESS: *Villa Léandre*

ARRONDISSEMENT: *18th*

CLOSEST MÉTRO STATION: *Lamarck–Caulaincourt*

Square Nadar

—— PARK

This leafy park was named for the French photographer and balloonist Gaspared-Félix Tournachon, known as Nadar. However the statue that overlooks the square is not of Nadar, but of François-Jean Lefebvre de la Barre – the last person in France to be executed for blasphemy in the 1700s (in part for failing to remove his hat during a Catholic procession).

The beautifully landscaped Square Nadar is also a dog-friendly park, which is not so easy to find in Paris. Everyone is welcome here, even sans dog. I like to come here to watch the dogs play and enjoy the incredible secret view of the Eiffel Tower, framed by the gaps in the trees.

ADDRESS: *Rue Saint-Éleuthère*

ARRONDISSEMENT: *18th*

CLOSEST MÉTRO STATION: *Lamarck–Caulaincourt or Pigalle*

Atelier Tholozé

—— CERAMICS

It was the arresting green eyes of a beautiful tabby cat that first drew me into this Montmartre ceramics workshop. Most days Elfo is perched next to the charming window display of small ceramic plates embossed with the Eiffel Tower and glazed coffee cups with delicate butterfly handles. The irony is that the gorgeous tabby who has become a mascot for the atelier doesn't belong to shop owner Anita Laginha. Instead, he's a neighbour's cat who, every morning without fail, reports to work on a purely volunteer basis (no kibbles exchanged).

Laginha's boutique stocks a wide range of handmade tableware and decorative ceramics, all handmade by Laginha and fired at her downstairs workshop. Inspired by her son, a *boulanger* (artisan baker), her mini croissant charms have a practical purpose as a *repose-couteau* (knife-rest) or a *fève*, a trinket hidden in a *galette des rois* (king's cake), traditionally baked to celebrate Epiphany (p 41). Laginha also holds casual ceramics classes throughout the week, with no strict schedules or internet forms: she encourages eager students to call.

ADDRESS: *18 Rue Tholozé*

ARRONDISSEMENT: *18th*

CLOSEST MÉTRO STATION: *Abbesses or Blanche*

Additional VENUE

B Rocante

—— ANTIQUES

Tricky to find on Google Maps because *brocante* means 'flea market' (and a map search will likely show every antique shop in Paris), B Rocante sources antiques from estate sales and auctions, and sells them for bargain prices. Despite its dusty appearance, B Rocante has a high turnover that makes it worth visiting on a regular basis. I've furnished my apartment with many objects from B Rocante, including antique mirrors, furniture and gilded candlesticks. The shop is also my go-to for collecting objects for photoshoot set design. The shop is sometimes closed while the owner is scouting for new stock, so call ahead to make sure it's open.

ADDRESS: *35 Rue Guy Môquet*

ARRONDISSEMENT: *17th*

CLOSEST MÉTRO STATION: *Brochant*

Additional VENUE

La Blouse de Lyon

—— CLOTHING

Many of today's archetypal clothing styles are descendants and variations of traditional French workwear. Take the *bleu de travail* (worker's jacket), a boxy jacket made from durable cotton twill canvas that's now a mainstay of popular brands such as A.P.C. There's also the Breton striped shirt, worn by French Navy sailors in the nineteenth century, which has become an icon of fashion houses including Chanel and Jean Paul Gautier. Even the iconic French beret (p 25) originated as functional headwear for shepherds in the French Pyrenees.

The Prussian blue facade of this store, established in 1937, is the first hint of its focus on traditional-style workwear. Current owners Gwendoline Van Opstal and Nicolas Le Jeune acquired La Blouse de Lyon in 2019 with a vision to expand its appeal beyond workers and craftspeople while preserving the essence of the shop's history. Wooden shelves and racks neatly display an extensive, curated selection of affordable accessories and clothing (with prices averaging €30–130), including traditional blouses, jackets, trousers and overalls crafted from robust materials like moleskin and denim, designed for durability and comfort. There is also a selection of shoes and clogs, which have been the choice of artisans for generations. Many of the products are produced in collaboration with legendary workwear manufacturers such as Le Laboureur, La Botte Gardiane and Lafont.

ADDRESS: *21 Rue Gérando*

ARRONDISSEMENT: *9th*

CLOSEST MÉTRO STATION: *Anvers*

Additional VENUE

Curiositas

—— GIFTS

The magpie in me cannot help but be drawn to this store's modern interpretation of the Victorian cabinet of curiosities. Every inch of the dark-wood shelves and display cases is filled with interesting objects such as minerals, fossils and butterfly specimens, all displayed in vintage apothecary jars and glass cloches. Often described as the mini Deyrolle (p 234) of the 18th arrondissement, Curiositas's unique artifacts have interesting origin stories and are responsibly sourced with certificates to confirm they're legally protected specimens. Some of the high-end objects like antique scientific instruments and rare taxidermy are expensive, with a €495 price tag for a wolverine skull. But for the not-so-serious collector, smaller gifts such as postcards and prints are €5–20.

ADDRESS: *7 Rue Ravignan*

ARRONDISSEMENT: *18th*

CLOSEST MÉTRO STATION: *Abbesses*

SHOPPING

Additional VENUE

Chez Virginie

——— CHEESE

When strolling the 18th I always stop to look in the window of Chez Virginie. Its display is the classic image of a little *fromagerie* (cheese shop) that you might find in a children's book, with overflowing displays of cheeses of every shape and size, each with a handwritten label.

This *fromagerie* is a family business that has been around since 1946 and is now in the good hands of Virginie Boularouah, a third-generation *maître fromagère-affineuse* (master cheesemonger). Chez Virginie is known for its speciality pure raw-milk cheeses, offering over 150 varieties from across France and beyond, such as the rare Corsican sheep's milk Brin d'Amour, Swiss summer truffle tomme, Italian truffle pecorino and Mont d'Or, a luxurious cow's milk cheese from the Jura Mountains. All cheeses are aged to perfection in-store.

ADDRESS: *54 Rue Damrémont*

ARRONDISSEMENT: *18th*

CLOSEST MÉTRO STATION: *Lamarck–Caulaincourt*

Additional VENUE

Marché aux Puces

—— FLEA MARKET

Located just outside the northern city limits, about 30 minutes from the city centre by métro, Marché aux Puces is one of the world's iconic and largest flea markets. Technically named Marché aux Puces de Paris Saint-Ouen, it spans seven hectares and features over 2000 stalls. Officially recognised in 1920, its origins date back to the late nineteenth century when *chiffonniers* (rag-and-bone men) scavenged discarded goods from Parisian garbage to resell. In 1885 authorities pushed these informal vendors to the outskirts of the city, where they began congregating in Saint-Ouen.

Today the Marché aux Puces is divided into 14 markets. My favourites are Marché Vernaison, with its labyrinthine layout and stalls hawking all manner of curios, and Marché Jules Vallès, known for bargain second-hand goods. There are also stalls and shops outside of the market buildings including vintage stores ripe for treasure hunting such as Beatnik and Ritchie Vintage.

There is not just shopping on offer, but also food. Stop for a snack at La Terrasse des Puces, known across Paris for its fried sardines and chips. The market is open daily but more vendors are open on weekends. Be on guard for pickpockets and don't walk down empty alleys on your own.

ADDRESS: *110–142 Rue des Rosiers*

ARRONDISSEMENT: *Saint-Ouen-sur-Seine*

CLOSEST MÉTRO STATION: *Porte de Clignancourt*

Additional VENUE

Arlette & Colette

BAKERY

Being asked by a Parisian one day where I had bought my bread was a proud rite-of-passage moment. The bread in question was from Arlette & Colette, which I think is the best bakery in Paris. But it all depends on how you like your bread. A *boulanger* (baker) will typically ask how well cooked you would like it – as if it were a steak – by asking, '*Bien cuite*?' ('Well done?').

Artlette & Colette is renowned for many of their breads including their *pain d'antan* (a rustic white loaf whose name means 'bread of yesteryear') and their seasonal breads with fruit and nuts. But the most popular variety is their signature baguette. Twice the size of the average breadstick, it resembles something between a *pain de pompagne* (country loaf) and a baguette.

ADDRESS: *4 Rue de La Jonquière*

ARRONDISSEMENT: *17th*

CLOSEST MÉTRO STATION: *Guy Môquet*

Armande

—— CAFÉ

Dining options in Parisian tourist hotspots can often be lacklustre and Montmartre is no exception, yet there are some gems to be found. Among them is Armande. After spotting their delicious-looking crab rolls in the window, I was pleased to discover that the sandwich did not disappoint, with its moreish combination of crab, apple, avocado and carrot. This kind of fresh and comforting creation is typical of the food made by former pastry chef Margaux Bellorgeya, who runs the café with her friend Sébastien Aubé. Every day Margaux prepares 10 dishes inspired by their respective travels and local seasonal ingredients, which are displayed in the window. Typical dishes include soft chicken kofta, Japanese eggplant, roasted carrots and devilled eggs. The consistently high standard of food has earned Armande its reputation as a gourmet refuge from Montmartre's more average tourist eateries.

ADDRESS: *26 Rue Tholozé*

ARRONDISSEMENT: *18th*

CLOSEST MÉTRO STATION: *Abbesses*

EAT & DRINK

Boris Lumé

—— BAKERY

With its Belle Époque facade, Boris Lumé looks like the archetypal French bakery. The trio of signboards above the entrance reading *boulangerie* (bakery), *confiserie* (confectionery) and *patisserie* (pastry shop) appear to advertise its specialties, but these actually describe the businesses of the heritage-listed building's previous owners. Pastry chef Boris Lumé and his Japanese baker wife Mihona Nishizawa continue to offer baguettes and croissants along with modern delights combining French and Japanese baking techniques (think matcha tarts). The meeting of cultures in Lumé's creations reflect the pair's heritage as well as his training under illustrious French pastry chefs, including Joël Robuchon and Cyril Lignac.

ADDRESS: *48 Rue Caulaincourt*

ARRONDISSEMENT: *18th*

CLOSEST MÉTRO STATION: *Lamarck–Caulaincourt*

Café de la Butte

—— BISTRO

Café de la Butte is a classic Parisian terrace restaurant, with its row of circular tables lined up beneath a pastel green awning. The menu features traditional bistro dishes such as *magret du canard* (seared duck breast) and slow-cooked beef cheeks reinterpreted by its chef-owner Mickey with more flavour than you can typically expect from traditional French fare (the secret is his addition of extra herbs and spices).

One of the hardest working restaurateurs in Paris, Mickey cooks and serves with the help of just one protégé in the kitchen six days a week. Closed Sundays.

ADDRESS: *71 Rue Caulaincourt*

ARRONDISSEMENT: *18th*

CLOSEST MÉTRO STATION: *Lamarck–Caulaincourt*

Café Dose

—— CAFÉ

Café Dose is a boutique micro-roastery chain with a handful of outposts tucked away in Paris's neighbourhoods. This location, next to Lamarck–Caulaincourt métro station, has big windows and an outside bench that's a real sun magnet. Sourced from certified sustainable growers in Colombia, Ethopia and beyond, then house-roasted in small batches, the coffee will satisfy connoisseurs, as will Café Dose's selection of homemade baked goods, including chunky cookies and carrot cake with a generous dollop of cream cheese icing. Café Dose also serves a delicious all-day brunch that includes avocado toast and savoury pancakes. Closed Sundays.

ADDRESS: *74 Rue Lamarck*

ARRONDISSEMENT: *18th*

CLOSEST MÉTRO STATION: *Lamarck–Caulaincourt*

La Cave des Abbesses

——— WINE BAR

This is a beloved little local wine bar and shop that has been a neighbourhood institution since the 1980s. An extension of family-owned wine business Les Cave Bourdin (established in 1962), La Cave des Abbesses is known for its diverse selection of over 300 wines sourced from the Loire Valley, Bourgogne, Bordeaux and beyond, with an emphasis on natural and biodynamic wines and traditional production methods. The staff are walking wine encyclopedias, always enthusiastic about making recommendations. To complement the wine selection, La Cave des Abbesses serves small plates including beautifully composed cheese and charcuterie platters, *rillettes* (a rich, savory spread made by slow-cooking meat in fat) and duck confit. The venue's small and intimate terrace looks onto the lively Rue des Abbesses (p 156), and is the perfect place to enjoy a leisurely *apéro* (p 43) in the late afternoon while people-watching in the heart of the 18th arrondissement.

ADDRESS: *43 Rue des Abbesses*

ARRONDISSEMENT: *18th*

CLOSEST MÉTRO STATION: *Abbesses*

Additional VENUE

Les Cinq Marches

——— CAFÉ

Named after the five steps leading down into this café, Les Cinq Marches is a charming retreat from the crowds of Montmartre. On the international menu are dishes including scones and tarts, Middle Eastern shakshuka (eggs in spicy tomato sauce) and pastrami sandwiches, all homemade using organic and locally sourced ingredients.

In the bathroom you will see a black-and-white photo of the premises in the nineteenth century – almost exactly the same as it looks today following a thoughtful renovation that retained original elements like the flooring, counter and vintage light fixtures. Large windows bathe the interior with sunlight and there's an intimate front terrace with seats nestled among climbing plants.

ADDRESS: *12 Rue Girardon*

ARRONDISSEMENT: *18th*

CLOSEST MÉTRO STATION: *Abbesses*

Additional VENUE

Les Crèmes

——— CAFÉ

Following a trip to Australia, Parisians Aiman Hemmade and Lou Bigand decided to open a café like the ones they enjoyed on their holiday and set about transforming a former hair salon into this characterful local meeting spot. The couple sourced all the reclaimed fittings and vintage furniture themselves including the counter, which they personally tiled.

The café is beloved for its specialty coffee, with non-dairy milk alternatives available, and the menu features Australian café staples with French flair such as the 'croque truffle' (toasted cheese sandwich with truffle). Located in a residential area of the 9th arrondissement, Les Crèmes offers a perfect escape from the crowds.

ADDRESS: *82 Rue Marguerite de Rochechouart*

ARRONDISSEMENT: *9th*

CLOSEST MÉTRO STATION: *Anvers*

EAT & DRINK

Additional VENUE

La Main Noire

—— CAFÉ

Founded by three friends who met in Melbourne, this Australian-style café nestles between the residential 17th arrondissement and touristic Montmartre. Its name means 'the black hand' and reflects the café's artisanal approach – everything is made by hand.

'Wellness lattes' are a specialty, with drinks including a sticky chai made by combining roasted whole spices with Rwandan black tea and honey; and a golden latte made with turmeric, ginger, wild spices and coconut oil. The seasonal food menu features Australian brunch mainstays such as scrambled eggs, a granola bowl and pancakes.

ADDRESS: *12 Rue Cavallotti*

ARRONDISSEMENT: *18th*

CLOSEST MÉTRO STATION: *La Fourche*

Marcelle

—— CAFÉ

In a city as densely populated as Paris, it's a true luxury to find a picturesque place to spend a moment in quiet solitude. Hidden in a less frequented part of Montmartre, the Villa Léandre (p 159) outpost of the Marcelle boutique café chain is a rare peaceful haven. Sitting at a terrace table on a sunny day, you really feel a sense of being immersed in the local community of the 18th arrondissement.

Marcelle offers a very good all-day international brunch menu including pancakes (savoury and sweet) and a rather decadent French toast with salted butter toffee sauce and bananas. My favourite is the 'breakfast egg in a hole' with eggs, avocado, sausages, bacon and baked beans.

ADDRESS: *1 Villa Léandre*

ARRONDISSEMENT: *18th*

CLOSEST MÉTRO STATION: *Lamarck–Caulaincourt*

DAY 3

KEY NEIGHBOURHOODS

PASSY

AUTEUIL

INVALIDES

This itinerary leans into the iconic Paris with photo opportunities that will make you scream, 'I'm in Paris!' Along with the most spectacular vantage points for viewing the Eiffel Tower, you will discover some well-kept local secrets. Charge up your camera and get ready to capture the most magical and FOMO-inducing holiday snaps.

BECOME PARISIAN (FOR THE CAMERA)

Esplanade du Trocadéro

ITINERARY

This itinerary is recommended on

WEDNESDAY
THURSDAY
FRIDAY
SATURDAY

TIPS

——— You will be visiting some locations that expect a certain formality, so **OPT FOR A SMART CASUAL OUTFIT** with leather shoes or elegant sandals.

——— You'll also want to **DRESS FOR THE CAMERA** on this photogenic itinerary.

——— **PRE-BOOKING YOUR TICKET** to climb to the roof of the **ARC DU TRIOMPHE** (p 185) can help to cut waiting times.

——— For peace of mind, **RESERVE A TABLE** for dinner at **BRASSERIE LIPP** (p 206).

DAY 3

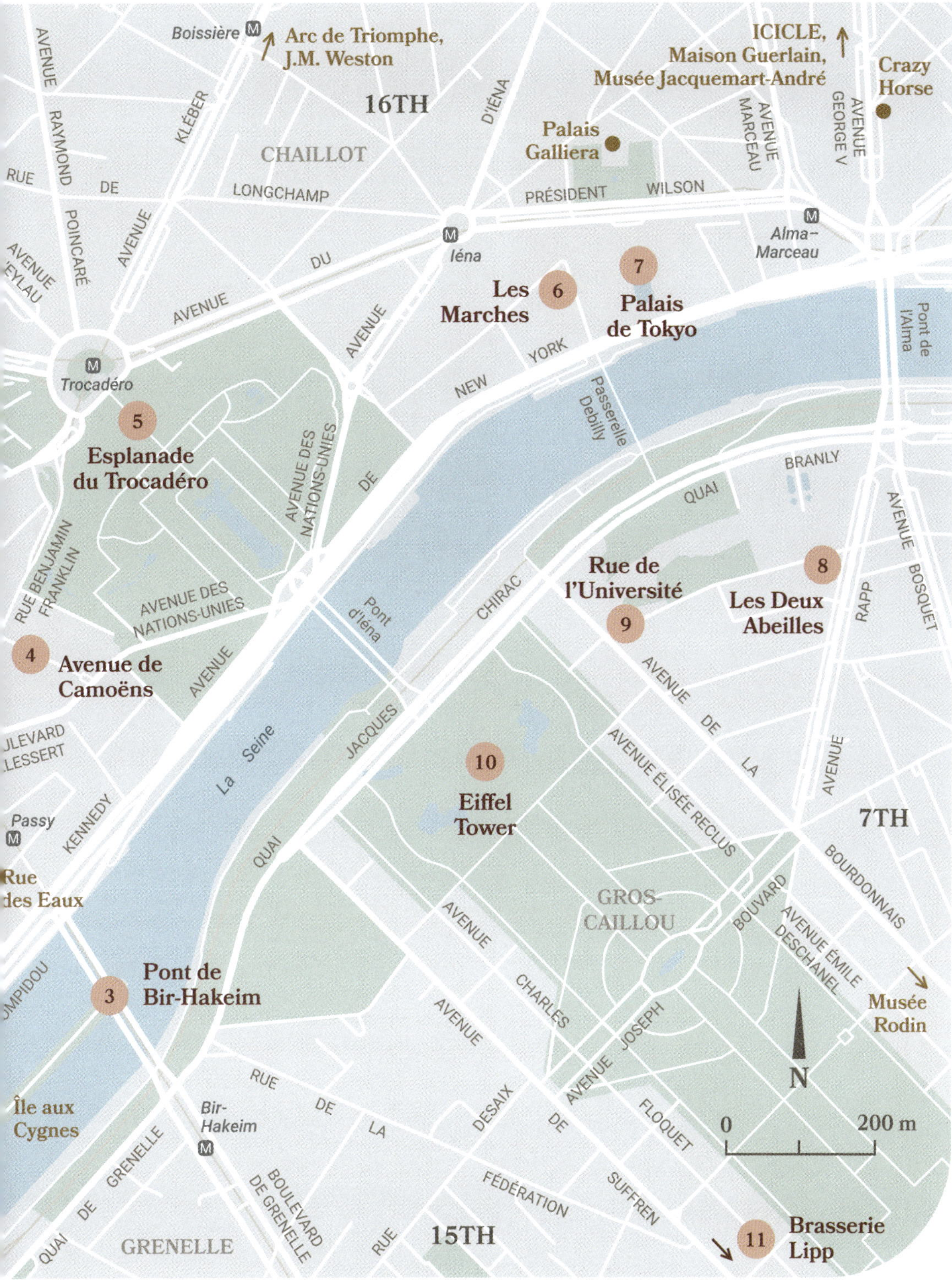
Boissière
Arc de Triomphe, J.M. Weston
ICICLE, Maison Guerlain, Musée Jacquemart-André
Crazy Horse
16TH
CHAILLOT
Palais Galliera
AVENUE RAYMOND POINCARÉ
AVENUE KLÉBER
D'IÉNA
AVENUE MARCEAU
AVENUE GEORGE V
RUE DE LONGCHAMP
PRÉSIDENT WILSON
AVENUE D'EYLAU
AVENUE DU
Iéna
Alma-Marceau
7
Palais de Tokyo
6
Les Marches
AVENUE
AVENUE
NEW YORK
Pont de l'Alma
Trocadéro
5
Esplanade du Trocadéro
Passerelle Debilly
AVENUE DES NATIONS-UNIES
DE
BRANLY
QUAI
AVENUE BOSQUET
RUE BENJAMIN FRANKLIN
AVENUE DES NATIONS-UNIES
8
Rue de l'Université
Les Deux Abeilles
RAPP
CHIRAC
Pont d'Iéna
9
4
Avenue de Camoëns
AVENUE
AVENUE DE LA
JACQUES
La Seine
10
Eiffel Tower
AVENUE ÉLISÉE RECLUS
AVENUE
7TH
Passy
KENNEDY
QUAI
Rue des Eaux
GROS-CAILLOU
BOUVARD
BOURDONNAIS
AVENUE ÉMILE DESCHANEL
AVENUE
CHARLES
3
Pont de Bir-Hakeim
AVENUE
Musée Rodin
AVENUE JOSEPH
N
RUE DE LA
DESAIX
DE
FLOQUET
0
200 m
Île aux Cygnes
Bir-Hakeim
GRENELLE
BOULEVARD DE GRENELLE
FÉDÉRATION
SUFFREN
QUAI DE GRENELLE
GRENELLE
RUE
15TH
11
Brasserie Lipp

ITINERARY

② Maison de Balzac

MORNING

——— Make your way to La Muette métro station in the 16th arrondissement and begin your day exploring ① **Rue de l'Annonciation** (p 204), its main shopping street lined with grocers, cheesemongers, specialty shops and bakeries where you can pick up a pastry to keep you going until breakfast or morning tea at your next stop.

① Rue de l'Annonciation

——— At the southern end of Rue de l'Annonciation, visit ② **Maison de Balzac** (p 193), the former house of celebrated French writer Honoré de Balzac that's now a museum dedicated to his work and life. The museum is a quiet retreat in the Passy neighbourhood, complete with an Eiffel Tower view. After viewing the exhibit, have a late breakfast or a drink at the maison's tearoom and relax in the garden terrace with its atmospheric ivy-covered wall – if the weather allows.

——— Your next destination is the ③ **Pont de Bir-Hakeim** (Bir-Hakeim Bridge, p 198). Take the secret route down the enigmatic long staircase of Rue des Eaux (p 199) that begins on Rue Raynouard, historically used to take livestock down to the water of the Seine. Then cross the two-level bridge and soak up the stunning Eiffel Tower views.

③ Pont de Bir-Hakeim

ITINERARY

AFTERNOON

—— Take Line 6 from Bir-Hakeim métro station to the Passy métro station, making sure to look out the left-side (west-facing) window as it passes back over the Pont de Bir-Hakeim to admire a delightfully unexpected view of the Eiffel Tower.

—— Exit the métro at Passy station and walk north on Rue de l'Alboni until you reach Boulevard Delessert, then head east to the bust of Portuguese poet Luís de Camões at the bottom of ④ **Avenue de Camoëns** (p 186). Head up the stairs behind the bust to enjoy another view of the Eiffel Tower, framed by Haussmann buildings (p 67) on either side of the avenue.

⑤ Esplanade du Trocadéro (above and right)

⑦ Palais de Tokyo

——— Continue to the north end of Avenue de Camoëns, then follow Rue Benjamin Franklin eastward until you reach the ⑤ **Esplanade du Trocadéro** (p 190), Paris's most iconic Eiffel Tower vantage point, where the geometric tiled walkway creates photogenic leading lines towards the iconic monument.

——— After enjoying the grandeur of Trocadéro, head east on Avenue du Président Wilson, then turn right and descend the stairs of Rue de la Manutention to ⑥ **Les Marches** (p 208) for a late brasserie lunch before it closes at 2.30 pm.

——— After lunch enter the grounds of the ⑦ **Palais de Tokyo** (p 197) art centre from its back entrance around the corner from Les Marches on Avenue de New York and admire the geometric fountain and huge bas-relief on the building's facade before you head inside to check out the current exhibition.

View of the Eiffel Tower from Paris Métro Line 6

ITINERARY

EVENING

——— Exit the Palais de Tokyo via its back entrance, then head east until Pont de l'Alma. Cross this bridge and continue south on Avenue Rapp, then turn right onto Rue de l'Université to arrive at Parisian teahouse **⑧ Les Deux Abeilles** (p 208). Stop here for an early evening snack, sampling some of Paris's best cakes and tarts as well as savoury options.

——— Continue to the west end of **⑨ Rue de l'Université** (p 199), where you can admire another dramatic view of the Eiffel Tower juxtaposed against Haussmann apartment buildings. From here you can continue into the Champ-de-Mars park to get a close-up view of the **⑩ Eiffel Tower** (p 188) from its base, but be particularly mindful of pickpockets operating in this touristy area, especially after dark.

⑨ Rue de l'Université

⑧ Les Deux Abeilles

⑪ Brasserie Lipp

⑩ Eiffel Tower

—— If time allows, climb the Eiffel Tower for a city view before dinner. Otherwise, arrange a taxi or Uber to ⑪ **Brasserie Lipp** (p 206) in Saint-Germain-des-Prés for dinner. This historical establishment is a Parisian institution serving traditional French cuisine in a classic brasserie atmosphere.

ATTRACTIONS

Additional VENUE

Arc de Triomphe
—— MONUMENT

As emblematic of Paris as the Eiffel Tower (p 188), the 50-metre-high (164-foot-high) Arc de Triomphe (technically the Arc de Triomphe de l'Étoile) at the western end of the Avenue des Champs-Élysées was commissioned by Napoleon Bonaparte in 1806. Completed in 1836, it was originally intended to honour French military victories with bas reliefs and high reliefs on the facades depicting key moments of the French Revolution and Napoleonic era. Among the large high reliefs on each of its four pillars is *Le Triomphe de 1910* (signifying the end of the Fifth Coalition during the Napoleonic Wars), showing Napoleon crowned by the Goddess of Victory.

In 1920, to honour France's fallen soldiers from the First World War, the remains of an unknown soldier were laid to rest underneath the Arc and an eternal flame was ignited. It is rekindled by veterans at 6.30 pm daily, and on Armistice Day (11 November) the French President lays a wreath here. Plaques have been added to commemorate France's role in more recent conflicts.

As the centrepiece of the Avenue des Champs-Élysées, the Arch has presided over France's most important parades, commemorations and celebrations for centuries, including Bastille Day parades, military victory marches and visits by popes and heads of states. It has also been the symbolic mass gathering place for other events that forever left their mark on the French psyche, such as the celebration of France's first FIFA World Cup victory in 1998 when the arch was illuminated with the names and images of the players; and the state funeral procession for French rock icon Johnny Hallyday in December 2017, when spectators turned out in huge numbers to cover every inch of the Avenue des Champs-Élysées.

Today visitors can explore its sculpted reliefs, attend the daily rekindling of the flame at the Tomb of the Unknown Soldier ceremony and even climb to the monument's rooftop terrace to experience one of Paris's most unforgettable views along the Axe Historique (p 74).

The entrance to climb up the Arc de Triomphe is accessed via an underground passage beneath Place Charles de Gaulle, which takes you inside the base of the arch where you'll find the ticket office and security checkpoint at the bottom of the spiral staircase. The 284-step staircase leads to the attic – a lift can carry you to this point, but you will need to climb 46 more steps to reach the rooftop terrace. I suggest allowing up to an hour for the entire experience, though due to its popularity you may need to factor in extra time for queuing, especially in summer and on weekends and public holidays. Aim for a weekday morning for a less hectic experience.

ADDRESS: *Place Charles de Gaulle*

ARRONDISSEMENT: *Paris Centre*

CLOSEST MÉTRO STATION: *Kléber or George V*

ATTRACTIONS

Avenue de Camoëns

—— STREET

While the secret is well and truly out about this Eiffel Tower viewing spot, this popular location for planned engagement photoshoots is still a beauty. Flanked by elegant Haussmann buildings, the narrow, cobblestone Avenue de Camoëns leads to a small terrace at its southern end that frames the Eiffel Tower (p 188) perfectly. Note the bust of Luís de Camõe, Portugal's greatest poet, at the bottom of the stairs.

ADDRESS: *Avenue de Camoëns*

ARRONDISSEMENT: *16th*

CLOSEST MÉTRO STATION: *Passy or Trocadéro*

Additional VENUE

Crazy Horse

—— CABARET

Emerging during the Belle Époque period of the late 1800s, Parisian cabaret venues established a tradition of risqué topless or nude performances such as the can-can at the Moulin Rouge. Crazy Horse is a more 'recent' addition to the scene, founded in 1951 among the ultra-chic couture houses of the day like Dior and Givenchy. The cabaret has always been linked with fashion, having collaborated throughout the decades with famous designers like Balenciaga (located next door), Karl Lagerfeld and Azzedine Alaïa (p 286).

The aesthetic of Crazy Horse makes it unique in the modern cabaret scene. All Crazy Horse dancers (Crazy Girls) must pass an extremely demanding selection process with strict physical proportion requirements. The cabaret's iconic choreography is highly technical and physically demanding, requiring months of intensive training to master.

In contrast to the grand productions and expansive stages of other Paris cabarets, Crazy Horse is an intimate and immersive space that makes you feel almost part of the 90-minute shows. A range of experience packages are offered with show-only tickets from €115 per person. More indulgent and expensive packages include Champagne, macarons and caviar.

ADDRESS: *12 Avenue George V*

ARRONDISSEMENT: *8th*

CLOSEST MÉTRO STATION: *Alma–Marceau*

ATTRACTIONS

Eiffel Tower

—— MONUMENT

There is perhaps no symbol more synonomous with Paris than the Eiffel Tower (Tour Eiffel), yet the tapered iron monument was never intended to be a permanent structure. Constructed between 1887 and 1889 for the 1900 world's fair, it was initially designed to be a temporary installation to commemorate the centennial of the French Revolution. Designed by engineer Gustave Eiffel and his team, the tower – so modern and daring for its time – faced criticism from artists and intellectuals who deemed it an eyesore. At the time, the 330-metre-high (1083-foot-high) tower was the world's tallest structure. Its intended lifespan was just 20 years, but it was initially preserved for utilitarian reasons (as a vital radio transmission tower) and the rest is history. The city now enforces strict building height regulations (with some rare exceptions like the Tour Montparnasse and developments in La Défense), limiting most structures to around 37 metres (120 feet), ensuring unobstructed views of the Eiffel Tower from every vantage point.

The real magic happens in the evening. Just after dusk, the Eiffel Tower projects a beam of light that can be seen across Paris. An electrical overhaul in 1985 saw 336 sodium-vapor lamps installed within the tower's structure, bestowing it with its now-signature golden hue. Then in 1999 for the millennium celebrations, 20,000 flashing bulbs were added, creating its iconic glittering effect. Nowadays, the tower sparkles for five minutes every hour on the hour from nightfall until 1 am (when the light beam is also turned off).

It's also possible to climb up into the tower. Three levels can be reached via stairs or lift. The first and second levels have a number of shops and restaurants, notably Michelin-starred restaurant Le Jules Verne on the second level. At the summit (third level), you'll find the Champagne Bar and Gustave Eiffel's restored office. Ticket prices vary (using the lift costs more) and should be booked in advance, especially on weekends.

ADDRESS: *Avenue Gustave Eiffel*

ARRONDISSEMENT: *7th*

CLOSEST MÉTRO STATION: *Bir-Hakeim or Trocadéro*

ATTRACTIONS

Esplanade du Trocadéro

—— ESPLANADE

Perched on the Right Bank, the Esplanade du Trocadéro is the most famous place in Paris from which to admire and photograph the Eiffel Tower (p 188). The grandeur and symmetry of nineteenth-century French architecture is exemplified by its magnificent design. The striking geometric floor tiling creates perfect leading lines towards the Eiffel Tower across the Seine, and the colonnaded wings of the Palais de Challiot cradle the green lawns and fountain of the Jardins du Trocadéro (Trocadéro Gardens) unfurling below.

On 10 December 1948 the United Nations General Assembly adopted the Universal Declaration of Human Rights within the Palais de Chaillot, giving the esplanade its nickname: the Esplanade of Human Rights.

ADDRESS: *Place du Trocadéro et du 11 Novembre*

ARRONDISSEMENT: *16th*

CLOSEST MÉTRO STATION: *Trocadéro*

Additional VENUE

Fondation Louis Vuitton

—— ART MUSEUM

French multinational luxury goods conglomerate LVMH invests significantly in the preservation and restoration of French artistic and cultural heritage. Opened in 2014 in the sprawling Bois de Boulogne public park, the nonprofit Fondation Louis Vuitton is one of the few privately owned and funded art spaces in Paris.

Designed by legendary Canadian-American architect Frank Gehry, the innovative deconstructivist building resembles a ship, with billowing glass sails and 12 enormous glass panels that allow natural light to flood the interior. Works in the permanent collection – including Jeff Koons's *Balloon Dog (Yellow)* – fall into four categories: contemplative, pop, expressionist and music and sound. The foundation also organises two major exhibitions annually (which have an entrance fee) with past exhibitions featuring artists such as Jean-Michel Basquiat, Egon Schiele and Olafur Eliasson. Beyond the exhibitions there are impressive indoor and outdoor spaces to explore, including a striking reflective pool surrounding the building that underscores its nautical theme.

ADDRESS: *8 Avenue du Mahatma Gandhi*

ARRONDISSEMENT: *16th*

CLOSEST MÉTRO STATION: *Porte Dauphine or Pont de Neuilly*

ATTRACTIONS

Additional VENUE

Île aux Cygnes

——— ISLAND

One of three picturesque islands in the heart of the Seine, Île aux Cygnes (Island of Swans) is a long and narrow artificial isle created in 1827 to protect the Pont de Grenelle (Grenelle Bridge). Only accessible to foot traffic (and bikes), making it perfect for a stroll, its tree-lined Allée des Cygnes (Path of Swans) extends the full length of the island, which is just 900 metres (0.5 mile) long and 21 metres (0.1 mile) wide.

Despite its name, there are no swans on the island. Its name is an homage to a now-vanished natural island that once existed further upstream in the Seine near the Champ-de-Mars, which had been home to swans gifted to the French monarchy. There are entrances on the Pont de Grenelle and the Pont de Bir-Hakeim (p 198). At the western end you'll find an unexpected surprise. Here stands a quarter-scale replica of the Statue of Liberty, which symbolically looks west toward the New York City original.

ADDRESS: *Île aux Cygnes*

ARRONDISSEMENT: *16th*

CLOSEST MÉTRO STATION: *Bir-Hakeim*

This is FREE

Maison de Balzac

—— MUSEUM

Dedicated to the life and works of French literary great Honoré de Balzac, Maison de Balzac (Balzac's House) is located in the modest house he lived in from 1840–47. In debt and seeking to hide from his creditors, he rented the five-room apartment on the top floor (in his housekeeper's name), which opens onto a lovely garden with Eiffel Tower views.

During the seven years he lived in this Passy neighbourhood home, he worked feverishly on *La Comédie Humaine* (*The Human Comedy*), his vast collection of interlinked novels and stories depicting French society in 1815–48. Among the 91 finished works was *Le Père Gorio* (*Father Goriot*, 1835); its story of a young person learning to navigate Parisian society was immediately relatable to me as a newcomer to Paris. Balzac was notoriously productive, writing up to 30 words per minute by quill from 1 am to 8 am every day. The coffee pot that sustained him (he drank up to 50 cups per day) is one of the personal objects preserved at his former home.

ADDRESS: *47 Rue Raynouard*

ARRONDISSEMENT: *16th*

CLOSEST MÉTRO STATION: *Passy*

Additional VENUE

Musée Jacquemart-André

—— ART MUSEUM

Édouard André was a wealthy nineteenth-century banker and art collector who in the late 1800s commissioned the construction of this mansion to house his growing art collection. An art-world love story, André met and married renowned portrait painter Nélie Jacquemart in 1881 and together they travelled extensively, acquiring artworks from Europe and Asia. In accordance with a plan made with her husband before his death in 1911, Nélie bequeathed the mansion and its collections to the Institut de France upon her own death the following year, stipulating that it be turned into a museum. The Musée Jacquemart-André opened to the public in 1913.

A prime example of the opulent Haussmann architecture (p 67) that characterised Paris in the late nineteenth century, the mansion is divided into several distinct areas including the lavishly decorated State Apartments featuring works by eighteenth-century painters such as François Boucher and Jean Siméon Chardin, and the scarlet-hued Library housing a Rembrandt. Every part of the house showcases opulent mosaics, carvings and frescos including the stunning fresco by Venetian painter Giovanni Battista Tiepolo depicting Henry III ascending to the French throne in 1574 that decorates the wall above the Winter Garden's grand staircase. The former dining room is now a café and restaurant called Le Nélie, which houses another significant Tiepolo fresco.

ADDRESS: *158 Boulevard Haussmann*

ARRONDISSEMENT: *8th*

CLOSEST MÉTRO STATION: *Monceau or Saint-Philippe-du-Roule*

Additional VENUE

Musée Rodin

—— ART MUSEUM

Some artworks are so ubiquitous that they are instantly recognisable to anyone with so much as a passing interest in art. Among them is *The Thinker* by Auguste Rodin. The artist created 28 full-size bronze castings of his most famous sculpture, but to see the original you need to visit the Musée Rodin (Rodin Museum).

The museum is housed in the Hôtel Biron, an eighteenth-century Rococo mansion where Rodin began renting rooms as a workspace in 1908. He fell in love with the building and its gardens, which inspired much of his work. When the French government acquired the property in 1911, Rodin negotiated a deal: he would donate his entire collection of sculptures, drawings and personal archives to the state in exchange for the right to live and work in the Hôtel Biron for the rest of his life. One of the first museums in France dedicated to a single artist, Musée Rodin officially opened in 1919.

Breaking conventions with idealised Greco-Roman sculpture, Rodin's works explore emotional themes of love, despair, struggle and introspection, and represent the human form with the imperfections of realism. My favourite is *The Kiss*, a marble sculpture taking centre stage in the main gallery that captures an intimate embrace of two lovers, inspired by *The Divine Comedy*, an Italian narrative poem by Dante Alighieri. Some of Rodin's most famous large-scale sculptures, including *The Thinker* and *The Gates of Hell*, are found in the garden, which fashion house Dior has a history of using as a venue for its haute couture shows.

ADDRESS: *77 Rue de Varenne*

ARRONDISSEMENT: *7th*

CLOSEST MÉTRO STATION: *Varenne*

Additional VENUE

Palais Galliera

—— FASHION MUSEUM & PARK

Containing a permanent collection of over 200,000 pieces, Palais Galliera (officially Musée de la Mode de la Ville de Paris) is Paris's first fashion museum. There are historical garments that offer a glimpse of eighteenth-century France's gilded glamour; important haute couture pieces by designers such as Coco Chanel, Christian Dior and Yves Saint Laurent; and countless photographs and original design sketches that document the design processes of the great French designers.

The museum was originally envisioned by Italian noblewoman and philanthropist Maria Brignole-Sale De Ferrari, the Duchess of Galliera, who commissioned the construction of the *palais* to house her extensive art collection. The building itself is magnificent with a rectangular shape and symmetrical design in the Beaux-Arts style. As you enter, an arcade encircles the palace's iconic wrought-iron door, while classical statues are made even more dramatic as the sun casts long shadows between the limestone columns.

A little local secret about Palais Galliera is that the garden at the rear of the building is a public park called Square du Palais-Galliera. This more discrete entrance is just opposite the Palais de Tokyo (p 197) on Avenue du Président Wilson and cannot be accessed via the museum itself. Lush with long-blooming flowers and anchored by a fountain dotted with bronze sculptures, the park is a peaceful retreat in the 16th arrondissement.

ADDRESS: *10 Avenue Pierre 1er de Serbie*

ARRONDISSEMENT: *16th*

CLOSEST MÉTRO STATION: *Iéna*

Palais de Tokyo

—— ART CENTRE

Built for the 1937 world's fair, Palais de Tokyo (Tokyo Palace) is now the largest centre of contemporary art in Europe, focusing on compelling temporary exhibitions. Named for the road separating the building from the Seine, which in the 1930s was called Avenue de Tokio (it has since been renamed Avenue de New York), the grand building was one of the first in the city to use steel and concrete; its minimalist exposed concrete facade contrasting with the ornate buildings surrounding it.

Exhibitions feature works in a variety of media – from paintings to performance art – and highlight both established and emerging talents. Past exhibitions have featured some of the most prominent names in contemporary art such as Yayoi Kusama, Takashi Murakami, Pierre Huyghe, Maurizio Cattelan and Santiago Sierra. The modern and expansive exhibition spaces also lend well to hosting fashion shows, and during the Paris fashion weeks the museum often hosts the shows of emerging and experimental designers, aligning with the innovative spirit of the venue.

To truly experience the building's grandeur, enter from Avenue de New York (technically the back entrance) and follow the steps up to the geometric fountain, juxtaposed by classical structures. From here there's a great view of the Eiffel Tower, framed by the museum's distinctive architecture. Continue up the stairs that lead to an arcade lined by fluted pillars. Covering the wall is a large bas-relief depicting scenes of human figures engaged in labour to represent industrial progress, technology and modernity. My favourite part of the museum is the set of stairs that lead from the rear of the building to the front entrance, where the shadows of the pillars create dramatic geometric contrasts. With large, open and smooth spaces so rare in this compact city, the rear of the Palais de Tokyo is often occupied by skateboarders, especially when the fountain is emptied.

ADDRESS: *13 Avenue du Président Wilson*

ARRONDISSEMENT: *8th*

CLOSEST MÉTRO STATION: *Iéna*

ATTRACTIONS

Pont de Bir-Hakeim

——— BRIDGE

Unveiled in 1905, the two-level Pont de Bir-Hakeim showcased the height of engineering at the time and is a shining example of Art Nouveau aesthetics, with cast-iron columns supporting the viaduct adorned with sculpted motifs. Originally named Passy Bridge, it was renamed in 1948 to honour the Free French Forces' stand at the Battle of Bir-Hakeim in Libya during the Second World War.

The Line 6 métro runs along the second level, unusual in a city where most métro lines are underground. Backdropped by the Eiffel Tower, it makes for a unique photo opportunity. The lower level is a road with pedestrian and bike paths that offer similarly dramatic Eiffel Tower views.

The bridge is a popular filming location – you might remember it from *Inception* (2010), while French audiences will know it from the 1975 film *Peur Sur la Ville*, which sees French actor Jean-Paul Belmondo walk atop a moving train. Following Belmond's death in 2021, the City of Paris named the central walkway of the bridge 'Promenade Jean-Paul Belmondo' – look for the sign illustrated with a still from the movie scene.

ADDRESS: *Boulevard de Grenelle*

ARRONDISSEMENT: *8th*

CLOSEST MÉTRO STATION: *Bir-Hakeim*

Additional VENUE

Rue des Eaux

—— STREET

I was walking in the Passy neighbourhood one day when I noticed a hidden set of stairs. Descending 63 metres (206 feet), this lane is unlike any other street in Paris. Historical records show that Passy residents used these stairs to take their livestock down to the Seine, but the street sign highlights Rue des Eaux as the 'Street of Waters'. This sign remembers the area's history as a mineral springs destination, a place Parisians visited during the 1700s for the waters' healing properties.

The stairs will take you down to Square Charles-Dickens, a shortcut to the Pont de Bir-Hakeim (p 198), and also to the Musée du Vin (Museum of Wine). Turning back to look at the entrance to the stairs from below, you'll see that the staircase is almost completely hidden, making you feel as if you've just passed through Platform 9¾ in a *Harry Potter* novel.

ADDRESS: *Rue des Eaux*

ARRONDISSEMENT: *16th*

CLOSEST MÉTRO STATION: *Passy*

Rue de l'Université

—— STREET

The western end of Rue de l'Université, near the Champ-de-Mars park, offers one of the city's most dramatic views of the Eiffel Tower. Standing at the intersection with Avenue de la Bourdonnais, the Haussmann apartment buildings (p 67) lining the narrow cobblestone street create a striking contrast with the monumental structure rising up from the Champ-de-Mars. Continue to the cul-de-sac at the western end of Rue de l'Université for uninterrupted Eiffel Tower views. Prepare to share the view with influencers and travel photographers, especially on weekends.

ADDRESS: *Rue de l'Université*

ARRONDISSEMENT: *7th*

CLOSEST MÉTRO STATION: *Alma–Marceau*

SHOPPING

Additional VENUE

ICICLE

——— FASHION

Founded in Shanghai in 1997, ICICLE's distinctive approach is rooted in the Chinese values of 敬天 (*Jing Tian* or reverence for nature), 爱人 (*Ai Ren* or kindness for others) and 惜物 (*Xi Wu* or cherishing what is given).

Well-known for its high-quality clothing and accessories that are made from the finest natural materials, the brand's signature products are timeless wardrobe staples including their cult cotton T-shirt in seasonal tones and signature trench coat made with ICICLE's patented DEW fabric, a blend of merino wool and silk that's naturally water repellent, wind resistant and exceptionally lightweight. Following a responsible production process designed to minimise waste, its garments and accessories are created to last as long as possible.

While ICICLE's origins are in China, its flagship store in Paris (opened in 2019) is a fashion destination in Europe. Occupying a nineteenth-century building and spanning four levels, it's a calming, minimalist space featuring natural materials like limestone and wood. Also integrated are a bookstore and a rotating series of contemporary art exhibitions often bridging Western and Chinese perspectives.

ADDRESS: *35 Avenue George V*

ARRONDISSEMENT: *Paris Centre*

CLOSEST MÉTRO STATION: *George V*

Additional VENUE

J.M. Weston

—— SHOES

For many Parisians, getting fitted for your first pair of J.M. Weston shoes is a coming-of-age moment.

The brand's origins date back to 1891 when Édouard Blanchard established a shoe factory in Limousin. After studying shoemaking in the United States, his son Eugène Blanchard integrated new techniques into his father's brand including the Goodyear welt method that allowed shoes to be resoled multiple times, extending their durability and longevity, and which – along with the highest quality materials such as French calf leather – have become the defining features of J.M. Weston shoes today. Signature models including the Mocassin 180 have remained staples since their inception, reinterpreted from season to season with different materials or in collaboration with designers.

Opened in 1922, the brand's first Paris boutique rapidly gained a loyal local clientele of professionals, intellectuals and aristocrats who resided in the affluent 8th arrondissement. It's said that whisky and cigars were served as gentlemen had their shoes fitted. Staff continue to fit shoes the traditional (snug) way, which allows the shoe to mould around the foot with wear and also prevents excessive creasing over the toe of the shoe.

ADDRESS: *98 Boulevard de Courcelles*

ARRONDISSEMENT: *8th*

CLOSEST MÉTRO STATION: *Ternes or Monceau*

SHOPPING

Additional VENUE

Maison Guerlain

—— PERFUME

Founded in 1828 and renowned for creating custom fragrances for the likes of Queen Victoria and Queen Isabella II, French perfume and beauty brand Guerlain established its flagship store on the prestigious Avenue des Champs-Élysées in 1914. Featuring marble floors, extravagant chandeliers and carved wood panelling, the original Art Deco–style interior was designed by Charles Méwès, architect of the Ritz Paris. In 2005, lauded US architect Peter Marino modernised the space by adding mirrored surfaces and minimalist lighting that now creates a striking contrast with the original decor.

Historical fragrances are displayed in 'perfume galleries' on the ground floor alongside the brand's current range, with bespoke services including personalised fragrance creation offered in the private salon upstairs.

The most influential member of the Guerlain dynasty was master perfumer Jacques Guerlain, who created iconic fragrances including Shalimar, L'Heure Bleue and Mitsouko. The brand is also known for its 1936 invention, the Rouge Automatique, a lipstick operated by a small lever, facilitating one-handed application. Cult fragrances produced by the brand more recently include La Petite Robe Noire, an ode to the little black dress that was released in 2012.

ADDRESS: *68 Avenue des Champs-Élysées*

ARRONDISSEMENT: *8th*

CLOSEST MÉTRO STATION: *George V or Franklin D. Roosevelt*

Additional VENUE

Maison Sarah Lavoine

—— GIFTS & HOMEWARES

I love Paris's *fond de court* (back of the courtyard) boutiques. Due to the lack of retail space in the city centre, many of the most interesting shops are located deep within a building's courtyard. The *fond de court* of 25 Rue de l'Annonciation (p 204) is home to eponymous French interior brand Maison Sarah Lavoine's 16th arrondissement outpost. The boutique has preserved the original exposed beam, glass ceiling and steel trusses, creating an open space that feels refreshingly airy as you enter.

Sarah Lavoine's designs are characterised by bold colours, organic forms and simple Parisian elegance. The range runs the gamut of soft upholstered furniture, vibrant tableware and home décor and patterned textiles. The most sought-after products are the 'blue Sarah' objects made in the brand's iconic blue shade, which is used as accents on its ceramics and décor. Also on offer is a ready-to-wear line of relaxed-chic clothing.

The boutique sells other French brands, too, including Parisian ready-to-wear brand Sézane and fine-jewellery boutique brand Pascale Monvoisin.

ADDRESS: *25 Rue de l'Annonciation*

ARRONDISSEMENT: *16th*

CLOSEST MÉTRO STATION: *La Muette*

SHOPPING

Rue de l'Annonciation

—— STREET

Once part of the historic village of Passy, Rue de l'Annonciation is a popular local shopping hub, perfect for getting a glimpse of Parisian life. Among the many shops to be found here are Huitres et Saumons de Passy, a beloved purveyor of fresh seafood and natural wines; gourmet grocery store Maison Gosselin; and Maison Sarah Lavoine (p 203), one of the boutiques of the renowned French interior designer known for her vibrant use of colour. There is also an outpost of French fashion brand Sézane, known for its vintage-inspired designs that embody the Parisian aesthetic of simple and effortless dressing. Called Le Petit Apartement, it's more intimate than Sézane's larger boutiques in the centre of Paris, offering a curated selection of the brand's collection.

ADDRESS: *Rue de l'Annonciation*

ARRONDISSEMENT: *16th*

CLOSEST MÉTRO STATION: *La Muette*

Additional VENUE

Tendance Raphia

GIFTS & HOMEWARES

Most Saturdays, you're likely to find the stall of Titiane and Nicolas Randrianarivony just outside Marché Couvert de Passy. Specialising in artisanal goods from Madagascar, the couple's stall – laden with straw hats, colourful textiles and handmade baskets – has been a neighbourhood institution for decades. In addition to importing handmade products, the stall owners also work with NGOs to help launch small businesses to support remote communities in Madagascar. The stall is generally found at this location between April and December. Titiane and Nicolas spend the rest of the year in Madagascar sourcing new wares.

ADDRESS: *Place de Passy*

ARRONDISSEMENT: *16th*

CLOSEST MÉTRO STATION: *La Muette*

Brasserie Lipp

—— BRASSERIE

Brasserie Lip may have become a tourist hot spot, but the high-quality French classics it dishes up keeps locals coming too. I like their herring and warm potato salad, *oeuf en gelée* (egg in aspic), *pâté en croûte* (pâté baked inside a pastry crust) and the classic *blanquette de veau* (a creamy veal stew with a white sauce, carrots and mushrooms, served with rice).

Brasserie Lipp is one of the last brasseries in Paris where you can witness career *garçons* (waiters) showcase the art of service. I'm always fascinated by the way they navigate between packed tables with an air of nonchalance, almost to the point of indifference to the customer, while they simultaneously charm diners with the same 'Franglish' jokes they have been repeating for decades.

ADDRESS: *151 Boulevard Saint-Germain*

ARRONDISSEMENT: *6th*

CLOSEST MÉTRO STATION: *Saint-Germain-des-Prés*

Additional VENUE

Les Choupettes de ChouChou

—— BAKERY

Les Choupettes de ChouChou is a Montmartre-born bakery that exclusively makes 'choupettes'. These are founder Sandra Schoukroun's take on French 'chou' pastry – a hollow pastry topped with powdered sugar that you can find in just about every Parisian bakery. Schoukroun (nicknamed ChouChou) had a childhood obsession with this sweet treat and decided to take these pastries to the next level by adding delicious fillings like vanilla, chocolate and coffee cream. Thus the choupette was born, and it looks as cute and tastes as good as the name sounds.

Les Choupettes de ChouChou has two locations in Paris, with the original at 27 Rue Durantin in the 18th arrondissement. Both boutiques are simple and cosy with an open-view kitchen where you can watch choupettes being made fresh and filled to order. This cute little snack starts from €1.25, but I challenge you to stop at just one.

ADDRESS: *24 Rue de l'Annonciation*

ARRONDISSEMENT: *16th*

CLOSEST MÉTRO STATION: *La Muette*

EAT & DRINK

Les Deux Abeilles

CAFÉ

Renowned for its cakes since 1985, Les Deux Abeilles (The Two Bees) is a gem of a tearoom located near the Eiffel Tower. Every day it displays a decadent array of sweet treats in the window, from chocolate fondant to cheesecake. I can't go past their lemon meringue tart – with its generous dollops of fluffy meringue piled high, it's almost too pretty to eat. Savoury tarts and salads are also available. The cosy interior is tightly packed with little white tables and chairs, with terrace seating during the warmer months looking onto the quieter residential end of Rue de l'Universite (p 199).

ADDRESS: *189 Rue de l'Université*

ARRONDISSEMENT: *7th*

CLOSEST MÉTRO STATION: *Alma–Marceau*

Les Marches

RESTAURANT

A good local French brasserie serving honest, traditional French food is hard to find even in Paris's residential neighbourhoods. Right next door to the Palais de Tokyo (p 197), Les Marches is hidden in plain sight. With simple folding tables, its modest appearance is part of its secret to maintaining a predominantly local clientele – tourists either overlook it or are intimidated by its lack of English menus. However, when lunchtime rolls around Les Marches's terrace is packed full of Parisians who come for its French comfort food dishes such as *steak frites* (steak and fries), *blanquette de veau* (white stew of veal) and *chou farci* (stuffed cabbage), served in generous portions at reasonable prices, and all in a laid-back, cosy setting.

ADDRESS: *5 Rue de la Manutention*

ARRONDISSEMENT: *16th*

CLOSEST MÉTRO STATION: *Iéna*

BRASSERIE

DAY 4

KEY NEIGHBOURHOODS

SAINT-GERMAIN-DES-PRÉS

LATIN QUARTER

Now that you've experienced the iconic Paris, it's time to ease into the Parisian lifestyle. This itinerary introduces you to Saint-Germain-des-Prés and the Latin Quarter, with plenty of people-watching opportunities in store. You will discover local hangouts and neighbourhood shops, observe and partake in Parisian leisure in the Jardin du Luxembourg and retrace the footsteps of American novelist Ernest Hemingway near Place de la Contrescarpe.

BECOME PARISIAN (WHEN NO-ONE'S WATCHING)

Jardin du Luxembourg

ITINERARY

This itinerary is recommended on

TUESDAY
WEDNESDAY
THURSDAY
FRIDAY
SATURDAY

TIPS

—— Some venues including museums and upscale shops expect a degree of formality, so **AVOID WEARING VERY CASUAL CLOTHING OR SPORTSWEAR.**

—— To **VISIT THE INSIDE OF THE PANTHÉON** (p 226) you'll need to get here before it closes at 6.30 pm.

—— **RESERVE A TABLE AT NARRO** (p 241) at least one or two days in advance.

—— This itinerary covers a fair distance; **CONSIDER RENTING AN ELECTRIC BIKE** for part of it (p 49).

SAINT-GERMAIN-DES-PRÉS — LATIN QUARTER

DAY 4

ITINERARY

MORNING

——— Make your way to Falguière or Montparnasse–Bienvenue métro station in the 15th arrondissement and start your day with a leisurely visit to ① **Musée Bourdelle** (p 225), an intimate and peaceful museum dedicated to the life and work of French sculptor Antoine Bourdelle. If you've yet to have breakfast, head to the museum's café, Café Rhodia, on the top floor.

② Brocante Hétéroclite

① Musée Bourdelle (above and opposite)

——— Walk to eclectic second-hand goods shop ② **Brocante Hétéroclite** (p 233) on Rue de Vaugirard to browse its second-hand wares.

——— Stroll along Rue du Cherche-Midi, popping into its small boutiques and vintage stores en route to ③ **Marie Thé** (p 240) for a cup of tea and a cake, if you're peckish.

③ Marie Thé

ITINERARY

AFTERNOON

——— Purchase some delicious bagel sandwiches at ④ **Bagels & Brownies** (p 236) on Rue Notre Dame des Champs for a lunchtime picnic in the famous Jardin du Luxembourg. If the weather isn't conducive to an alfresco lunch, eat in at the next stop.

——— Head east towards the gardens on Rue de Fleurus and drop by ⑤ **Bread & Roses** (p 238) on the corner of Rue Madame to pick up some of their delectable desserts for your picnic. Or eat here, with savoury dishes also available.

④ Bagels & Brownies

⑤ Bread & Roses

⑥ Jardin du Luxembourg (above and right)

—— Enter the ⑥ **Jardin du Luxembourg** (p 223) and find a quiet bench to enjoy your lunch. Then explore the park, making sure to visit the beautiful Medici Fountain and the pétanque courts.

—— Leave the park via the north exit at the Odéon Theatre and head north to explore ⑦ **Cour du Commerce Saint-André** (p 221), ⑧ **Rue de Buci** (p 228) and ⑨ **Place de Furstemberg** (p 227) – the bustling shopping streets of Saint-Germain-des-Prés. Pop into charming boutiques such as perfumery ⑩ **Le Labo** (p 235) and ⑪ **Compagnie Française des Poivres & des Épices** (p 234) at Place Furstemberg, which stocks spices sourced from all over the world.

—— Walk to the café ⑫ **Bar de la Croix Rouge** (p 237) at 2 Place Michel Debré and people-watch over a coffee break.

—— Head north on Rue de Grenelle, taking your time to pop into the trendy fashion boutiques along the way. Continue north to ⑬ **Deyrolle** (p 234) on Rue du Bac and immerse yourself in its impressive collection of ethically sourced and historical taxidermy animals. Then grab a chocolate mousse just up the street at ⑭ **Chapon** (p 239).

ITINERARY

EVENING

——— Take a taxi or Uber or rent a bike to the Latin Quarter to admire the striking neoclassical architecture of the ⑮ **Panthéon** (p 226), the mausoleum housing the remains of some of France's most distinguished citizens including Voltaire and Marie Curie. Return another day to visit inside, as it closes at 6.30 pm (6 pm October to March).

⑯ Place de la Contrescarpe (above and opposite)

Wall of Philippe II Augustus

——— Walk down Rue Clovis and note the Wall of Philippe II Augustus – the oldest remaining twelfth-century medieval city wall of Paris – surreally sandwiched between nineteenth-century apartment buildings. Then follow Rue du Cardinal Lemoine south and peek into the hidden courtyard of the former house of Irish novelist James Joyce at 71 Bis Rue du Cardinal Lemoine (the gate looks locked, but it opens automatically as you approach). Then explore the famous ⑯ **Place de la Contrescarpe** (p 227), immortalised by the writings of Ernest Hemingway, who lived nearby for many years.

——— Head north on Rue du Cardinal Lemoine for a memorable dinner at contemporary French restaurant ⑰ **Narro** (p 241). Reserve ahead.

55

Cour du Commerce Saint-André

Additional VENUE

Beaupassage

—— ARCADE

Beaupassage ('beautiful passage') is a picturesque open-air arcade in the heart of the Rue du Bac area. Its historical layering comes from the transformation and linking of a seventeenth-century Récollets convent and an early twentieth-century Renault garage into a single passage. The convent – founded under Henry IV and rebuilt in 1614 by Marie de' Medici – is preserved at 83–85 Rue du Bac as a historical monument. The former Renault garage's vast brick-and-iron hall now forms Beaupassage's industrial-style plaza and houses art installations, cafés and restaurants including L'Allénothèque, French chef Yannick Alléno's flagship restaurant; Pierre Hermé Café, a chic salon by the eponymous pastry chef; and Certified Café, one of my favourite local haunts that serves high-quality, hand-brewed coffees in its minimalist space, always buzzing with Left-Bank locals.

ADDRESS: *53 Rue de Grenelle*

ARRONDISSEMENT: *7th*

CLOSEST MÉTRO STATION: *Rue du Bac*

Cour du Commerce Saint-André

—— STREET

Connecting Boulevard Saint-Germain and Rue Saint-André-des-Arts, the Cour du Commerce Saint-André is one of many hidden passageways in the 6th arrondissement. Established in 1776, the passage traces the perimeter of the twelfth-century defensive walls constructed by King Philippe-Auguste and contains a number of charming cafés and shops including Le Procope, said to be Paris's oldest café. Opened in 1686, its former patrons include Voltaire, Jean-Jacques Rousseau and Benjamin Franklin. The entrance to the passage on Boulevard Saint-Germain is a stunning stone archway decorated by Greco-Roman sculptures, its wrought-iron grills and balconies are typical of late eighteenth-century design. The original cobblestone street, laid in the eighteenth century, remains intact, as does the glass canopy.

ADDRESS: *Cour du Commerce Saint-André*

ARRONDISSEMENT: *6th*

CLOSEST MÉTRO STATION: *Odéon*

ATTRACTIONS

Jardin du Luxembourg

—— GARDEN

The green jewel of the 6th arrondissement, this garden owes its origins to Marie de' Medici – widow of King Henry IV and mother of King Louis XIII. In 1612, nostalgic for the lush gardens of her native Florence, she purchased an old *hôtel particulier* (urban mansion) and surrounding land owned by François de Luxembourg to build a palace and create a grand garden. Modelled after Florence's Palazzo Pitti, the Palais du Luxembourg now houses the French Senate.

The northern section of the garden adheres to traditional French garden principles of symmetry and geometry; its central axis is dominated by the Grand Bassin (a large octagonal pond encircled by manicured lawns), flowerbeds and tree-lined promenades. Over 100 statues are scattered throughout the gardens including representations of French queens and allegorical figures – even a miniature version of the Statue of Liberty is hidden among the trees. The southern section of the garden incorporates English garden design with its winding paths, small grottos and secluded benches where locals like to eat their lunch or read the newspaper.

The most iconic part of the garden is the baroque Medici Fountain built in 1630 with its statue group depicting the mythological figures of Polyphemus, Galatea and Acis. The fountain is the domain of the park's charmingly impertinent resident wild ducks, whose fluffy offspring delight visiting children each spring. There's a designated pitch for *pétanque* (also known as boules) in the southwestern corner of the park; visit on a weekday morning to watch locals play.

The garden is also known for its heavy (but moveable) steel green seats known as Sénat seats.

ADDRESS: *Rue de Vaugirard (main entrance)*

ARRONDISSEMENT: *6th*

CLOSEST MÉTRO STATION: *Odéon*

This is FREE

Musée Bourdelle

—— MUSEUM

Dedicated to the life and work of renowned French sculptor Antoine Bourdelle, this museum is one of Paris's best kept secrets. Along with preserving Bourdelle's original studio, the museum houses a collection of over 500 of his works encompassing marble, plaster and bronze pieces, as well as his personal collection of works by contemporaries including Eugène Delacroix and Auguste Rodin.

The small museum is a delightful maze of interconnected spaces including the Street-side Garden dotted with large sculptures. The Sculpture Studio is my favourite – showcasing works in various stages of completion alongside unfinished models and sketches, it gives the impression that the sculptor himself might enter at any moment and shoo you out so he can continue his work in peace. Continue through the Inner Garden with its flowering trees and enter the double doors into the Plaster Casts Hall, which houses temporary exhibitions.

On the second floor you will find a charming café, La Rhodia, serving a mix of French and Latin American dishes. It's named for Bourdelle's daughter, Rhodia, whose apartments formerly occupied this space. The inside of the laid-back café is decorated beautifully with vintage furniture and the balcony seating overlooks the gardens.

ADDRESS: *18 Rue Antoine Bourdelle*

ARRONDISSEMENT: *15th*

CLOSEST MÉTRO STATION: *Falguière*

Panthéon

— MONUMENT

Situated atop the Montagne Sainte-Geneviève (Mount Saint Geneviève) in the Latin Quarter, the Panthéon is one of Paris's most historically significant monuments. This is not simply because of its architectural beauty – defined by its soaring Corinthian columns, magnificent sculptural relief and massive dome reminscent of Donato Bramante's Tempietto of the Church of San Pietro in Montorio, Rome – but also because it is the final resting place of some of France's most important historical figures.

Commissioned by King Louis XV in 1744 as a gesture of gratitude for his recovery from illness, the Panthéon was initially conceived as a church dedicated to Saint Genevieve, the patron saint of Paris. During the French Revolution it was secularised and repurposed as a mausoleum to honour distinguished French citizens, with a new inscription added on its facade: *Aux grands hommes la patrie reconnaissante* ('To great men, the grateful homeland').

Inside the Panthéon, the majestic dome rises 83 metres (272 feet) above you, presiding over the classical and Gothic architecture, and nineteenth-century artworks narrate scenes from the lives of Saint Genevieve, Joan of Arc and historical kings Charlemagne and Clovis. Suspended from the dome is the Foucault Pendulum, an experiment devised by physicist Léon Foucault in 1851 to demonstrate the Earth's rotation.

Descending into the crypt, you'll find the final resting places of France's most illustrious figures including writers Voltaire and Victor Hugo, scientist Marie Curie (the first woman to be interred here) and, more recently, American-born entertainer and civil rights activist Josephine Baker.

ADDRESS: *Place du Panthéon*

ARRONDISSEMENT: *5th*

CLOSEST MÉTRO STATION: *Cardinal Lemoine*

Place de Furstemberg

—— SQUARE

A secluded square hidden within the narrow streets of Saint-Germain-des-Prés, Place de Furstemberg was built in the seventeenth century on the grounds of the Abbaye de Saint-Germain-des-Prés – one of the oldest and most influential abbeys in Paris. This explains its enclosed layout with just two entrances at either end.

Haussmann buildings with tall windows and wrought-iron balconies surround the square, and at its centre are four paulownia trees. Romantic nineteenth-century painter Eugène Delacroix lived and worked on Rue de Furstemberg during the later years of his life. His former home and studio are now preserved as the Musée National Eugène-Delacroix at 6 Rue de Furstemberg.

ADDRESS: *Rue de Furstemberg*

ARRONDISSEMENT: *6th*

CLOSEST MÉTRO STATION: *Saint-Germain-des-Prés*

Place de la Contrescarpe

—— SQUARE

The northern end of Rue Mouffetar opens to the lovely Place de la Contrescarpe, a square surrounded by café terraces. During the warmer months it's abuzz with local activity well into the long evenings. Created in the seventeenth century, the square takes its name from a military term: a *contrescarpe* is the exterior wall of a ditch or fort. The name reflects the area's location near the former medieval fortifications of Paris, which were demolished in the seventeenth century.

The square and its surrounding streets were once home to famous writers and intellectuals – Ernest Hemingway lived just a short walk away at 74 Rue du Cardinal Lemoine and he wrote about Place de la Contrescarpe in his 1964 memoir, *A Moveable Feast*. The area evolved into a bohemian centre of the Left Bank in the twentieth century with university crowds congregating in its numerous cafés and bars.

ADDRESS: *Place de la Contrescarpe*

ARRONDISSEMENT: *5th*

CLOSEST MÉTRO STATION: *Place Monge*

Rue de Buci

—— STREET

Dating back to the Middle Ages, Rue de Buci is one of the city's oldest streets. Named after Simon de Buci, a prominent magistrate in fourteenth-century Paris, it has a long history as a market street and is still lined with shops and cafés with colourful awnings today.

Rue de Buci and the surrounding Saint-Germain-des-Prés area became synonymous with Paris's bohemian culture in the nineteenth and early twentieth centuries, with artists, writers and musicians including Pablo Picasso, Ernest Hemingway and Jean-Paul Sartre frequenting its cafés and bars. Popular venues on the curving street include the historic Café le Buci, student-favourite panini shop Pastavino and artisan bakery Maison Thevenin.

ADDRESS: *Rue de Buci*

ARRONDISSEMENT: *6th*

CLOSEST MÉTRO STATION: *Mabillon or Odéon*

Additional VENUE

Rue Mouffetard

—— STREET

Rue Mouffetard is one of the oldest and best preserved medieval streets in Paris and it remains authentically local. This historical road follows the route of an ancient Roman road that connected Lutetia (the Gallo-Roman predecessor to Paris) to Italy; today it winds its way through the heart of the 5th arrondissement. The street became a bustling commercial centre in the Middle Ages, serving as the main road leading out of Paris to the south. The area was historically a working-class district filled with butchers, artisans and market vendors, and Rue Mouffetard grew into a popular food market street during the seventeenth to nineteenth centuries. Today the charming serpentine cobblestone street buzzes with the energy of market stalls, cosy cafés and specialty shops housed in centuries-old buildings.

ADDRESS: *Rue Mouffetard*

ARRONDISSEMENT: *5th*

CLOSEST MÉTRO STATION: *Censier–Daubenton*

Additional VENUE

Barthélemy

—— CHEESE

Whether or not you're a cheese connoisseur, it's difficult to walk past renowned cheesemonger Barthélemy without stopping to stare into its window filled with every type of cheese imaginable. Owner Nicole Barthélemy sources the finest selection of cheeses from across France directly from small producers that observe traditional cheesemaking methods and pay meticulous attention to aging and presentation. Its reputation for quality saw Barthélemy Fromagerie appointed as an official supplier to the Élysée Palace in the 1970s.

Every product in the *fromagerie* (cheese shop) is lovingly presented with a handwritten label that details its name, origin and *affinage* (aging). Expert staff behind the marble-topped counter assist customers with the all-important choice of the right cheese for the occasion.

Among Barthélemy's expansive offerings are a wide variety of rare cheeses from remote regions of France. On one visit I discovered the Fontainebleau, a mousse-like cheese made from cow's milk and cream and piped into little cups. It's commonly eaten with fruit as a dessert.

ADDRESS: *51 Rue de Grenelle*

ARRONDISSEMENT: *7th*

CLOSEST MÉTRO STATION: *Rue du Bac*

Additional VENUE

Big Band Poterie

POTTERY

Paris has always been resistant to foreign trends, yet *poterie* (pottery) cafés have become a hit among Parisians who don't have the resources or space in the city's notoriously small apartments to pursue pottery as a hobby at home.

One of the only studios that allows for walk-in customers, Big Band Poterie gives you access to all the tools to make your own ceramic souvenir of your trip to Paris from scratch. Big Band Poterie is also the first studio to charge by weight rather than time, so you can take as long as you like to perfect your masterpiece. You will need to leave your creation here for a few days to dry and be fired, or you can arrange for the store to ship it to your home address.

ADDRESS: *57 Rue Saint-André des Arts*

ARRONDISSEMENT: *6th*

CLOSEST MÉTRO STATION: *Mabillon or Odéon*

Additional VENUE

Le Bon Marché

——— DEPARTMENT STORE

One of the world's first department stores, Le Bon Marché is a symbol of Parisian elegance and innovation. Founded in the 1830s as a novelty shop, the business was acquired in 1852 by Aristide Boucicaut, the son of a milliner, who together with his wife Marguerite transformed it into the first modern department store. Innovations introduced by the couple – including fixed pricing, home delivery, seasonal sales and the option to return goods – were a huge success, leading to the construction of a new building completed in 1872 with assistance from the engineering firm Gustave Eiffel (of Eiffel Tower fame). By 1888 Le Bon Marché occupied the entire block.

The innovative use of steel and glass in the building's construction created a sense of openness and light – the grand central atrium, with its skylights and elegant ironwork, remains one of its most striking features. Following a devastating fire in 1915 that destroyed the annex housing what is now La Grande Épicerie, the building was rebuilt in Art Deco style and reopened in 1923.

Since 1984 Le Bon Marché has been owned by luxury conglomerate LVMH, which has enhanced the department store's prestige as a curated space for high-end goods and experiences. Don't miss La Grande Épicerie de Paris – the grand food hall stocked with rare ingredients, luxury food products and fine wines.

ADDRESS: *24 Rue de Sèvres*

ARRONDISSEMENT: *7th*

CLOSEST MÉTRO STATION: *Sèvres–Babylone*

Brocante Hétéroclite

—— BRIC-A-BRAC

Brocante Hétéroclite means 'miscellaneous flea market', which is apt since there are always new curiosities displayed outside. Owner Dominique Ekman loves treasure hunting for unusual and rare objects, and her finds – from kitchenwear to vintage tools – are diverse and often unexpected. Her shop is not so much a place to look for something in particular as an opportunity to discover something interesting and unusual that you never knew you wanted. Pieces I have picked up here over the years include vintage tin madeleine moulds, a retro enamel hole punch and a vintage BIC Criterium drafting pencil – all of which came with fascinating stories. Best of all, items are reasonably priced, though it sometimes takes a little convincing for Dominique to sell them to you.

ADDRESS: *111 Rue de Vaugirard*

ARRONDISSEMENT: *6th*

CLOSEST MÉTRO STATION: *Falguière*

SHOPPING

Compagnie Française des Poivres & des Épices

——— SPICES

In recent years Paris has seen a resurgence of specialty shops focusing on a single product category. Among them are a number of *épiceries* (spice shops) that aim to re-create the charm and authenticity of *épiceries* once found all over Paris during the nineteenth and twentieth centuries.

Compagnie Française des Poivres & des Épices (French Company of Peppers & Spices) specialises in high-quality peppers and spices sourced from around the globe. Though the shop only opened in 2019, its nineteenth-century-inspired interior with wooden shelving and antique-style spice containers evokes a bygone era. The location opposite the picturesque Place de Furstemberg (p 227) gives the small boutique an intimate and hidden-away feel, like it's waiting to be discovered on a serendipitous walk.

ADDRESS: *7 Rue de Furstemberg*

ARRONDISSEMENT: *6th*

CLOSEST MÉTRO STATION: *Saint-Germain-des-Prés or Mabillon*

Deyrolle

——— TAXIDERMY

Known for its extensive collection of taxidermy animals, Deyrolle is like a mini natural museum, with its specimens meticulously preserved in the same scientific spirit as those of Paris's public museums. Founder Jean-Baptiste Deyrolle was an entomologist (a biologist who studies insects) and his shop, opened in 1831, originally specialised in butterflies, beetles and other insects, as well as tools and equipment for naturalists. His grandson, Émile Deyrolle, expanded the business in the 1870s, creating educational materials including charts used in French schools for teaching natural sciences, geography and anatomy. By the mid-nineteenth century the shop had moved to its current premises – a two-storey building with space to house its growing collection. During this period Deyrolle became a global supplier of taxidermy and natural history specimens, exporting items to universities, museums and collectors worldwide.

Deyrolle is now known the world over for its extensive collection of taxidermy animals, from

exotic species to common wildlife. Each has a documented history verifying that it was legally and ethically sourced – typically from zoos and wildlife sanctuaries where the animals died from natural causes. Specimens are also sourced from collections, museums and private estates –all intended for education, not as trophies or status symbols. Deyrolle adheres to the Convention on International Trade in Endangered Species of Wild Fauna and Flora (CITES), which regulates the trade of wild animals and plants to ensure it doesn't threaten their survival.

Taxidermy lions, zebras, tigers and even a giraffe are displayed in the middle room, and walls and cabinets are filled with butterflies, beetles and insects, making for a surreal atmosphere. It's no wonder Deyrolle has inspired artists and filmmakers throughout history including surrealist Salvador Dalí and director Wes Anderson.

ADDRESS: *46 Rue du Bac*

ARRONDISSEMENT: *6th*

CLOSEST MÉTRO STATION: *Rue du Bac*

Le Labo

PERFUMERY

Le Labo (The Lab) was founded in New York, but this perfume brand (which also makes hair, face and grooming products and candles) has many indelible connections with France. Founders Fabrice Penot and Eddie Roschi both have French backgrounds, and the brand prioritises French-sourced ingredients and observes traditional French artisanal perfume-making methods. So its Paris boutiques feel like a natural fit. Featuring raw, exposed architecture complemented by vintage furniture and hot-rolled steel fixtures, the Saint-Germain-des-Prés branch was the first to open in Paris. The lab-like set-up is not just for aesthetics; this is where fragrances are hand-blended at the time of purchase and finished off with a customised label with your name or a personal message.

Le Labo's woody, smoky Santal 33 is popular among Paris's creative industry, but the Paris boutique also offers an exclusive scent, Vanille 44, which aims to distill the essence of Paris with top notes of citrus and bergamot and base notes of vanilla and musk.

ADDRESS: *6 Rue de Bourbon le Château*

ARRONDISSEMENT: *6th*

CLOSEST MÉTRO STATION: *Saint-Germain-des-Prés or Mabillon*

EAT & DRINK

Additional VENUE

Au Babylone

——— BISTRO

Near Le Bon Marché (p 232), this cherished family-owned neighbourhood restaurant has been serving traditional country-style French cuisine (lunch only) at reasonable prices since 1951. From its mustard facade to its checked tablecloths typical of mid-twentieth-century Parisian bistros, everything about this relaxed restaurant feels nostalgic. Classic dishes include *harengs pomme à l'huile* (smoked herring with potatoes), roast veal and *gâteau aux pommes* (apple tart), with a three-course lunch menu including a beverage costing just €25.

ADDRESS: *13 Rue de Babylone*

ARRONDISSEMENT: *7th*

CLOSEST MÉTRO STATION: *Sèvres–Babylone*

Bagels & Brownies

——— BAGELS

Paris isn't known for its bagels; at least it wasn't until Bagels & Brownies came along in 1999. Following her travels in the United States, owner Sylvie Baruch was inspired to introduce the bagel to Paris. Named after North American cities, her bagels are assembled-to-order with an interesting range of ingredients. My favourite is the Phoenix, a moreish combination of avocado, two types of cheese, tomato, cream cheese and mustard.

There is also a delicious selection of sweet treats including an extremely satisfying cheesecake (a family recipe passed down from Sylvie's grandmother), mini jam donuts and, of course, brownies. It's takeaway only – perfect for enjoying in the nearby Jardin du Luxembourg (p 232).

ADDRESS: *12 Rue Notre Dame des Champs*

ARRONDISSEMENT: *6th*

CLOSEST MÉTRO STATION: *Rennes*

Bar de la Croix Rouge

CAFÉ

Quintessential Parisian café Bar de la Croix Rouge is a local favourite, evidenced by the frequent invitations I receive from my fashion industry colleagues to meet here. Meaning 'red cross', its name is a reference to the major intersection opposite the bar historically called the Carrefour de la Croix Rouge, now officially called Place Michel Debré.

The café is known for its *tartines* (open-faced sandwiches) named after the streets of the neighbourhood, including the Saint-Sulpice plate, which features tuna and tomato on toast.

The terrace sits on the lively intersection, providing the perfect vantage point for watching the world go by.

ADDRESS: *2 Place Michel Debré*

ARRONDISSEMENT: *6th*

CLOSEST MÉTRO STATION: *Sèvres-Babylone*

Bread & Roses

—— BAKERY

This bakery café near the Jardin du Luxembourg (p 223) has lured me many a lunchtime for its excellent signature pastrami bun. The display window is always meticulously arranged with breads, pastries, tarts and quiches that are baked offsite. Purchase some treats to take away or grab a table in the seating area; its muted colours give it a clean and airy feel.

ADDRESS: *62 Rue Madame*

ARRONDISSEMENT: *6th*

CLOSEST MÉTRO STATION: *Saint Placide*

Chapon

CHOCOLATE

With its colourful packaging depicting the flora and fauna of faraway destinations (reflecting the origins of its chocolate), the Chapon *chocolaterie* has always captured my imagination.

Known for its single-origin chocolates (with cacao beans sourced from a single identifiable location), the brand was founded in the 1980s by Patrice Chapon, a former pastry chef and ice cream maker for Buckingham Palace in London. Chapon created his brand upon his return to France, seeking to keep the entire chocolate-making process in-house, from roasting the cocoa beans to tempering and moulding the chocolate, which was not common among Parisian chocolatiers at the time.

Chapon chocolate is found in many stores around Paris, but it's only at the Chapon boutiques where you can experience the interesting chocolate mousse bar – a counter where you can sample a bowl of single-origin chocolate mousse.

ADDRESS: *69 Rue du Bac*

ARRONDISSEMENT: *6th*

CLOSEST MÉTRO STATION: *Rue du Bac*

EAT & DRINK

Marie Thé

—— CAFÉ

It was the collection of novelty teapots in the window that first attracted me to this unassuming little *salon de thé* (tearoom). During the cooler months you can sit next to the big windows and soak up the winter sun, and in summer there's a lively terrace shaded by green parasols. Against the back wall is a bookshelf displaying homemade tarts, quiches, crumble and cakes – all fine accompaniments to the vast tea menu. Comforting homemade dishes such as stuffed vegetables and tagines are also on offer.

Owner Lola is full of energy – even during the lunch rush she always makes time to joke and chat with customers. It seems to me that locals come here for her as much as for the food.

ADDRESS: *102 Rue du Cherche-Midi*

ARRONDISSEMENT: *6th*

CLOSEST MÉTRO STATION: *Vaneau*

Narro

—— RESTAURANT

A rare gourmet gem in the Latin Quarter, the popularity of Narro – particularly among Japanese visitors – can predominantly be attributed to Hakuba-born chef Kazuma Chikuda. His contemporary French dishes reflect the harmonious balance of flavours, reverence for ingredients and attention to detail that characterise Japanese cuisine. Each dish is a pleasure both to the eyes and the tastebuds, with a closer look revealing the simplicity of the ingredients.

A pan-seared scallop dish is enlivened by edible chrysanthemum puree and kiwifruit vinaigrette, and vegetables are elevated by balanced combinations such as white asparagus with wild garlic gnocchi and fermented blood orange.

There's alfresco terrace seating under a forest-green awning, while exposed brick walls and wooden floors make for cosy indoor seating.

ADDRESS: *72 Rue du Cardinal Lemoine*

ARRONDISSEMENT: *5th*

CLOSEST MÉTRO STATION: *Cardinal Lemoine*

Additional VENUE

Le Saigon d'Antan

—— RESTAURANT

After all my years in Paris I've found very few Asian restaurants to recommend. Le Saigon d'Antan is one of them. This simple and relaxed Vietnamese restaurant dishes up high-quality food from its minuscule kitchen with surprising speed – perfect for hungry visitors looking for a quick and tasty meal. The pho (rice-noodle soup) is as good as any I have tasted anywhere in the world. Their roast duck and fried beef noodles are another personal favourite.

ADDRESS: *24 Rue Monsieur le Prince*

ARRONDISSEMENT: *6th*

CLOSEST MÉTRO STATION: *Cluny La Sorbonne*

DAY 5

KEY NEIGHBOURHOODS

SAINT-GEORGES
ROCHECHOUART FAUBOURG-MONTMARTRE
MARAIS

Paris's reputation for amazing vintage shopping is well deserved. The city is full of vintage and second-hand clothing shops catering to every shopper's desires. This itinerary takes you to two of the city's best second-hand clothing enclaves – in the 9th arrondissement and the Marais – interspersed with café stops and sightseeing.

DAY OF VINTAGE

ITINERARY

This itinerary is recommended on

TUESDAY
WEDNESDAY
THURSDAY
FRIDAY

TIPS

Slip a **COLLAPSIBLE SHOPPING BAG** into your handbag to stow new purchases.

BRING SOME SNACKS to keep you going during your afternoon vintage shop-hopping.

If you're planning to dine at Vivant 2 (p 273), **BOOK AT LEAST A WEEK IN ADVANCE** and wear something smart to comply with the unofficial dress code.

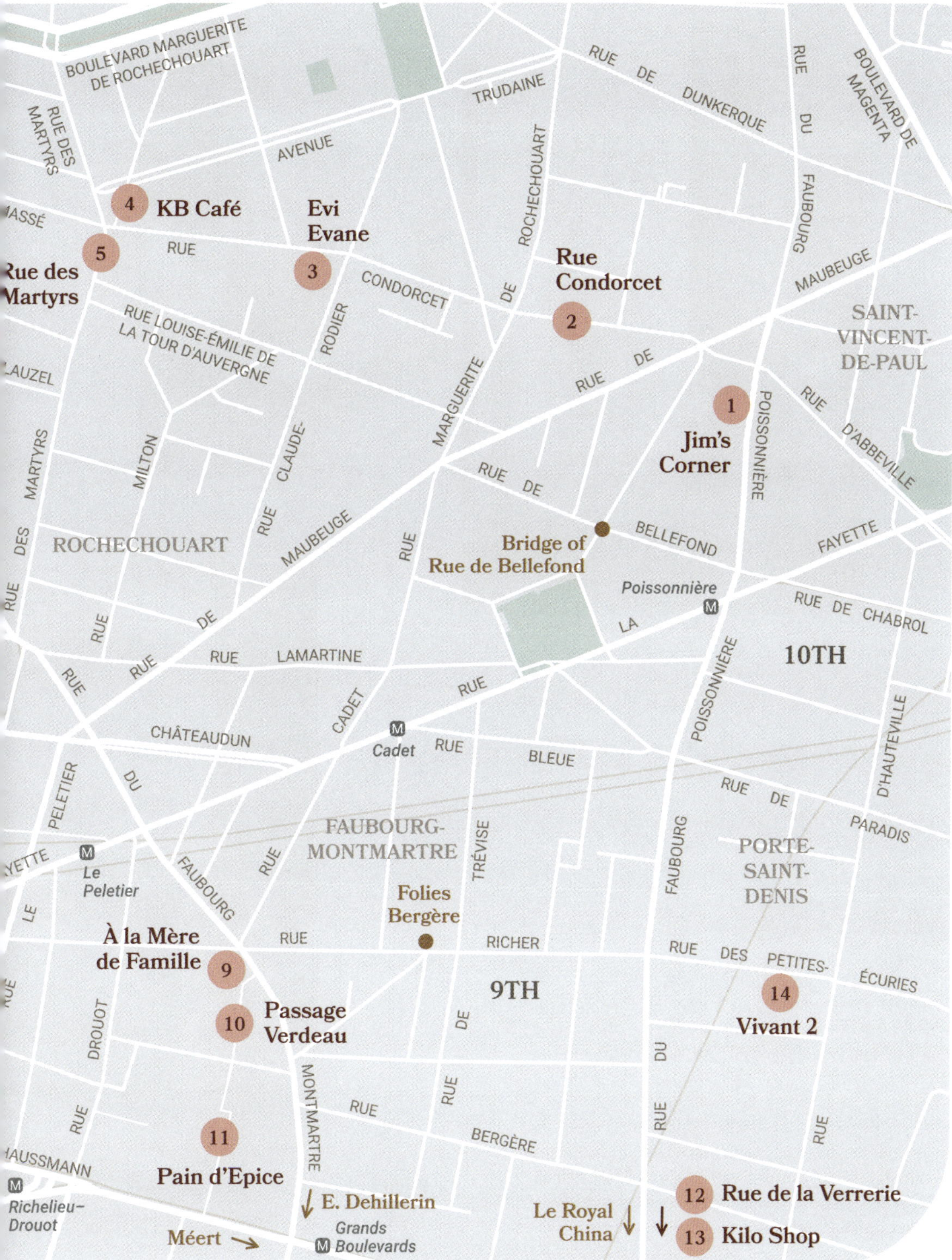
BOULEVARD MARGUERITE DE ROCHECHOUART
RUE DES MARTYRS
TRUDAINE
AVENUE
RUE DE DUNKERQUE
RUE DU FAUBOURG POISSONNIÈRE
BOULEVARD DE MAGENTA
4 KB Café
Evi Evane
3
5
Rue des Martyrs
RUE CONDORCET
ROCHECHOUART
DE
Rue Condorcet
2
MAUBEUGE
SAINT-VINCENT-DE-PAUL
RUE LOUISE-ÉMILIE DE LA TOUR D'AUVERGNE
RODIER
RUE DE MAUBEUGE
1
Jim's Corner
RUE D'ABBEVILLE
MARGUERITE
MILTON
RUE CLAUDE-
RUE DE BELLEFOND
Bridge of Rue de Bellefond
ROCHECHOUART
FAYETTE
Poissonnière
RUE DE CHABROL
RUE LA
10TH
RUE LAMARTINE
CADET
CHÂTEAUDUN
Cadet
RUE BLEUE
D'HAUTEVILLE
RUE DE PARADIS
PELETIER
FAUBOURG-MONTMARTRE
TRÉVISE
PORTE-SAINT-DENIS
Le Peletier
RUE DU FAUBOURG
Folies Bergère
RUE RICHER
RUE DES PETITES-ÉCURIES
À la Mère de Famille
9
10
Passage Verdeau
9TH
14
Vivant 2
DROUOT
MONTMARTRE
RUE BERGÈRE
11
Pain d'Epice
HAUSSMANN
Richelieu–Drouot
E. Dehillerin
Grands Boulevards
Méert
Le Royal China
12 Rue de la Verrerie
13 Kilo Shop

ITINERARY

① Jim's Corner

③ Evi Evane

MORNING

—— Alight at Poissonnière métro station in the 9th arrondissement and have a hearty breakfast at ① **Jim's Corner** (p 269), a laid-back Australian-style café on Rue du Faubourg Poissonnière offering all-day brunch.

—— Turn left onto ② **Rue Condorcet** (p 266) and check out the vintage shops dotted along the street including Chezel Vintage and Retro Chic as well as Merguiller, which is just off Rue Condorcet on Rue Marguerite de Rochechouart.

② Rue Condorcet (above and right)

—— If all this shopping has worked up the munchies, grab a snack at Greek delicatessen ③ **Evi Evane** (p 269) on Rue Condorcet – I recommend their fluffy puff pastries. Then order a coffee at ④ **KB Café** (p 270) on Avenue Trudaine; looking onto Place Lino Ventura at the top of Rue des Martyrs, it's the perfect vantage for people-watching in the heart of the 9th arrondissement.

ITINERARY

AFTERNOON

——— Head south on ⑤ **Rue des Martyrs** (p 259) and browse its many local boutiques and specialty shops for treasures. Then turn west on Rue Clauzel and explore ⑥ **Place Saint-Georges** (p 258), the heart of the New Athens district and a prime example of the Greek Revival architecture in this neighbourhood.

⑦ La Petite Charlotte

⑥ Place Saint-Georges

——— Have lunch at ⑦ **La Petite Charlotte** (p 272) near Place Saint-George, which offers a daily two- or three-course lunch featuring classic, comforting French dishes such as homemade terrine and the classic pork chop.

——— Walk to the ⑧ **Musée de la Vie Romantique** (Museum of Romantic Life, p 255). Dedicated to the Romantic era that shaped Paris in the nineteenth century, it houses an extensive collection related to the French novelist best known as George Sand, and other authors and artists of the Romantic era. Take a break at the tearoom in the property's former greenhouse.

⑨ À la Mère de Famille

——— Take a leisurely stroll southeast on Rue du Faubourg Montmartre (or take a bike or taxi) to ⑨ **À la Mère de Famille** (p 268), the oldest chocolate shop in Paris. Browse its Aladdin's cave of offerings, from chocolates in beautifully decorated boxes to colourful candied fruits.

——— Turn right into the ⑩ **Passage Verdeau** (p 257) and begin your journey through the trio of connected *passages couverts* (covered arcades) of the 9th arrondissement. While browsing their charming boutiques, don't miss ⑪ **Pain d'Epice** (p 263) in Passage Jouffroy, a magical toyshop specialising in miniatures for dollhouses. If you need a break, there are many cafés inside the passages.

⑪ Pain d'Epice

RUE DE TURENNE
MARIA LUND

⑫ Rue de la Verrerie

⑬ Kilo Shop

EVENING

—— When you've finished exploring the covered passages take a taxi or Uber or a hired bike to ⑫ **Rue de la Verrerie** (p 267) for some of the city's best thrift shopping. Don't miss ⑬ **Kilo Shop** (p 262), where second-hand pieces are sold by weight.

—— If time permits, return to your hotel to refresh and change for dinner at chic French restaurant ⑭ **Vivant 2** (p 273) in the 10th arrondissement, where the masterful kitchen brigade can be observed via the open kitchen behind the bar. Book at least one week ahead.

Additional VENUE

Bridge of Rue de Bellefond

——— ROAD BRIDGE

One of my favourite things about Paris is the way it seamlessly exists on multiple levels. Sometimes when wandering at street level, you might find yourself on a bridge you didn't notice you had climbed, looking down on rooftops below. This is the feeling I got when I first stumbled upon the 'bridge' of Rue de Bellefond. I was so taken by its multi-dimensional charm that I often use it as a backdrop in photoshoots.

The 'bridge' of Rue de Bellefond is one of two road bridges of this kind, both located in the north of Paris. On sunny days you'll often find young people hanging out on the stairs that lead up to the bridge on either side.

ADDRESS: *Cnr Rue de Bellefond and Rue Pierre Samard*

ARRONDISSEMENT: *Paris Centre*

CLOSEST MÉTRO STATION: *Poissonnière*

Additional VENUE

Folies Bergère

—— THEATRE

With its striking gold and white Art Deco facade, the Folies Bergère holds profound cultural significance in Paris. Opened in 1869, it transitioned from a *café-théâtre* (tiny theatre with tables for drinks) to the world's first major music hall in 1886, pioneering lavish productions known for their glamorous costumes, illusionists and even early striptease (it introduced the first fully nude female performer in 1912). The Folies Bergère stage became the launchpad for stars such as Maurice Chevalier (seen in the 1958 film *Gigi*) and singer Josephine Baker, whose risqué banana-skirt dance, though tame by today's standards, remains famous. The music hall was greatly influential in Parisian art and culture, and was even immortalised in Édouard Manet's famous painting *A Bar at the Folies-Bergère*.

Today, the Folies Bergère continues to host many notable concerts and shows throughout the year. The extravagant gold and red auditorium is spacious and seats over 1500 guests, with ticket prices starting at €29.

ADDRESS: *32 Rue Richer*

ARRONDISSEMENT: *9th*

CLOSEST MÉTRO STATION: *Le Peletier*

Additional VENUE

Musée National Gustave Moreau

—— ART MUSEUM

When painter Gustave Moreau, an important figure in the Symbolist movement, passed away in 1898 he bequeathed his four-storey house to the city on the condition that it be transformed into a museum to preserve his paintings, sculptures and other works. The Musée National Gustave Moreau opened in 1903 and in accordance with his wishes, the haphazard display has never been changed, making a visit feel like truly stepping back in time.

Among the museum's highlights is the second-floor studio designed by architect Albert Lafon, where Moreau's large-scale paintings such as *The Suitors*, along with unfinished works, are displayed. The remarkable helical staircase winding up to the third floor is a masterpiece in itself; also designed by Lafon in collaboration with Moreau, its delicate wrought-iron balustrade is decorated with intricate motifs in the Art Nouveau style. Positioned centrally in the room, it serves as a vantage point to view the monumental paintings as you climb.

ADDRESS: *14 Rue Catherine de la Rochefoucauld*

ARRONDISSEMENT: *9th*

CLOSEST MÉTRO STATION: *Trinité–d'Estienne d'Orves*

Musée National Gustave Moreau

This is FREE

Musée de la Vie Romatique

—— MUSEUM

A natural fit the for the City of Love, The Musée de la Vie Romantique (Museum of Romantic Life) is dedicated to preserving and showcasing the art, literature and culture of the Romantic era that shaped nineteenth-century Paris. It's housed in the former residence of Dutch painter Ary Scheffer, who hosted luminaries such as Amantine Lucile Aurore Dupin de Francueil (best known by her pen name, George Sand), Frédéric Chopin, Eugène Delacroix and Charles Dickens. The mansion was converted into a museum in 1987.

The museum houses an extensive collection related to French novelist, memoirist and journalist George Sand including portraits, personal belongings and furnishings that re-create the ambiance of her living spaces. Also on display are paintings by Ary Scheffer and his contemporaries, as well as sculptures, manuscripts and other artifacts emblematic of the Romantic era.

With pastel green shutters, arched windows and wrought-iron details, the main house is a suitably romantic setting. The museum also spreads across twin glasshouses that served as Scheffer's studios. A cobblestone courtyard leads to a serene garden adorned with lilacs, roses and wisteria, providing a tranquil retreat from the busy city. The garden hosts a delightful tearoom in a former greenhouse run by Rose Bakery, which has cafés in several Parisian museums.

ADDRESS: *16 Rue Chaptal*

ARRONDISSEMENT: *9th*

CLOSEST MÉTRO STATION: *Pigalle or Blanche*

HÔTEL CHOPIN
HOTEL
HOTEL

Passages Couverts of the 9th Arrondissement

—— ARCADES

Forming a straight line across three blocks in the lively Grands Boulevards district of the 9th arrondissement, a trio of well-preserved, interconnected *passages couverts* (covered arcades) provide a glimpse into the city's vibrant nineteenth-century culture and commerce.

Opened in 1799, Passage des Panoramas is one of the oldest covered arcades in Paris. Named after the panorama paintings exhibited in rotundas at its entrance, the arcade features glass ceilings, ornate metalwork and elegant shopfronts capturing the neoclassical style of the era. A haven for collectors, the arcade is lined with antique shops, stamp dealers and small restaurants.

Passage Jouffroy was the next to be added, across Boulevard Montmartre to the north. Built in 1847, Passage Jouffroy marked a new era in arcade construction with its innovative use of iron and glass. It was one of the first passages to incorporate central heating, making it a luxurious destination.

Also opened in 1847, Passage Verdeau was designed as a continuation of the Jouffroy arcade. Known for its antique and vintage offerings, Passage Verdeau attracts collectors and enthusiasts of photography, rare books and antique furniture.

Historical establishments that continue to operate today include Passage Jouffroy's Librairie Gribaudo Vandamme, a bookshop known for its beautiful dark-wood book displays lining the arcade. The arcades are also known for their toy and hobby stores including The Toy Box, which specialises in figurines from popular comic books such as the TinTin series, and Pain d'Epice (p 263), which specialises in dollhouse accessories.

ADDRESS: *Rue du Faubourg Montmartre (for Passage Verdeau)*

ARRONDISSEMENT: *9th*

CLOSEST MÉTRO STATION: *Grands Boulevards*

Place Saint-Georges

SQUARE

Place Saint-Georges is a picturesque circular square located in a part of the 9th arrondissement that is less frequented but rich in history and local charm. Established in 1824, it's a focal point of the Nouvelle Athènes (New Athens) district and was a source of inspiration for artists and intellectuals of the Romantic era including composer and pianist Frédéric Chopin, writer Victor Hugo and painter Eugène Delacroix.

The square is surrounded by elegant nineteenth-century Haussmann buildings (p 67) that have housed many prominent French personalities. This includes the neo-Gothic and neo-Renaissance Hôtel de la Païva, the residence of Esther Lachmann, known as La Païva, a prominent courtesan of the era. Next door is the Hôtel Dosne-Thiers, once the home of former President Adolphe Thiers and later rebuilt as Bibliothèque Thiers, a library with extensive collections relating to the First French Empire. At the heart of the square stands the Monument to Paul Gavarni, a nineteenth-century caricaturist known for his depictions of Parisian life.

Other notable aspects of Place Saint-George include an eponymous café with its distinctive bright-red awning and parasols. The café's terrace spills out onto the square, offering a prime location to view the architecture while sipping coffee among locals. The Saint-Georges métro station was integrated into the courtyard of a building on the square, making its inconspicuous entrance and curved staircase leading underground seem like a secret passage.

ADDRESS: *Place Saint-Georges*

ARRONDISSEMENT: *9th*

CLOSEST MÉTRO STATION: *Saint-Georges*

Rue des Martyrs

—— STREET

In the centre of South Pigalle, chic Rue des Martyrs stretches for nearly a kilometre (0.6 mile) from the northern end of the 9th arrondissement near Montmartre down to the Notre-Dame-de-Lorette church. From the top of the street, looking down, the street winds down into the south of Paris, and is lined with charming shops including tearoom Rose Bakery and the Right-Bank branch of the Quatrehomme cheesemonger. There are also many picturesque streets leading off from Rue des Martyrs to explore, such as Rue Condorcet (p 266), which is home to a number of independent boutiques including vintage shops.

ADDRESS: *Rue des Martyrs*

ARRONDISSEMENT: *9th*

CLOSEST MÉTRO STATION: *Abbesses, Pigalle or Notre-Dame-de-Lorette*

Additional VENUE

E. Dehillerin

KITCHENWEAR

Renowned for the exceptional quality of its cooking supplies, E. Dehillerin was founded in 1820 by Eugène de Hillerin near Les Halles, which at the time was known for its food markets. Long popular among French chefs and cooking enthusiasts, the store gained global recognition thanks to the late American TV chef and author Julia Child, whose groundbreaking 1961 book, *Mastering the Art of French Cooking*, included references to the importance of high-quality cookware, much of which she purchased at E. Dehillerin.

Not much has changed behind the store's emerald green facade since Julia Child's era, with handwritten stock lists available for customers to use to locate items they need.

ADDRESS: *18–20 Rue Coquillière*

ARRONDISSEMENT: *Paris Centre*

CLOSEST MÉTRO STATION: *Poissonnière*

Galeries Lafayette

Additional VENUE

Galeries Lafayette

—— DEPARTMENT STORE

Now Europe's largest department store chain, Galeries Lafayette began its life in 1893 as a small shop founded by two Alsatian cousins with a vision of creating a grand retail space in Paris. By 1906 the store had grown significantly, leading to the construction of the iconic flagship building on Boulevard Haussmann. Architect Ferdinand Chanut and glass artist Jacques Grüber designed its spectacular Art Nouveau glass dome in 1912, which remains a symbol of Galeries Lafayette to this day.

The flagship department store offers seven hectares of shopping and dining, with an A-to-Z of luxury fashion and beauty brands represented. It also has an underground floor dedicated to wellness with a range of wellness therapies, fitness classes and beauty treatments available.

One of the best kept secrets of the Galeries Lafayette is its expansive rooftop terrace, which, unbeknownst to many tourists and Parisians alike, is open to the public. Soak up panoramic views of Paris, spanning the Eiffel Tower, Montmartre and the rooftop of the Opéra Garnier.

ADDRESS: *40 Boulevard Haussmann*

ARRONDISSEMENT: *9th*

CLOSEST MÉTRO STATION: *Chaussée d'Antin–La Fayette*

Kilo Shop

—— SECOND-HAND CLOTHING

I've lost count of the times I have asked one of my younger employees where they got their oversized trench coat or cowboy boots and their answer was Kilo Shop. This chain of second-hand shops, where clothes are sold by weight, is sacred ground for Parisian youth.

Kilo Shop has many locations in Paris, but the best known are the outposts in the Marais. There is the classic Kilo Shop, where you will find an enormous assortment of second-hand clothing from jeans, knits and coats to handbags and jewellery. Then there is Kilo Shop Kawaii (kawaii means 'cute' in Japanese), which offers a more eclectic and playful selection of ruffles, bows and animal motifs, often aligned with Y2K trends and anime. Clothes are divided into four price categories (€20–50 per kilo), denoted by different coloured tags.

ADDRESS: *65 and 67 Rue de la Verrerie*

ARRONDISSEMENT: *Paris Centre*

CLOSEST MÉTRO STATION: *Hôtel de Ville*

Pain d'Epice

—— MINIATURES

Nestled in the heart of Passage Jouffroy (p 257), Pain d'Épice is a charming boutique known for its enchanting collection of quality handcrafted miniature dollhouse accessories and vintage-inspired toys. Named for the French word for gingerbread, the store is filled with beautifully crafted dollhouses ranging from classic Victorian styles to contemporary designs. Countless dollhouse accessories are also carefully displayed in glass cases. From a teeny Parisian café terrace with micro coffee cups to chalkboards with handwritten prices and ornate Haussmann buildings (p 67) that fit in the palm of your hand, the miniatures encapsulate the essence of French life, architecture and traditions throughout history. In a nod to the city's fashion legacy, there are even miniature dressmaker's mannequins, sewing machines and bolts of fabric.

ADDRESS: *29 Passage Jouffroy*

ARRONDISSEMENT: *9th*

CLOSEST MÉTRO STATION: *Grands Boulevards*

Additional VENUE

Printemps

—— DEPARTMENT STORE

Opened in 1865, Printemps is one of Paris's five historic *grands magasins* (department stores). It's an iconic landmark in the shopping hub of the 9th arrondissement, with its multicoloured stained-glass dome and an ornate Belle Époque facade adorned with intricate carvings, ironwork and mosaics.

The location on Boulevard Haussmann – which was dramatically transformed as part of Baron Haussmann's ambitious urban renewal project (p 67) – was key to its success. Printemps founders Jules Jaluzot and Jean Alfred Duclos seized the opportunity to establish a retail venture in a burgeoning district and their bet well and truly paid off.

The seven floors of Printemps offer every category of goods, from beauty and fashion to homewares and children's clothing, but my favourite is the seventh floor, called 7eme Ciel (7th Heaven). This spectacular area of the department store was unveiled in 2021, along with the restoration of the 1910 Binet Dome, which had been closed for more than 50 years. Contrasting with the multi-coloured Charras Dome, which contains the store's brasserie, the Binet Dome features a transparent glass dome and Eiffel Tower–style metal framework. Linking the two domes is what was once intended to be an ephemeral bridge, the Pond d'Argent. This has also been restored, now dedicated to second-hand luxury and designer items. Rare and unique vintage designer pieces by luxury brands such as Balenciaga, Gucci and Fendi fill the floor, often with providence tags listing the year and season when the piece graced the runway. The Pont d'Argent also opens to Printemps's beautiful rooftop terrace that looks out onto the rooftops of Paris.

ADDRESS: *64 Boulevard Haussmann*

ARRONDISSEMENT: *9th*

CLOSEST MÉTRO STATION: *Havre–Caumartin*

SHOPPING

Rue Condorcet

STREET

A quiet street leading off the famous Rue des Martyrs (p 259), Rue Condorcet houses trendy boutiques including a small cluster of vintage shops. Notable shops include Chezel Vintage, offering a highly curated selection of clothing and accessories including rare pieces from designers such as Yves Saint Laurent, Chanel, Burberry and Dior; and Retro Chic, where I often see second-hand Chanel bags and shoes at reasonable prices. Merguiller is another wonderful vintage shop just off Rue Condorcet, around the corner on Rue Marguerite de Rochechouart, which offers clothing and accessories from the early 1900s to the 1980s by French designers including Courrèges, Hermès and Mugler.

Other charming shops on Rue Condorcet include Bloc de l'Est, a vintage furniture boutique that specialises in refurbished 1960s armchairs, sofas and benches; and second-hand bookstore Poches with its double arched windows and resident ginger cat.

ADDRESS: *Rue Condorcet*

ARRONDISSEMENT: *9th*

CLOSEST MÉTRO STATION: *Anvers*

Rue de la Verrerie

—— STREET

Known for its historic architecture and proximity to cultural landmarks, Rue de la Verrerie is also home to the Bazar de l'Hôtel de Ville (BHV), a large department store offering a wide range of products from fashion to homewares, as well as an excellent range of second-hand clothing stores.

Popular vintage shops include chains Free'p'Star, an affordable chain famous for its €1 bin; and Hippy Market, a colourful retro bazaar meticulously organised by theme. Other notable shops include Vintage by Ramin, a no-frills vintage shop with rock-bottom prices; and Tilt Vintage, which carries a wide variety of second-hand pieces from the 1960s–1990s.

ADDRESS: *Rue de la Verrerie*

ARRONDISSEMENT: *Paris Centre*

CLOSEST MÉTRO STATION: *Hôtel de Ville*

À la Mère de Famille

CHOCOLATE

Established in 1761, À la Mère de Famille is the oldest chocolate store in Paris and it's everything you hoped it would be. Its corner facade is a stunning example of eighteenth-century design with handpainted gold lettering on deep forest-green wood panels, and large display windows meticulously arranged with mountains of chocolates, candied fruits and other delights. Inside, antique glass display cases overflow with all kinds of handcrafted chocolates, ganache, truffles and countless sweets of every shape and colour.

Originally opened as a small *épicerie* (grocery store), owner Pierre-Jean Bernard's store gained a loyal clientele for its chocolates, caramels, pralines, jams and candied fruit, which were luxurious treats at the time. Bernard's widow took over in 1807 and gave the store its current name, which means 'to the mother of the family'. It became one of the first Parisian *chocolateries* to adopt the practice of presenting chocolates in beautifully decorated boxes and, to this day, the gift boxes of À la Mère de Famille are luxurious, often tied with a signature orange ribbon.

Under the helm of the Dolfi family, who took over in 2000, À la Mère de Famille has opened many new locations in Paris, always faithfully replicating the historical look of the flagship store. They have also expanded the product line to over 1500 products with recent additions including chocolate-coated marshmallow bars and chocolate-coated tiles with flaked almonds known as 'almond cracks'.

ADDRESS: *35 Rue du Faubourg Montmartre*

ARRONDISSEMENT: *9th*

CLOSEST MÉTRO STATION: *Le Peletier*

Jim's Corner

—— CAFÉ

The traditional French breakfast is coffee and buttered baguette with jam or *tartine* (a term also used to describe 'something on toast'). But this small café with distinctive orange awnings serves the classic Australian bacon and egg roll courtesy of its New Zealand–born chef and co-owner, who previously worked in Sydney.

This Aussie influence is clear in the cosy café's laid-back atmosphere, which makes me nostalgic for my favourite local cafés back in Australia. Jim's Corner takes their bacon and egg rolls seriously: the egg is perfectly cooked with a runny yolk and the caramelised bacon is slow-roasted. They have also recently upgraded the classic roll into the 'breakfast BLT', complete with lettuce, tomato and avocado.

ADDRESS: *127 Rue du Faubourg Poissonnière*

ARRONDISSEMENT: *9th*

CLOSEST MÉTRO STATION: *Poissonnière*

Evi Evane

—— DELI

If you have worked up an appetite while shopping on Rue des Martyrs (p 259) and Rue Condorcet (p 266), the fluffy puff pastries piled up in the window of Greek delicatessen Evi Evane may be just the thing to cure your craving. The deli is a sister-venue to Evi Evane restaurant in the 6th arrondissement. Both venues are run by sisters Maria and Dina Nikolaou, who hail from the Greek village of Kyrtoni. Their deli offers a large selection of homemade salads and sandwiches. My favourites are the savoury filo pastries stuffed with meat, spinach or cheese.

ADDRESS: *49 Rue Condorcet*

ARRONDISSEMENT: *9th*

CLOSEST MÉTRO STATION: *Anvers*

EAT & DRINK

KB Café

—— CAFÉ

While some people come to KB Café for the house-roasted coffee and tasty scones, most come here to work – or to be seen working. The café has tried to discourage digital nomads by covering up powerpoints and switching off their wi-fi on weekends, but it hasn't stopped the laptop crowd from piling into the shared bench seating and long window bar to work alongside fellow freelancers, from filmmakers editing on huge Macbooks to writers feverishly typing their manuscripts – myself included.

ADDRESS: *53 Avenue Trudaine*

ARRONDISSEMENT: *9th*

CLOSEST MÉTRO STATION: *Pigalle*

Additional VENUE

Méert

—— CHOCOLATE

One of the most beautiful chocolate shops in Paris, Méert's elegant Pompeian-style gold and dark-green design is a beautiful representation of the original boutique in the northern French city of Lille, which was established by legendary chocolatier Sieur Delcourt in 1761. The brand didn't gain its current name until Michael Paulus Gislinus Méert took over the original shop in 1849 and created the legendary Meert *gaufre* (waffle). Unlike a traditional thick waffle, Méert's handmade oblong-shaped waffles are smaller and flatter – more like a soft, crumbly biscuit – and are stuffed with a sweet filling. These days there are many delectable filling flavours from which to choose, including its signature speculoos (a spiced Flemish biscuit), lemon, chestnut and the traditional Madagascar vanilla.

While the Paris store only opened in 2010, Méert is intimately intertwined with French history. Méert's former patrons include general Charles de Gaulle, who loved its brioches, and its caramels are said to have been the favourite of Mozart.

ADDRESS: *16 Rue Elzevir*

ARRONDISSEMENT: *Paris Centre*

CLOSEST MÉTRO STATION: *Chemin Vert*

La Petite Charlotte

—— BISTRO

Just a few minutes up the road from the Nouvelle Athènes (New Athens) area of the 9th arrondissement, traditional French bistro La Petite Charlotte is named after the chef's wife. I can't help but make the connection with the cosy feel of the eponymous song by Swiss French-language singer Henri Dès about little Charlotte who wants nothing but to bake a cake.

The short à la carte menu (including a homemade terrine) is complemented by daily specials like the quintessential pork chop (which most people order). Meals are simple but delicious and affordable, with a two-course lunch offered for just €20. La Petite Charlotte also operates a gourmet takeaway sandwich shop across the street at lunchtime.

ADDRESS: *47 Rue Notre Dame de Lorette*

ARRONDISSEMENT: *9th*

CLOSEST MÉTRO STATION: *Saint-Georges*

Additional VENUE

Le Royal China

—— CHINESE

When a craving for Chinese food strikes in Paris, the place to go is Le Royal China, a legendary Cantonese restaurant serving all the classics. My favourite is the roast pork and Peking duck, and the sizzling eggplant is juicy and bursting with flavour. Delicious cold side dishes like peanut and celery salad and black mushroom salad remind me of dinner at my grandparents' home in China. Le Royal China also specialises in dim sum – steamed, fried or baked – and handmade rice noodle dishes. Through the street-facing window you can see the open kitchen, where chefs expertly slice up roast duck and pork, and make dumplings by hand, with steam billowing from the bamboo steamers behind them.

ADDRESS: *85 Rue Beaubourg*

ARRONDISSEMENT: *Paris Centre*

CLOSEST MÉTRO STATION: *Arts et Métiers*

Vivant 2

—— RESTAURANT

French restaurant Vivant 2 was established in 2011 by chef, restaurateur and wine merchant Pierre Jancou. It owes its popularity not only to its food and expertly curated wine list – including many natural wines – but for its contagious energy and ambiance. Making the best of its typically small Parisian venue size, the open galley kitchen is right behind the marble bar, allowing diners to observe chef Robert Mendoza and his staff at work.

The contemporary French menu focuses on small, seasonal plates designed to be shared, with signature dishes including whole-roasted broccoli served atop a vibrant green mole sauce and a refined take on the classic steak tartare using fresh watercress.

ADDRESS: *43 Rue des Petites Écuries*

ARRONDISSEMENT: *10th*

CLOSEST MÉTRO STATION: *Poissonnière*

DAY 6

KEY NEIGHBOURHOODS

BERCY

ODÉON

BELLEVILLE

To me, Paris seems to spin counterclockwise. Instead of big malls and chain stores displacing small independent businesses, this is a city where everything big and efficient just can't seem to compete with the small and traditional. This itinerary takes you to the intersection of old and new, where historic makers and purveyors of fine goods rub shoulders with a new generation of entrepreneurs reimagining French heritage for today's consumers.

DAY OF ARTISANS

Superstitch MFG Paris

ITINERARY

This itinerary is recommended on

TUESDAY
WEDNESDAY
THURSDAY
FRIDAY
SATURDAY

TIPS

——— You may want to **PACK SOME SNACKS** to keep you going while browsing local boutiques.

——— **A COLLAPSIBLE BAG OR CHIC BACKPACK MAY COME IN USEFUL** for carrying purchases comfortably.

——— **A BOOKING IS RECOMMENDED** for dining at **SARDEGNA A TAVOLA** (p 305).

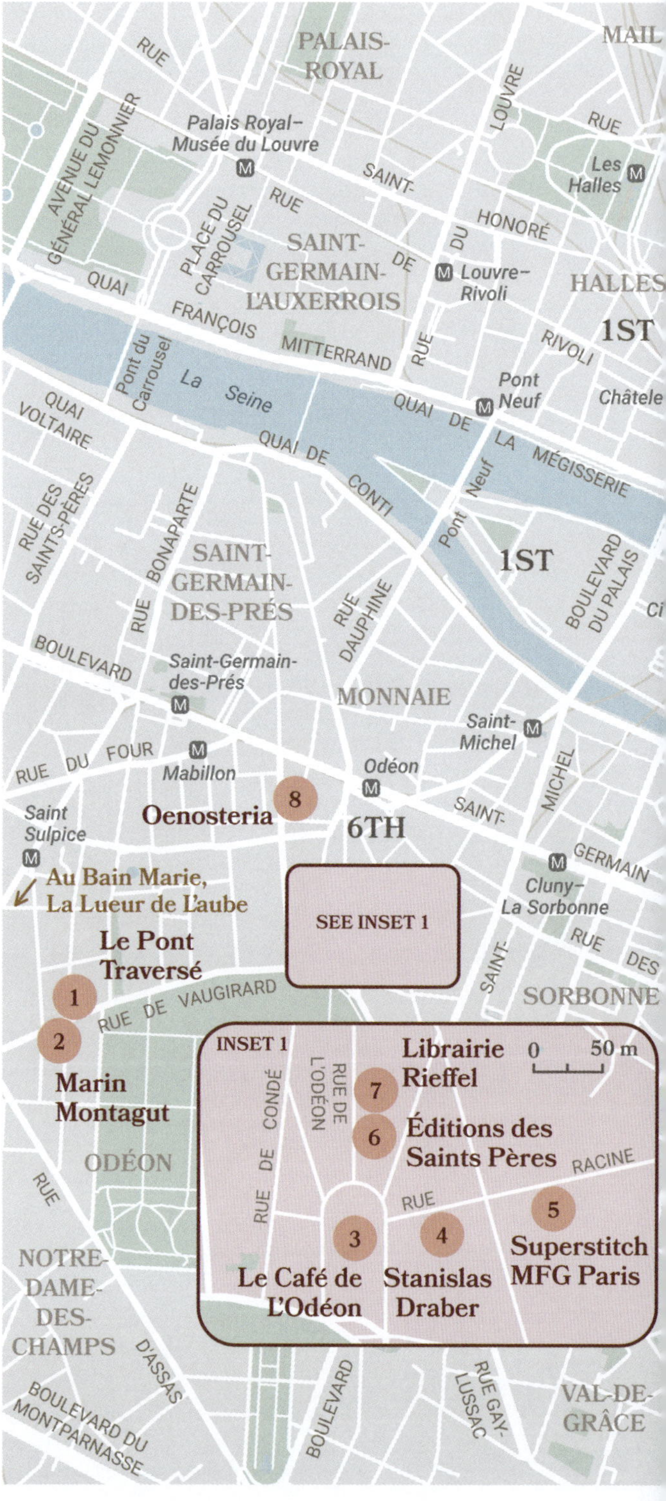

DAY 6

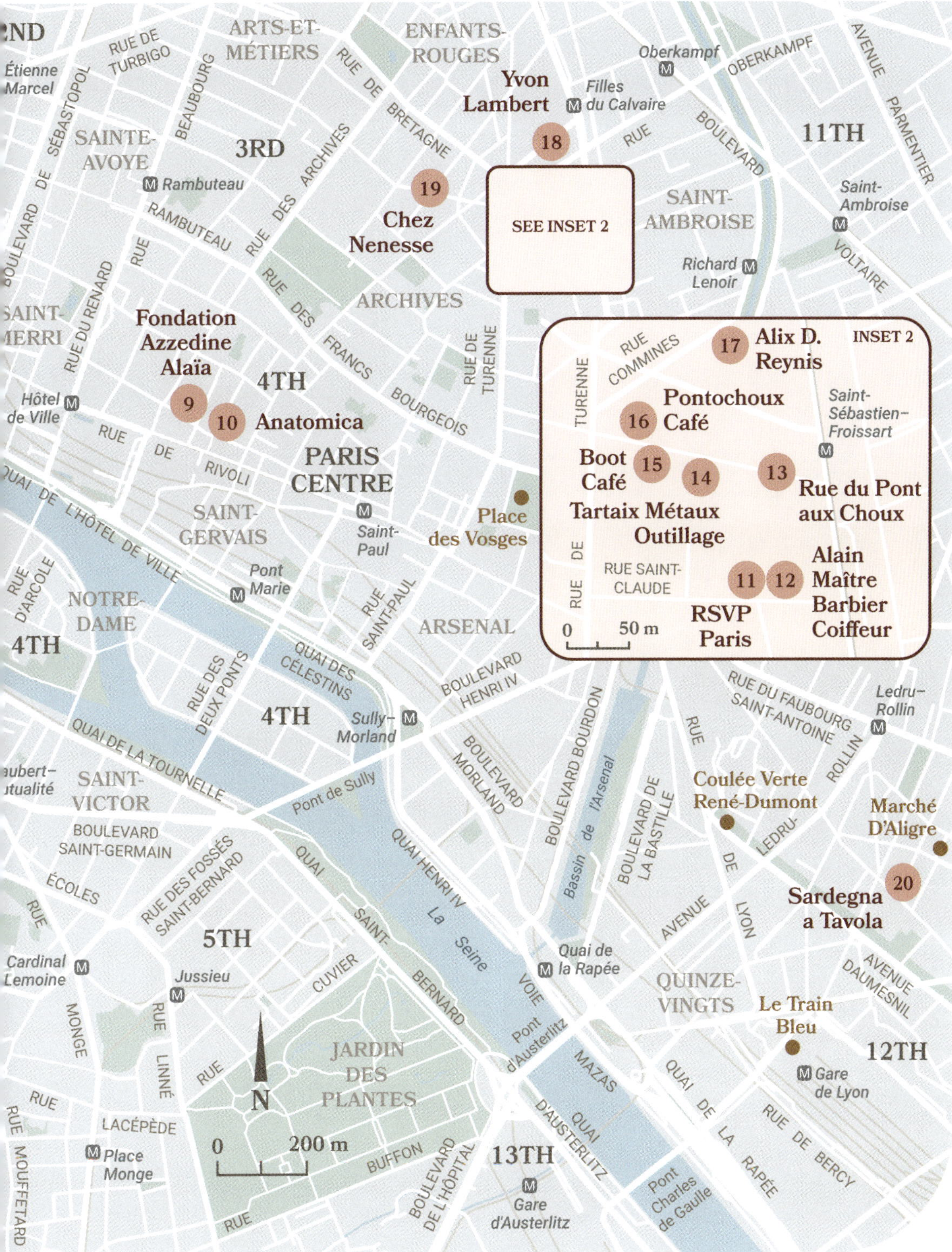
Yvon Lambert
18
19
Chez Nenesse
SEE INSET 2
Fondation Azzedine Alaïa
9
10
Anatomica
INSET 2
17
Alix D. Reynis
16
Pontochoux Café
15
Boot Café
14
Tartaix Métaux Outillage
13
Rue du Pont aux Choux
11
12
Alain Maître Barbier Coiffeur
RSVP Paris
0 50 m
20
Sardegna a Tavola
Place des Vosges
Coulée Verte René-Dumont
Marché D'Aligre
Le Train Bleu
0 200 m
N
3RD
4TH
11TH
5TH
12TH
13TH
PARIS CENTRE
ARTS-ET-MÉTIERS
ENFANTS-ROUGES
SAINTE-AVOYE
ARCHIVES
SAINT-AMBROISE
SAINT-GERVAIS
NOTRE-DAME
ARSENAL
SAINT-VICTOR
QUINZE-VINGTS
JARDIN DES PLANTES
Oberkampf
Filles du Calvaire
Rambuteau
Saint-Ambroise
Richard Lenoir
Saint-Sébastien–Froissart
Hôtel de Ville
Saint-Paul
Pont Marie
Sully–Morland
Ledru-Rollin
Quai de la Rapée
Cardinal Lemoine
Jussieu
Place Monge
Gare de Lyon
Gare d'Austerlitz
La Seine
Bassin de l'Arsenal
Pont de Sully
Pont d'Austerlitz
Pont Charles de Gaulle
RUE DE TURBIGO
BOULEVARD DE SÉBASTOPOL
BEAUBOURG
RUE RAMBUTEAU
RUE DES ARCHIVES
RUE DE BRETAGNE
RUE OBERKAMPF
BOULEVARD
AVENUE PARMENTIER
VOLTAIRE
RUE DU RENARD
RUE DES FRANCS BOURGEOIS
RUE DE TURENNE
RUE COMMINES
TURENNE
RUE DE
RUE SAINT-CLAUDE
RUE DE RIVOLI
QUAI DE L'HÔTEL DE VILLE
RUE D'ARCOLE
RUE SAINT-PAUL
QUAI DES CÉLESTINS
RUE DES DEUX PONTS
BOULEVARD HENRI IV
BOULEVARD BOURDON
BOULEVARD MORLAND
BOULEVARD DE LA BASTILLE
RUE DU FAUBOURG SAINT-ANTOINE
ROLLIN
LEDRU-
RUE DE LYON
AVENUE
AVENUE DAUMESNIL
QUAI DE LA TOURNELLE
BOULEVARD SAINT-GERMAIN
ÉCOLES
RUE
RUE DES FOSSÉS SAINT-BERNARD
QUAI SAINT-BERNARD
QUAI HENRI IV
CUVIER
VOIE MAZAS
QUAI D'AUSTERLITZ
QUAI DE LA RAPÉE
RUE DE BERCY
MONGE
RUE LINNÉ
RUE LACÉPÈDE
RUE MOUFFETARD
BUFFON
BOULEVARD DE L'HÔPITAL

ITINERARY

MORNING

——— Take the métro to Saint-Sulpice in the 6th arrondissement and have breakfast at the stunning Art Nouveau café ① **Le Pont Traversé** (p 304), then head south on Rue Madame to visit ② **Marin Montagut** (p 294), an eclectic shop filled with whimsical gifts embellished with the owner's charming illustrations.

② Marin Montagut

① Le Pont Traversé

③ Le Café de L'Odéon

—— Head east towards Odéon, taking the opportunity to stroll through the Jardin du Luxembourg (p 233), then have a coffee break on the sunny terrace or in the stunning foyer of ③ **Le Café de L'Odéon** (p 300).

—— Continue east to Rue Racine, browsing local boutiques along the way, especially the flower shop ④ **Stanislas Draber** (p 295) and the workshop and boutique of Parisian specialist denim brand ⑤ **Superstitch MFG Paris** (p 297), where the on-site workshop is filled with rare vintage sewing machines used to create made-to-order denim garments.

④ Stanislas Draber

⑤ Superstitch MFG Paris

ITINERARY

AFTERNOON

——— Backtrack on Rue Racine and turn north to explore Rue de l'Odéon, visiting ⑥ **Éditions des Saints Pères** (p 292), which specialises in republishing the original manuscripts of beloved books; and second-hand bookshop ⑦ **Librairie Rieffel** (p 292).

——— Have lunch at tucked-away Italian restaurant ⑧ **Oenosteria** (p 302) on Rue Grégoire de Tours, which offers fresh and vibrant Tuscan cuisine.

⑧ Oenosteria

⑥ Éditions des Saints Pères

Catch a taxi or Uber to the Marais and visit the ⑨ **Fondation Azzedine Alaïa** (p 286), the former home and atelier of Tunisian-French designer Azzedine Alaïa, which is now a museum dedicated to showing his work and extensive personal collections.

Head east to visit ⑩ **Anatomica** (p 290), a menswear brand on Rue du Bourg Tibourg that seeks to revive the simplicity and elegance of traditional French fashion. Its high-quality knits and coats are also popular among Parisian women.

⑪ RSVP Paris

⑨ Fondation Azzedine Alaïa

Wander north, taking a right and then a left onto Rue Vieille du Temple, and browse trendy boutiques en route to Rue Saint-Claude, where you'll find modern French leathergoods brand ⑪ **RSVP Paris** (p 294) and cult barber shop ⑫ **Alain Maître Barbier Coiffeur** (p 284).

Continue north to historic ⑬ **Rue du Pont aux Choux** (p 289) to browse independent boutiques and workshops including tool shop ⑭ **Tartaix Métaux Outillage** (p 298). Take a coffee break at ⑮ **Boot Café** (p 300) or ⑯ **Pontochoux Café** (p 303) if it's Monday and Boot Café is closed.

ITINERARY

⑱ Yvon Lambert

⑲ Chez Nenesse (above and opposite)

EVENING

——— On nearby Rue Commines visit the boutique of ⑰ **Alix D. Reynis** (p 290), a ceramicist and bespoke jewellery designer. Rue Commines connects with Rue des Filles du Calvaire, home to bookshop and art gallery ⑱ **Yvon Lambert** (p 299).

——— Have dinner at ⑲ **Chez Nenesse** (p 301), a traditional French restaurant in the Marais that pairs a cosy atmosphere with homemade French dishes. If you are in the mood for vibrant Sardinian food instead, try family restaurant ⑳ **Sardegna a Tavola** (p 305).

8€
16€
19€
8€

Alain Maître Barbier Coiffeur

—— BARBER

Alain Maître Barbier Coiffeur is more than just a barbershop. It's also a mini private museum with nostalgic furnishings including 1950s ceramic basins and barber chairs, and an impressive collection of grooming tools from various eras. The retro posters and photographs covering the walls were all collected by Mr Alain, the master barber himself.

Alain offers traditional barber techniques including straight-razor shaves, hot towel treatments and classic haircuts, which he revived in the 1980s when these traditional techniques were declining. Alain has always run his business solo, without an assistant, and represents it well in his 1950s personal style.

Over the years Alain has garnered an international following, having appeared in numerous books and articles and attracting fans passionate about traditional *barberie* (barbershops) as well as vintage style and history. His services are strictly by appointment only (call or pop in to book).

ADDRESS: *8 Rue Saint-Claude*

ARRONDISSEMENT: *Paris Centre*

CLOSEST MÉTRO STATION: *Saint-Sébastien–Froissart*

Additional VENUE

Coulée Verte René-Dumont

—— PARK

Parks and gardens appear in some unexpected places in Paris. Built on top of a former railway viaduct, the Coulée Verte René-Dumont is a great example.

Also known as the Promenade Plantée (Plant-filled Walk), this elevated linear park was constructed along the decommissioned Vincennes railway line, which until 1969 connected the city's Bastille Station to the eastern suburbs of Vincennes. Transformed into a lush urban amenity by architect Philippe Mathieux and landscape designer Jacques Vergely, the Coulée Verte René-Dumont officially opened in 1993, making it the world's first elevated linear park. The main elevated section stretches from just south of Place de la Bastille to Jardin de Reuilly, a distance of about 1.5 kilometres (1 mile), and continues all the way to Bois de Vincennes, roughly a 4.7-kilometre (3-mile) journey in total. With many hidden alcoves, pergolas, fountains and views to be discovered along the way, it's worth taking your time.

ADDRESS: *Avenue Daumesnil*

ARRONDISSEMENT: *12th*

CLOSEST MÉTRO STATION: *Bastille*

Fondation Azzedine Alaïa
—— ART MUSEUM

The Fondation Azzedine Alaïa is a small private museum hidden in the Marias that showcases the works of Tunisian-French fashion designer Azzedine Alaïa, as well as his extensive personal collections of fashion, art and design. The intimate venue regularly holds thought-provoking temporary exhibitions that traverse the world of fashion and art.

A legend in the fashion industry, Alaïa is remembered for his body-sculpting designs. Unlike most of his contemporaries – including Yves Saint Laurent, Jean Paul Gaultier and Giorgio Armani, who were household names – Alaïa shied away from the spotlight and avoided the traditional fashion seasons that necessitated creating many collections each year. He held only a handful of shows, which had special meaning. All of them were raging successes.

Alaïa developed a love affair with Paris and France after moving here from Tunisia in the 1950s and he wished to have his life's work preserved and showcased at his home in the Marais, where he lived

and worked until his death in 2017. Alaïa was also an insatiable collector, with his collection including tens of thousands of designer pieces by Cristóbal Balenciaga, Madame Grès, André Courrèges, Comme des Garçons and Martin Margiela. This enormous collection is being progressively curated into temporary exhibitions, often drawing parallels between Alaïa's own works and those that he collected.

On the second floor, Alaïa's atelier is preserved just as it was before his passing, in a state of activity with garments in the process of being sewn onto dress form mannequins (which were moulded on the body of his muse, supermodel Naomi Campbell) and racks full of prototypes. Alaïa made everything himself, from patterns to prototypes, and he was always experimenting.

The historic building housing the fondation is something to be admired: a stunning glass-ceilinged exhibition space and courtyard enclosed by seventeenth-century buildings with their own glass canopy. There is also a bookshop with a curated selection including tomes related to Alaïa's work as well as other rare and limited editions on fashion, art, design and photography.

Alaïa is said to have been extremely warm and generous, often gathering his friends around him and cooking and caring for them. Traces of those friendships can be found all over his former home, including portraits of Alaïa created by his friends to honour their bond; one such example is the emblematic portrait by artist Julian Schnabel incorporating broken plates.

The fondation's Italian restaurant is inspired by Alaïa's love of cooking, and the long table around which he would gather with friends remains in the kitchen where it always was.

ADDRESS: *18 Rue de la Verrerie*

ARRONDISSEMENT: *Paris Centre*

CLOSEST MÉTRO STATION: *Hôtel de Ville*

Additional VENUE

Place des Vosges

——— SQUARE

One of my favourite places in Paris, the beautiful Place des Vosges is the city's oldest planned square. Almost completely enclosed by seventeenth-century apartment buildings set above vaulted arcades, the square is entered through grand-arched entrances to the north and south, giving the impression of entering another world when you walk through to its manicured lawns.

Commissioned by King Henry IV and completed in 1612, the Place des Vosges is unique in its absolute symmetry and inspired many other squares across Europe including Covent Garden in London.

Place des Vosges is the site of many historical events – even some aristocratic duels in the seventeenth and eighteenth centuries. French musketeer Charles de Batz de Castelmor, also known as d'Artagnan (who inspired the Alexandre Dumas novel, *The Three Musketeers*), was known to frequent the area and is rumored to have participated in duels himself.

Victor Hugo lived on the square while writing parts of *Les Misérables* and *The Hunchback of Notre-Dame*. His home on the second floor of Hôtel de Rohan-Guéménée at 6 Place des Vosges has been preserved as the Maison de Victor Hugo museum.

The arcades of the square are populated with boutiques, antique shops, specialty stores and cafés, including historic Carette. Less crowded than the Trocadéro and Montmartre branches, this is my favourite of Carette's trio of Parisian outposts.

ADDRESS: *Place des Vosges*

ARRONDISSEMENT: *Paris Centre*

CLOSEST MÉTRO STATION: *Chemin Vert*

Place des Vosges

Rue du Pont aux Choux

—— STREET

I love the name of this street, which means 'Bridge of Cabbages', in the Marais. It was named in the sixteenth century after a small bridge that crossed a city drain in an area once known for cabbage cultivation. In the eighteenth century, the street's reputation for artisanship took hold, thanks to Manufacture de Pont aux Choux, a French *faience* (tin-glazed earthenware) and porcelain factory established in 1743. Today the street is home to a number of diverse independent workshops, boutiques and cafés, including the pint-sized Boot Café (p 300), set in a former cobbler's workshop.

ADDRESS: *Rue du Pont aux Choux*

ARRONDISSEMENT: *Paris Centre*

CLOSEST MÉTRO STATION: *Saint-Sébastien–Froissart*

Anatomica

—— MENSWEAR

Loved by customers for its functional, well-made clothes, Anatomica has been a Parisian retail institution since 1994. Founder Pierre Fournier, who is as revered as the boutique itself, has made significant contributions to men's fashion over the years through the establishment of several influential Parisian boutiques. Globe and Hémisphère, two multi-brand stores he founded in the 1970s, played key roles in popularising American casualwear in Europe.

At Anatomica, Fournier seeks to revive traditional French fashion that he has seen disappearing from men's wardrobes – a reversible raglan coat, Shetland sweater and *pantalon à pont* (button-fly trousers) are staple styles. Though technically a menswear boutique, it is also frequented by stylish Parisian women for its high-quality unisex knits and outerwear.

Alix D. Reynis

—— HOMEWARES

Alix D. Reynis is a Paris-based designer of porcelain tableware, bespoke jewellery and other forms of decorative art. Her understated style is inspired by neoclassical French design and eighteenth-century decorative arts, with subtle references to architectural motifs, including Corinthian columns and ornate friezes, often seen on the rims of her teacups and the bases of her egg cups. All products are handcrafted using traditional methods at workshops across the country – particularly in Limoges, the home of fine French porcelain.

With its charming wood furniture and shelves filled with delicate white porcelain objects, the Marais boutique feels like a chic Parisian apartment. There is another boutique in Saint-Germain-des-Prés at 22 Rue Jacob.

ADDRESS: *14 Rue Commines*

ARRONDISSEMENT: *Paris Centre*

CLOSEST MÉTRO STATION: *Filles du Calvaire or Saint-Sébastien–Froissart*

Anatomica's offerings also include footwear, notably American shoe brand Alden's 'modified last' style – originally designed in the mid-twentieth century as an orthopaedic shoe. Anatomica collaborates closely with Alden to curate designs that align with its philosophy of comfort and fit. Unusually for a Parisian footwear store, Fournier tends to recommend sizing up for comfort.

Handwritten signs hung over the counter warn customers that they are not always right at Anatomica – Fournier's fastidiousness may baffle new clients, but the proof is in the pudding as Anatomica has a fiercely loyal clientele.

ADDRESS: *14 Rue du Bourg Tibourg*

ARRONDISSEMENT: *Paris Centre*

CLOSEST MÉTRO STATION: *Hôtel de Ville*

Additional VENUE

Au Bain Marie

KITCHENWEAR

The large shop window filled with eclectic tableware, whimsical animal figurines and audacious *barbotine* (ceramic) plates and soup tureens shaped like hens, cabbages and lobsters foreshadow the Aladdin's cave of kitchenwear you'll find at Au Bain Marie.

Conceived by culinary journalist, stylist and qualified architect Aude Clément in 1977, Au Bain Marie's house brand is inspired by decorative and entertaining objects from the eighteenth and nineteenth centuries. There is whimsy and fun in every object, from barbotine cat salt-and-pepper shakers to butter dishes topped with little rabbits.

The shop's antiques collection includes many rare and interesting pieces with glass display cases full of every type of utensil you can imagine, including a collection of travelling kits from the eighteenth century. Aude has received and accepted many requests from museums around the world to borrow and exhibit her rare pieces.

ADDRESS: *59 Boulevard Raspail*

ARRONDISSEMENT: *6th*

CLOSEST MÉTRO STATION: *Rue du Bac*

SHOPPING

Éditions des Saints Pères

—— BOOKS

The 6th arrondissement has long been a hub of intellectual and literary activity, making it a natural fit for this French publishing house specialising in high-quality facsimiles (reproductions) of original manuscripts by some of the world's most celebrated authors. While technically called Éditions des Saints Pères, the shop is best known as Le Coup Papier (The Letter Opener), which it uses on its signage.

Often marked up with the author's handwritten notes and edits, manuscripts including *Notre-Dame de Paris* by Victor Hugo and *Madame Bovary* by Gustave Flaubert are transformed into beautiful literary objects by owners Jessica Nelson and Nicolas Tretiakow. The reproduction of *Alice's Adventures in Wonderland* by Lewis Carroll is particularly precious – originally intended as a birthday gift, the manuscript is fully illustrated. The shop is a lovely little refuge with cosy wood shelves and rolling library ladders.

ADDRESS: *19 Rue de l'Odéon*

ARRONDISSEMENT: *6th*

CLOSEST MÉTRO STATION: *Odéon*

Librairie Rieffel

—— BOOKS

Popular with the student population of Saint-Germain-des-Prés, independent bookshop Librairie Rieffel sells a broad range of second-hand titles at reasonable prices. Large display windows featuring stacks of books alongside eclectic objects give the bookshop an old-world vibe and the interior is packed floor-to-ceiling with books and vintage postcards.

Operating for over a century, Librairie Rieffel gained its name from its 1960s owner, Mr Riefell, whose family continues to preserve its traditional neighbourhood bookshop feel. Titles range from poetry and literature to children's books and textbooks, mostly in French but also some in English, sourced from all over Paris. Current owner Adrien Delbes remarked to me that he spends so much time searching for books that he hardly has time to read them.

ADDRESS: *15 Rue de l'Odéon*

ARRONDISSEMENT: *6th*

CLOSEST MÉTRO STATION: *Odéon*

Additional VENUE

La Lueur de L'aube

— JEWELLERY

Japanese jeweller Makiko Akiyama studied jewellery-making in Japan and Paris before opening this boutique on a quiet corner of Rue du Cherche-Midi in 2016. La Lueur de L'aube doubles as boutique and atelier, with Akiyama and her employees often seen creating their delicate lost-wax-casted pieces (metal objects cast from wax models) at the workstation by the window.

Handmade on-site, the brand's jewellery is inspired by nature with pieces featuring intricate branches of coral and delicate folded leaves. Display cabinets decorated with treasures you might find on the forest floor make the store feel like a fairy cabin in the woods. La Lueur de L'aube brand also crafts bespoke pieces by special order.

ADDRESS: *77 Rue du Cherche-Midi*

ARRONDISSEMENT: *6th*

CLOSEST MÉTRO STATION: *Rennes or Vaneau*

Additional VENUE

Marché d'Aligre

— MARKET

There are many famous markets in Paris, but for a truly local experience – which is reflected in the reasonable prices – head to Marché d'Aligre. Despite the out-of-the-way location, Parisians come from all over the city for its fresh produce, especially fruits and vegetables, as well as its flea market.

The market's history dates back to 1779 and is closely tied to the growth of the historically working-class neighbourhood of Faubourg Saint-Antoine. Open daily except Mondays, it consists of the covered Marché Beauvau, where you will find butchers and fishmongers, and an outdoor section, with fresh fruit and vegetable vendors taking over the Place d'Aligre. In the centre of the outdoor market is the flea market with stalls run by both professional antique dealers and locals selling preloved wares. Here you can find just about anything from homewares and tools to old books and vintage clothing.

ADDRESS: *Place d'Aligre*

ARRONDISSEMENT: *12th*

CLOSEST MÉTRO STATION: *Ledru–Rollin*

SHOPPING

Marin Montagut

—— GIFTS

Marin Montagut's whimsical giftshop can perhaps best be described as something between the Weasleys' Wizard Wheezes joke shop from *Harry Potter* and your grandmother's house. Every inch of the walls and display cabinets are adorned with charming and curious objects such as cups, cards, aprons and ceramic adornments – all painted, embroidered or printed with Montagut's distinctive vintage-inspired illustrations. My favourite part of the store is the 'magic window', where intricate paper cut-outs are arranged in layers to create a 3D effect, like an old theatre set.

Originally from the south of France, Montagut shares his *coup de foudre* (love at first sight) of Paris through his love-themed creations and emblems of Parisian charm. All made in his Paris studio, they reflect the blissfully naive wonder and romanticism of discovering Paris for the first time.

ADDRESS: *48 Rue Madame*

ARRONDISSEMENT: *6th*

CLOSEST MÉTRO STATION: *Rennes*

Marin Montagut (above and opposite, top left)

RSVP Paris

—— HANDBAGS

Paris is rich in both heritage and contemporary brands that continue the great French tradition of *maroquinerie* (leathergoods). Founded in 2015, RSVP Paris has become known globally for its minimalist handbag designs, quality craftsmanship and limited production model – just 500 numbered pieces are produced in each style.

Epitomising the brand's savoir faire, RSVP handbags and small leathergoods typically have minimal embellishments and hardware, often limited to its signature double-brass-magnet closure, allowing the carefully selected leather – sourced from renowned French tanneries – to shine.

ADDRESS: *8 Rue Saint-Claude*

ARRONDISSEMENT: *Paris Centre*

CLOSEST MÉTRO STATION: *Saint-Sébastien–Froissart*

Stanislas Draber

—— FLOWERS

When passing by Stanislas Draber's flower shop, I can't help but admire its rich wooden facade, often covered in seasonal flowers. Stepping inside, you are transported to the eclectic greenhouse of a country cottage, with grand flower bouquets in ornate urns filling every corner and editions of French poet Charles Baudelaire's *Les Fleurs du Mal* (*The Flowers of Evil*) displayed around the store.

Stanislas's flowers are strictly seasonal, sourced from local growers near Paris and in the south of France. Wrapped in crisp white paper and with a brown card secured by a long pearl-head hat pin, his beautiful bouquets are among my gifting go-tos. I've been lucky to receive a few of them myself.

ADDRESS: *19 Rue Racine*

ARRONDISSEMENT: *6th*

CLOSEST MÉTRO STATION: *Odéon*

SHOPPING

Superstitch MFG Paris

—— DENIM

Having originally trained in milling and turning, it was Arthur Leclercq's love of mechanics and fascination with using vintage sewing machines to make denim that inspired him to launch his own denim label in 2017. Superstitch has since become known the world over for its limited range of high-quality denim products made in Japan and Paris.

An incredible depth of research and development goes into every Superstitch product, from the fabric woven in small Japanese factories by shuttle loom to the buttons and trimmings, and even the threads – all meticulously directed by Leclercq. All Superstitch jeans are personally fitted and hemmed in-store using one of Leclercq's legendary Union Special hemming machines. The boutique and workshop are lined with original vintage sewing machines from Leclercq's collection – an homage to the golden era of denim from the 1940s to the 1970s.

Superstitch also offers a made-to-order service, allowing clients to choose their fabric, trimmings and jeans style to have a unique piece created in the Paris atelier. No fewer than 13 different sewing machines are used to create each piece, which the store can ship to you (there's a waiting list).

In 2025 Leclercq established the Superstitch weaving operation, which uses the first vintage Japanese shuttle loom operated outside Japan to weave traditional selvedge denim.

Full disclosure, Arthur Leclercq is my partner, but it would be remiss of me not to include Superstitch in this guide.

ADDRESS: *13 Rue Racine*

ARRONDISSEMENT: *6th*

CLOSEST MÉTRO STATION: *Odéon*

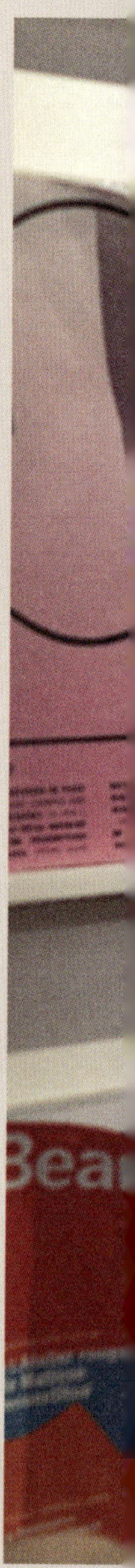

Tartaix Métaux Outillage

—— ARTISAN TOOLS

Tartaix is not your average tool shop. Founded in 1919, it has been serving professionals and artisans for over a century. In its early years it specialised in raw metals like brass, steel and copper, later expanding to offer specialised tools and accessories. Tartaix still specialises in cutting metals to client-specified dimensions and has a clientele of jewellers, sculptors, metalworkers and interior and set designers from all over Paris.

An impressive wooden cabinet of drawers stretches from floor to ceiling and wall to wall, with handwritten labels describing each drawer's contents, from metals and screws to nuts and bolts of every shape and size.

ADDRESS: *13 Rue du Pont aux Choux*

ARRONDISSEMENT: *Paris Centre*

CLOSEST MÉTRO STATION: *Filles du Calvaire*

Yvon Lambert

BOOKS

Established in 1967 by art dealer and collector Yvon Lambert, this self-titled space was initially a gallery showcasing works by prominent artists such as Cy Twombly, Sol LeWitt and Jean-Michel Basquiat. Closed in 2014, it was reborn in 2017 in partnership with Lambert's daughter Ève in its current location.

The 200-square-metre (650-square-foot) venue seamlessly integrates a bookshop, publishing house and gallery. The front of the store serves as the bookshop with an extensive collection of books on contemporary art, photography and design including out-of-print titles, exhibition catalogues and limited-edition publications. An inner gallery space and courtyard host rotating exhibitions, artist talks and community events.

The venue's minimalist frontage, designed by architect Dominique Perrault, features glazed-metal framed windows interspersed with recessed sections of the wall where the name of the shop is printed small and elegantly, intended as a modern reinterpretation of Haussmann architecture (p 67).

ADDRESS: *14 Rue des Filles du Calvaire*

ARRONDISSEMENT: *Paris Centre*

CLOSEST MÉTRO STATION: *Filles du Calvaire*

EAT & DRINK

Boot Café

—— CAFÉ

Boot Café is a charming little hole-in-the wall in the Marais, with colourful stools and tables lined up outside beckoning you to stop for a coffee in the sun. Hinting at the café's former life, its old blue facade still says *cordonnerie* (cobbler). The interior is tiny, homely and eclectic, with white-tiled walls and wooden fittings from the original cobbler shop.

Locals come for the atmosphere as well as the coffee, which is sourced from renowned Parisian micro-roaster Belleville Brûlerie. While the Marais has become the capital of cafés in Paris, Boot Café is among the most frequently recommended.

ADDRESS: *19 Rue du Pont aux Choux*

ARRONDISSEMENT: *Paris Centre*

CLOSEST MÉTRO STATION: *Saint-Sébastien–Froissart*

Le Café de l'Odéon

—— CAFÉ

Taking over the Place de l'Odéon between April and October, the expansive terrace café of the Odéon – Théâtre de l'Europe (also known as the Odéon Theatre) buzzes with locals sipping cool drinks in the sun and long into the evening (the café is open until midnight). On offer are wines from small producers alongside a short, modern French food menu that changes daily but often includes creative salads and grilled fish.

When the terrace is closed in the winter months, it's time to head inside to the Café de l'Odéon located in the grand foyer of the theatre. The café chairs and tables are arranged between majestic columns, statues of French playwrights Pierre Corneille and Jean-Baptiste Racine and paintings by Pierre-Nicolas Beauvallet and Pierre Joseph Lafontaine. The café also occupies the first floor, where you can look over the stone railings onto the intricate mosaic floor below.

ADDRESS: *Place de l'Odéon*

ARRONDISSEMENT: *6th*

CLOSEST MÉTRO STATION: *Odéon*

Chez Nenesse

—— RESTAURANT

If there's one restaurant in Paris that you need to visit on a Thursday, it's traditional French restaurant Chez Nenesse. For decades, Thursday has been the only day of the week when they serve *frites* (French fries) – and these are some of the best *frites* you will taste in Paris.

On the menu every day are traditional French country-style comfort dishes like herring and warm potato salad, and homemade foie gras on toast. With simple wooden tables and tartan tablecloths, the traditional decor reflects the restaurant's wonderfully laid-back simplicity.

ADDRESS: *17 Rue de Saintonge*

ARRONDISSEMENT: *Paris Centre*

CLOSEST MÉTRO STATION: *Filles du Calvaire*

EAT & DRINK

Oenosteria

——— RESTAURANT

You're unlikely to stumble upon this charming Italian restaurant because it it hidden away on the tiny Rue Grégoire de Tours, which connects Boulevard Saint Germain and Rue des Quartre Vents. In summer I come here to enjoy a simple plate of prosciutto and melon on the steps of the restaurant, while in winter I am lured inside by the cosy indoor space and smell of toasted garlic wafting in from the small open kitchen.

Behind the bar you'll often find tough-as-nails Italian chef Monica Luciani, who I once saw taking off down the street in pursuit of a man who had swiped a customer's wallet (she caught the thief, who was arrested by passing police). Her softer side shines in her food: one taste of her handmade strozzapreti pasta, often served with a caramelised onion sauce or with fresh broccoli, and you can taste the love put into it. True to Italian culinary principles, the ingredients are of the highest quality; the burrata is flown in from Italy and served the same day.

Hot tip: it's often possible to enjoy a late lunch here on a weekday afternoon after most other restaurants close at 2.30 pm.

ADDRESS: *40 Rue Grégoire de Tours*

ARRONDISSEMENT: *6th*

CLOSEST MÉTRO STATION: *Odéon*

Oenosteria

Pontochoux Café

—— CAFÉ

An intimate retreat in the lively Marais district, this laid-back specialty coffee shop features a minimalist design with floor-to-ceiling windows, raw wooden beams and rustic wooden tables and stools. The sister establishment of the Pontochoux Japanese curry restaurant next door, the café serves Japanese green teas such as hojicha and sencha in addition to classic espresso coffees. It also offers unique creations such as their 'akitonick', a refreshing blend of orange juice, tonic water, spices and coffee made with beans from Denmark's Coffee Collective; and sweet treats with Japanese flavours including hojicha canelés and black sesame madeleines.

ADDRESS: *18 Rue du Pont aux Choux*

ARRONDISSEMENT: *Paris Centre*

CLOSEST MÉTRO STATION: *Saint-Sébastien–Froissart*

EAT & DRINK

Le Pont Traversé

—— CAFÉ

With its intricately embellished Art Nouveau exterior dominating the corner of Rue de Vaugirard and Rue Madame, gluten-free coffee shop Le Pont Traversé (The Crossed Bridge) is difficult to miss. In summer, chairs line the pavement and are filled with locals.

This cosy local meeting place is full of history. The first clue that Le Pont Traversé wasn't always a coffee shop is the lettering above the door that says 'Livres' (Books) – a remnant from its era as a bookshop founded by surrealist poet Marcel Béalu in 1973 and specialising in rare books and first editions. With notable customers including former French President François Mitterrand, the bookshop's name – carried on by the café – paid homage to a rare 1921 collection of stories by French writer Jean Paulhan. Before the bookshop, the site was a butcher's shop, with carved ox heads and handpainted advertising panels still visible on the bright blue exterior.

In 2021 Le Pont Traversé was reopened as a minimalist contemporary café by Frédérique Jules – founder of the Noglu chain of gluten-free restaurants, which have a number of locations in Paris and New York. It serves an entirely gluten-free selection of food and drinks for breakfast and lunch on weekdays, brunch on weekends and dinner on select evenings. There is always a delicious window display of gluten-free homemade pastries and desserts.

ADDRESS: *62 Rue de Vaugirard*

ARRONDISSEMENT: *6th*

CLOSEST MÉTRO STATION: *Rennes*

Sardegna a Tavola

RESTAURANT

With its unassuming green facade and handpainted sign, Sardegna a Tavola mightn't look like one of the city's most loved restaurants, but this Sardinian restaurant is a Paris institution.

Established in 1997 by Tonino Simbula and his wife Angela, the restaurant has changed little since then, including the exceptional quality of its food. A celebration of traditional Sardinian home-cooking, the menu includes fresh seafood, lamb, goat and pork, flavoured with wild herbs. My favourite experiences here have been dining with a group, sharing heaped platters of fried sardines with wild vegetables; bruschetta with fragrant olive oil and sweet cherry tomatoes; and seafood spaghetti generously packed with fresh crab, crayfish and bottarga (salted and cured fish roe pouch). Surrounded by shelves packed with various types of pasta, wine and spicy jams, dining here feels like a big Italian family dinner, when pasta is passed around and lively conversation fills the room.

ADDRESS: *1 Rue de Cotte*

ARRONDISSEMENT: *12th*

CLOSEST MÉTRO STATION: *Ledru-Rollin*

Additional VENUE

Le Train Bleu

RESTAURANT

Le Train Bleu is a legendary Belle Époque restaurant inside the Gare de Lyon train station. With the station serving as a major gateway for millions of visitors arriving in Paris for the 1900 world's fair, the restaurant was intended to welcome them in style. In 1963 it was renamed after the luxurious overnight train that transported Parisian elites to the French Riviera.

Featuring extravagant chandeliers, gilded woodwork and 41 painted murals depicting French landscapes and cities, the design and décor of Le Train Bleu beautifully encapsulates the romance of early twentieth-century train travel. In 2019 Chanel creative director Karl Lagerfeld re-created its evocative dining hall for the Chanel Cruise 2020 collection show.

Naturally the cuisine is French with signature dishes including foie gras with brioche and chutney, decadent seafood platters bursting with lobster and oysters and slow-roasted leg of lamb.

ADDRESS: *Gare de Lyon, Place Louis Armand*

ARRONDISSEMENT: *12th*

CLOSEST MÉTRO STATION: *Gare de Lyon*

DAY 7

KEY NEIGHBOURHOODS

ÎLE DE LA CITÉ

ÎLE SAINT-LOUIS

MARAIS

The sun is to Paris as paint is to a canvas, transforming it with new colours across the seasons. Sunshine is a precious commodity in Paris and locals love to *prendre le soleil* (take the sun) when it's available. This is done on sprawling café terraces, on balconies and on the lawns of Paris's many parks – which, as soon as there is sun, instantly fill with reading, picnicking and napping Parisians. This itinerary showcases the city's best outdoor experiences, beautiful terraces, hidden gardens and secret spots.

DAY IN THE SUN

Joli

ITINERARY

This itinerary is recommended on

MONDAY
SUNDAY

when many other Parisian venues are closed

TIPS

—— This day out is **BEST ENJOYED DURING THE WARMER MONTHS** between March and October, **WHEN ALFRESCO VENUES ARE OPEN.**

—— Wear clothing you don't mind sitting on the ground in or **BRING A LIGHTWEIGHT PICNIC BLANKET.**

—— **RESERVE YOUR ACCESS TIME** to Notre-Dame (p 320) online **IN ADVANCE**, to reduce waiting time.

—— **CALL AHEAD** to ensure Chalet de l'Oasis (p 330) is open on the night you plan to dine.

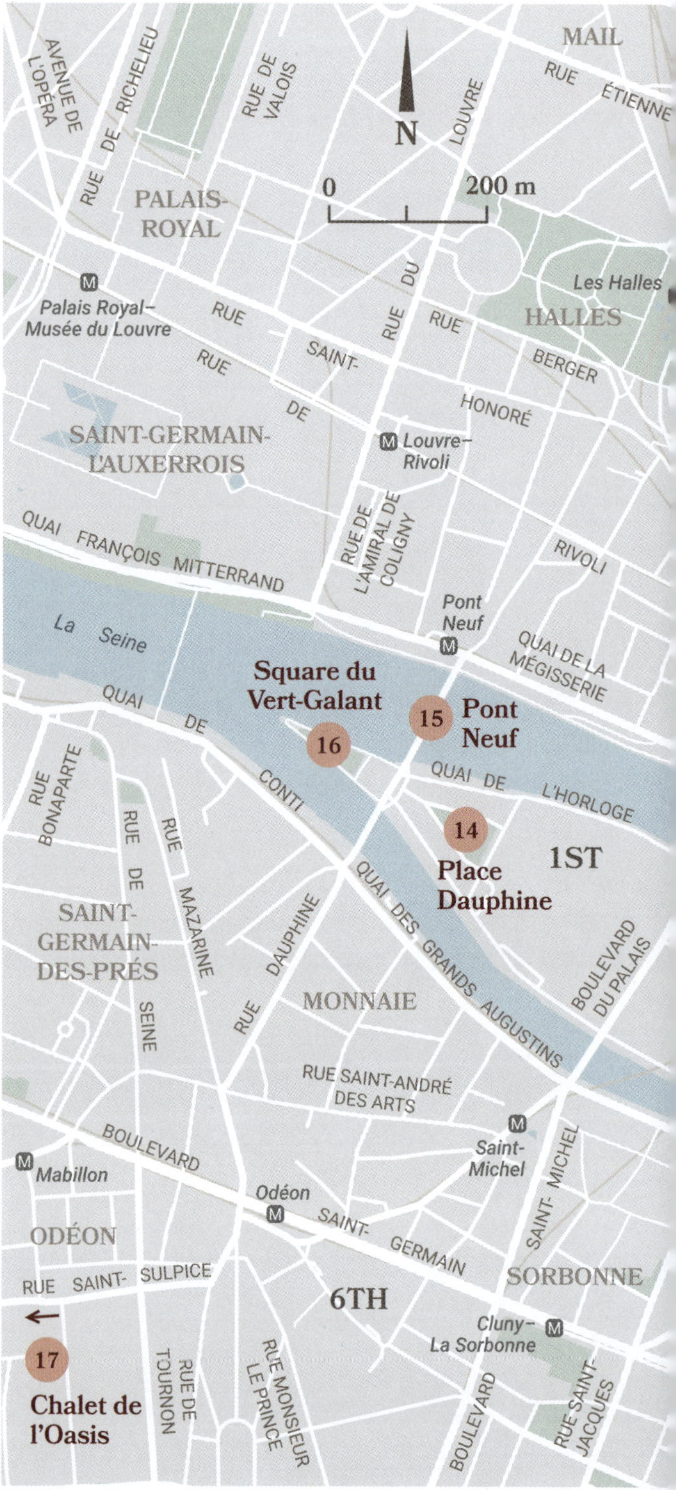

DAY 7

1
46 & 3rd
2
Partisan Café Artisanal
3
Jardin Anne Frank
4
Rue des Francs-Bourgeois
5
Christophe Lassalle's stall
6
Joli
7
8
The Bouillon of Paris
Marché des Enfants Rouges
9
Caractère de Cochon
10
Île Saint-Louis
11
Square Barye
12
Île de la Cité
13
Notre-Dame de Paris
Passage du Grand Cerf
Le Carreau du Temple
Rougier&Plé
Best Tofu
Cimetière du Père-Lachaise
Quai de la Photo
BONNE-NOUVELLE
2ND
1ST
3RD
4TH
5TH
ARTS-ET-MÉTIERS
ENFANTS-ROUGES
SAINTE-AVOYE
PARIS CENTRE
SAINT-MERRI
ARCHIVES
SAINT-GERVAIS
NOTRE-DAME
ARSENAL
SAINT-VICTOR
Arts et Métiers
Étienne Marcel
Rambuteau
Châtelet
Hôtel de Ville
Saint-Paul
Pont Marie
Sully–Morland
Maubert–Mutualité
Cité
RUE TURBIGO
RUE RÉAUMUR
RUE ÉTIENNE MARCEL
RUE DE BRETAGNE
BOULEVARD DU TEMPLE
BOULEVARD DE SÉBASTOPOL
RUE SAINT-DENIS
RUE BERGER
RUE BEAUBOURG
RUE DU TEMPLE
RUE PASTOURELLE
RUE DES ARCHIVES
RUE RAMBUTEAU
RUE DES QUATRE FILS
RUE VIEILLE DU TEMPLE
RUE DE TURENNE
RUE DU RENARD
RUE DU PARC ROYAL
PLACE DES VOSGES
AVENUE VICTORIA
QUAI DE GESVRES
RUE DE RIVOLI
RUE DE LOBAU
QUAI DE L'HÔTEL DE VILLE
QUAI AUX FLEURS
RUE D'ARCOLE
RUE DE LA CITÉ
Pont Notre-Dame
RUE DES NONNAINS D'HYÈRES
RUE SAINT-ANTOINE
RUE SAINT-PAUL
QUAI DES CÉLESTINS
Pont Marie
RUE SAINT-LOUIS EN L'ÎLE
RUE DES DEUX PONTS
QUAI DE MONTEBELLO
RUE LAGRANGE
RUE DES BERNARDINS
QUAI DE LA TOURNELLE
Pont de la Tournelle
La Seine
Pont de Sully
BOULEVARD HENRI IV
BOULEVARD MORLAND

MORNING

—— Make your way to Arts et Métiers métro station in Paris Centre and have breakfast across the road at popular local brunch spot ① **46 & 3rd** (p 333). Its delicious pancakes and breakfast sandwiches are worth the wait for a table on weekends.

—— Need another coffee? Head southwest along Rue de Turbigo and find a spot in the sun on the long benches of ② **Partisan Café Artisanal** (p 333) to people-watch while sipping a cup of their house-roasted Italian blend or single-origin coffee.

③ Jardin Anne Frank

① 46 & 3rd (above); ② Partisan Café Artisanal (opposite)

—— Head south to ③ **Jardin Anne Frank** (p 319) and enter the park via the inconspicuous dead-end street Impasse Berthaud, which gives no clue of the pretty garden that lies behind it. Wander through the garden and admire the famous horse-chestnut tree that was grown from a graft of the very tree that Holocaust victim Anne Frank wrote about in her famous diary.

ITINERARY

AFTERNOON

——— Head east towards ④ **Rue des Francs-Bourgeois** (p 324) and visit its trendy boutiques and galleries. If you're lucky, you might come across the street stall of artist ⑤ **Christophe Lassalle** (p 326), whose charming illustrations of Parisian scenes are peppered with his unique humour.

——— Have a light lunch in the sun at nearby ⑥ **Joli** (p 332), a café that takes over the manicured gardens of Parisian history museum Musée Carnavalet during summer. If you're visiting in winter, head to ⑦ **The Bouillon of Paris** (p 329) located inside the Marché des Enfants Rouges for simple but tasty French dishes such as charcuterie and roast chicken and potatoes.

⑧ Marché des Enfants Rouges

④ Rue des Francs-Bourgeois

⑤ Christophe Lassalle's stall

⑪ Square Barye

——— Pick up cheese, charcuterie, bread and wine at ⑧ **Marché des Enfants Rouges** (p 326) on Rue de Bretagne for an afternoon picnic on the Seine. Make sure to visit ⑨ **Caractère de Cochon** (p 330) for their popular *jambon-beurre* (ham and butter) sandwiches.

⑨ Caractère de Cochon

——— Take a taxi to ⑩ **Île Saint-Louis** (p 318), one of two small natural islands in the middle of the Seine, and find a place on the tip of the lower level of ⑪ **Square Barye** (p 324) overlooking the river for a picnic in the afternoon sun. If you're visiting in summer, you will likely be immersed in the energy of picnicking Parisians, who love a languid outdoors *apéro* (p 43). You might feel more comfortable with a picnic blanket, but locals often just sit on the paved ground, letting their legs dangle over the water.

EVENING

—— Cross the Pont Saint-Louis to ⑫ **Île de la Cité** (p 318) to visit ⑬ **Notre-Dame de Paris** (p 320); the famous cathedral reopened in 2024 following a devastating fire in 2019. It's open until 7 pm on weekdays and 7.30 pm on weekends.

—— Make your way to the western end of Île de la Cité, taking a slightly long route past the magnificent wisteria-covered facade of the Au Vieux Paris d'Arcole restaurant en route to ⑭ **Place Dauphine** (p 322), the beautiful triangular square tucked beside one of the city's most iconic bridges, ⑮ **Pont Neuf** (p 323).

⑮ Pont Neuf

⑬ Notre-Dame de Paris (above); ⑰ Chalet de l'Oasis (opposite)

—— Cross Pont Neuf, where the stately statue of King Henry IV on horseback hides the secret entrance to ⑯ **Square du Vert-Galant** (p 325). Behind the statue, dual entrances to an enigmatic staircase are marked by two lampposts. Follow it down to the square and wander out to its western tip where a large willow tree offers a shady spot to soak up the golden-hour river views.

—— Take a taxi or Uber to ⑰ **Chalet de l'Oasis** (p 330) in Parc de Saint-Cloud for dinner, allowing up to 40 minutes in traffic. Ask the driver to take the route past the Eiffel Tower and enjoy the view as you drive along Quai Jacques Chirac. Enjoy a classic French meal and view of Paris as the sun sets. If it's winter and Chalet de l'Oasis is closed, dine at any one of the fantastic restaurants in this guide.

Additional VENUE

Le Carreau du Temple

—— CULTURAL CENTRE

This nineteenth-century clothing market turned cultural centre and event space has two distinct personalities. One is during fashion week, when this area of the Marais is choked by photographers, fashion show attendees and fans hoping to catch a glimpse of their favourite celebrities attending the Valentino show that is typically held here. At other times, this striking cast-iron-and-glass structure with its large arched windows is much more peaceful.

In the twelfth century, Le Carreau du Temple was part of the estate of the Knights Templar – a powerful Catholic military order of elite warriors known for their role in the Crusades. The Knights Templar had a significant presence in Paris in the area now called the Marais, including a vast fortress. The order was disbanded in 1307 and their structures eventually demolished, yet the parks and streets where the Templar estate sat still bear the name 'du Temple' as a historical reminder.

The Templar estate was repurposed over the centuries, becoming the Temple Market in the seventeenth century, which sold used clothing and textiles. In 1863 the old wooden market structures were replaced by the current market hall, designed by Baron Haussmann (p 67) and renamed after the tiles used on the roof of the old market (Carreau du Temple means 'Tile of the Temple'). After falling into decline, it was renovated in 2014 and has since hosted countless runways shows including Valentino's all-pink autumn/winter 2022 show, and Louis Vuitton's autumn/winter 2022 menswear show – the final collection of the late creative director Virgil Abloh shortly after his death. The Carreau du Temple also hosts exhibitions, performances, vintage markets and festivals throughout the year.

ADDRESS: *4 Rue Eugène Spuller*

ARRONDISSEMENT: *Paris Centre*

CLOSEST MÉTRO STATION: *Temple*

Additional VENUE | This is FREE

Cimetière du Père-Lachaise

—— CEMETERY

The leafy, 44-hectare Cimetière du Père-Lachaise (Père-Lachaise Cemetery) is the final resting place of some of the most iconic figures in French and world history, from legendary French singer Édith Piaf to composer Frédéric Chopin and The Doors frontman Jim Morrison.

The cemetery's most prolific tomb, however, belongs to Irish playwright and author of *The Picture of Dorian Gray*, Oscar Wilde. Wilde's grave is marked by a winged sphinx-like sculpture by American-British sculptor Jacob Epstein, which created controversy at the time, particularly for its 'unnaturally sized' male genitalia, which led to alterations, coverings and finally its removal in a 1961 act of vandalism.

Over the years, fans have left love letters to Wilde in the form of graffiti and lipstick marks from kissing the sculpture's face, which led to the 2011 installation of protective glass around the monument. Visitors have since taken to writing messages directly on the glass, a defiant act that is perhaps a worthy tribute to both Wilde's life and the creation of his tombstone.

Wilde lived the last three years of his life in Paris following his conviction in England for 'gross indecency' (effectively being gay), for which he was imprisoned from 1895–97. The day of his release he decamped to France, assumed the nom de plume Sebastian Melmoth and lived out his final years in poverty and obscurity before dying of meningitis in 1900. He was initially buried at Cimetière de Bagneux outside Paris and was moved to Père-Lachaise in 1909. In 2017 he was among 50,000 men to be retrospectively pardoned in the United Kingdom for homosexual acts.

ADDRESS: *Boulevard de Ménilmontant*

ARRONDISSEMENT: *20th*

CLOSEST MÉTRO STATION: *Père Lachaise*

Le Carreau du Temple

ATTRACTIONS

Île de la Cité

—— ISLAND

Paris was born on this island in the heart of the Seine during Roman times, and there are remnants of Roman structures including forums, baths, temples, theatres and an amphitheatre still visible here today.

Aside from being the seat of Notre-Dame de Paris (p 320), the island's other important sites include the Gothic royal chapel Sainte-Chapelle; the city's oldest bridge, Pont Neuf (p 323); and the atmospheric Place Dauphine (p 322). It's also home to the Marché aux Fleurs Reine-Elizabeth-II (Flower Market of Queen Elizabeth II), made up of various greenhouse-like pavilions in Art Nouveau style – expected to be fully renovated by 2028.

ADDRESS: *Île de la Cité*

ARRONDISSEMENT: *Paris Centre*

CLOSEST MÉTRO STATION: *Cité*

Île Saint-Louis (this page and opposite, top left and bottom left)

Île Saint-Louis

—— ISLAND

Whether you're looking at it from the Left Bank or the Right Bank, the view of Île Saint-Louis is a real-life French fantasy. Its neatly lined Haussmann buildings (p 67) reach the very edge of the island, each almost identical with their pale brick walls descending into the water, making the island feel like a floating village.

Originally two islets used for cattle grazing and storing wood, Île Saint-Louis was transformed into a single island and developed into a residential area for the Parisian elite under the reign of Louis XIII. With its *hôtels particuliers* (urban mansions) and impeccably planned streets, Île Saint-Louis is one of the city's more bourgeois historic neighbourhoods. French poet Charles Baudelaire resided at Hôtel de Lauzun (a *hôtel particulier* or private mansion), where he wrote parts of his seminal 1857 work, *Les Fleurs du Mal* (*The Flowers of Evil*).

ADDRESS: *Île Saint-Louis*

ARRONDISSEMENT: *Paris Centre*

CLOSEST MÉTRO STATION: *Pont Marie*

Jardin Anne Frank

—— PARK

This small, peaceful garden tucked inconspicuously behind the Centre Pompidou modern art museum (closed for refurbishment until 2030) is dedicated to German-born Jewish teenager Anne Frank, who documented her life in hiding during the Holocaust.

The park is situated on the site of the Hôtel de Saint-Aignan, a seventeenth-century mansion housing the Musée d'Art et d'Histoire du Judaïsme (Museum of Jewish Art and History), which explores Jewish culture, history and the impact of the Second World War on Jewish communities.

The garden famously contains a horse-chestnut tree, grown from a graft of the tree that Anne Frank wrote about in her diary. This part of the park is particularly picturesque with its distinctive semicircular pergola covered in rose bushes.

ADDRESS: *14 Impasse Berthaud*

ARRONDISSEMENT: *Paris Centre*

CLOSEST MÉTRO STATION: *Rambuteau*

This is FREE

Notre-Dame de Paris
—— CATHEDRAL

The world watched in horror in 2019 as a fire devastated one of the world's oldest and most famous cathedrals, leading to the collapse of its spire and significant damage to the roof and upper walls. Restoration began almost immediately and Notre-Dame de Paris (known simply as Notre-Dame) reopened to the public in 2024.

Victor Hugo's 1831 novel *Notre-Dame de Paris* (known in English as *The Hunchback of Notre-Dame*) is largely responsible for the global fame of this cathedral, with Disney introducing it to a new generation with its 1996 animated film adaption. Hugo's book was the impetus for the restoration of the cathedral in the 1840s, cementing its place as a national treasure.

The construction of Notre-Dame commenced in 1163 and took almost 200 years. Largely completed by 1345, its facade is decorated with countless intricate sculptures illustrating biblical narratives and theological themes such as the 'Portal of Last Judgement' depicting figures being led to Heaven or Hell, the 'Portal of the Virgin' portraying scenes of the life of the Virgin Mary and the 'Portal of Saint Anne' depicting scenes from the childhood of Christ. The most recognisable feature is the twin towers housing the cathedral's bells; its design influenced numerous other cathedrals across Europe. The interior of the cathedral features soaring ribbed vaults, flying buttresses and three luminous rose windows that bathe the cathedral in light.

General entrance is free, but it's worth reserving your access time online to reduce your waiting time. Guided tours are also available.

ADDRESS: *6 Paris Notre-Dame*

ARRONDISSEMENT: *Paris Centre*

CLOSEST MÉTRO STATION: *Cité*

Additional VENUE

Passage du Grand Cerf

——— ARCADE

One of the city's tallest covered arcades, the Passage du Grand Cerf (Passage of the Great Stag) was constructed between 1825–27 on the site of the former Hôtel du Grand Cerf, from which its name is derived. Innovative for its time, the arcade was designed for both commercial and residential use with apartments located on the third floor. To allow for all this, it is over 11 metres (36 feet) high and topped by a beautiful glass ceiling that allows natural light to flood the passage. The grand main entrance on Rue Saint Denis features a stone arch crowned with intricate carvings of a broken pediment adorned with neo-Baroque volutes and fruit garlands – a traditional symbol of abundance. Many of the wood-panelled shops retain their original pictorial shop signs (including many references to stags), even if the original function of the shop has changed.

These days Passage du Grand Cerf is home to quirky artisanal stores including homewares store Rickshaw, impressively stocked yarn shop Lil Weasel and Tricote Moi un Tattoo (Knit me a Tattoo), an embroidery shop offering bespoke service.

ADDRESS: *145 Rue Saint Denis*

ARRONDISSEMENT: *Paris Centre*

CLOSEST MÉTRO STATION: *Étienne Marcel*

ATTRACTIONS

Place Dauphine

——— SQUARE

A legacy of King Henry IV's ambition to modernise Paris, Place Dauphine was one of Paris's first planned squares. Despite its central location on the western end of Île de la Cité (p 318), this square is partly hidden by the surrounding buildings, making it easy to miss. It is therefore frequented mainly by locals, who meet at its various cafés or relax in the neat park at its centre, which gives it a village atmosphere in the centre of Paris.

Place Dauphine has made some famous cameos including in Woody Allen's 2011 film *Midnight in Paris*, in which stars Owen Wilson and Marion Cotillard share a scene filmed at Restaurant Paul, located at 15 Place Dauphine. The square's unique shape and layout also make it a visually spectacular place for events: Louis Vuitton's men's runway show has been held here several times.

ADDRESS: *Place Dauphine*

ARRONDISSEMENT: *Paris Centre*

CLOSEST MÉTRO STATION: *Pont Neuf*

Pont Neuf

—— BRIDGE

Famed for being the city's oldest standing bridge, Pont Neuf has weathered over 400 years of Parisian history since its 1606 completion. Composed of two separate spans – one joining the Left Bank to the Île de la Cité (p 318) and the other joining the island to the Right Bank – its arches have starred in countless films. My own love of the bridge deepened after seeing *Les Amants du Pont-Neuf* (*The Lovers on the Bridge*), a 1991 French film starring Juliette Binoche that follows the love story of two vagrants living on the bridge while it was closed for renovation.

When I had a small office on Rue de Savoie on the Left Bank, I would cross Pont Neuf every day, admiring its ornate lampposts, fantastical *mascarons* (stone-carved masks) and semicircular seating areas where you can pause and enjoy the view. Where the Pont Neuf crosses the western tip of Île de la Cité, you'll see the statue of King Henry IV astride a horse; behind it is the entrance to pretty Square du Vert-Galant (p 325).

ADDRESS: *Pont Neuf*

ARRONDISSEMENT: *Paris Centre*

CLOSEST MÉTRO STATION: *Pont Neuf*

This is FREE | Additional VENUE

Quai de la Photo

—— ART CENTRE

A recent addition to the Paris art scene, this floating art centre built on a custom-designed, permanently docked barge focuses on exhibiting photographic works. Showcasing the works of both well-known and emerging photographers, its exhibitions are free to visit. The centre's restaurant offers a unique view of the Seine, with a large terrace open from May to October, making it a great spot for a drink.

ADDRESS: *9 Port de la Gare*

ARRONDISSEMENT: *13th*

CLOSEST MÉTRO STATION: *Quai de la Gare*

ATTRACTIONS

Rue des Francs-Bourgeois

STREET

Lined with boutiques, perfumeries and art galleries, Rue des Francs-Bourgeois is one of the central streets of the Marais. Connecting Place des Vosges to Rue des Archives, it is renowned for its well-preserved *hôtels particuliers* (urban mansions) including Hôtel de Soubise. Now dedicated to preserving the history of Paris as the Archives Nationales and Musée Carnavalet, the museum building also has a café, Joli (p 332), in its hedge-lined gardens that operates in summer.

ADDRESS: *Rue des Francs-Bourgeois*

ARRONDISSEMENT: *Paris Centre*

CLOSEST MÉTRO STATION: *Hotel de Ville, Rambuteau or Saint-Paul*

Square Barye

SQUARE

Seen from a distance, the leafy, triangle-shaped Square Barye, with its elevated terraces, creates the illusion of a giant ship's prow afloat on the Seine. Named after Antoine-Louis Barye, a celebrated Romantic sculptor known for his animal statues, this park at the eastern tip of Île Saint-Louis (p 318) serves as a mini-open-air museum of his work. Its centrepiece is a monument honouring Barye, which incorporates a number of replica sculptures including *Theseus Fighting the Centaur Bianor*, and sculpture pair *L'Ordre* (Order) and *La Force* (Strength).

ADDRESS: *2 Boulevard Henri IV*

ARRONDISSEMENT: *Paris Centre*

CLOSEST MÉTRO STATION: *Sully–Morland*

Square du Vert-Galant

SQUARE

The two sections of Pont Neuf (p 323) meet at the stately monument of King Henry IV on horseback at the western end of Île de la Cité (p 318). Just behind the statue, marked by two lampposts at either end, is a narrow opening in the pavement where a pair of stone staircases descends into obscurity. When you reach the bottom, you will find yourself in Square du Vert-Galant, the pretty park at the western end of the island that looks out towards the Pont des Arts.

There is yet another secret within this somewhat secret park. Instead of entering the park via the swinging gate, take a stroll on the walkway on either side to the very tip of the park where the branches of an old willow tree dip into the Seine. This is Paris's most spectacular picnic spot, with a private view of the river.

ADDRESS: *Square du Vert-Galant*

ARRONDISSEMENT: *Paris Centre*

CLOSEST MÉTRO STATION: *Pont Neuf*

Christophe Lassalle's Stall

ILLUSTRATIONS

On Rue des Francs-Bourgeois (p 324), in the centre of the Marais, you can often find the stall of illustrator Christophe Lassalle. His postcard-sized artworks in ink and watercolour capture the essence of Parisian life – Haussmann apartment buildings (p 67), bistros with red awnings lit by streetlights and Paris's idiosyncratic Art Nouveau cast-iron streetlamps and métro signs. Lasalle's illustrations are peppered with his dry humour. His detailed studies of Parisian rubbish bins, for example, highlight how their style and colour is strictly controlled by the city to blend in with the Art Nouveau mood. I'm also a fan of his series of Stormtroopers hugging cats. Prices are very reasonable, typically €10–20.

ADDRESS: *Rue des Francs-Bourgeois*

ARRONDISSEMENT: *Paris Centre*

CLOSEST MÉTRO STATION: *Saint-Paul*

Marché des Enfants Rouges

MARKET

Established in 1615, the city's oldest covered market was named after a nearby orphanage – the Hôpital des Enfants Rouges (Hospital of the Red Children) – where children wore red uniforms. While the orphanage is long gone, the market continues to provide fresh food to the Marais with its operation stretching back more than 400 years to the reign of Louis XIII. When it fell into disuse in the 1990s and was in danger of being closed, locals banded together to push for its restoration and it was reopened in 2000.

The market's tightly packed food stalls and small eateries – with counter seating or small terraces – leave just enough space to walk between them. Almost every kind of produce can be found here, from meat and seafood to fresh vegetables, flowers and spices. The eateries in the market are diverse and international including Moroccan, Italian, French, Lebanese and good ol' burgers. The Japanese restaurant Chez Taeko is reputed as serving the best karaage (Japanese fried chicken) in town. Always buzzing, it's a great place to get a glimpse of everyday Parisian life.

ADDRESS: *39 Rue de Bretagne*

ARRONDISSEMENT: *Paris Centre*

CLOSEST MÉTRO STATION: *Filles du Calvaire*

Additional VENUE

Rougier&Plé

STATIONERY & ART SUPPLIES

Founded in 1854 by Abel Rougier, who aimed to provide high-quality materials to craftspeople and artists, Rougier&Plé became a go-to destination for art supplies in Paris. Today Rougier&Plé boasts over 20,000 products, from paints, canvases and drawing tools to craft and framing supplies. Here you will find historic French art brands like Sennelier oil paints – favoured by artists including Paul Cézanne, Pablo Picasso and Henri Matisse, the brand's paints are still widely used by French art schools and professional artists.

To visit Rougier&Plé is also to view one of Paris's important art installations. To mark the store's 170th anniversary in 2024, French artist Daniel Buren (the artist behind the *Colonnes de Buren* at the Palais-Royal, p 119) was commissioned to redesign the facade. Buren's installation for Rougier&Plé, titled *En Partant d'un Triangle, Travail in Situ, 2024* (*Starting From a Triangle, in Situ Work, 2024*), features his signature black-and-white stripes, complemented by vibrant colours.

ADDRESS: *15 Boulevard des Filles du Calvaire*

ARRONDISSEMENT: *Paris Centre*

CLOSEST MÉTRO STATION: *Filles du Calvaire*

Additional VENUE

Vide-Greniers of Paris

GARAGE SALE

If I were to impart one local secret for second-hand shopping in Paris, it's to visit the city's *vide-greniers*. Translated as 'emptying attics', they're the Parisian version of the neighbourhood garage sale. As Parisians predominantly live in apartment buildings with no garage, the sale of pre-loved household items and second-hand books happens at these community-organised sidewalk markets held on weekends. Local businesses also get involved to take advantage of the foot traffic, with many restaurants setting up snack stations where you can pick up a hot chocolate or Nutella crepe as you browse the wares. I have found some of my favourite vintage clothing pieces at *vide-greniers*, all at affordable prices.

Visit vide-greniers.org for a calendar of upcoming *vide-greniers* and *brocantes* (flea markets) in Paris and across France. As *vide-greniers* are mostly outdoors, they are generally more frequent in the warmer months, between March and September.

EAT & DRINK

Additional VENUE

Best Tofu

—— DELI

Authentic Chinese food is not easy to come by in Paris, where flavours from Africa and the Middle East dominate over Asian imports. I often feel nostalgic for a traditional Chinese breakfast – as a child I remember my grandfather heading out at 6 am every morning in search of *youtiao* (a kind of long savory donut) and soy milk before they would sell out. So imagine my excitement to discover that this quintessential Chinese breakfast is served at Best Tofu, a small delicatessen that also specialises in tofu-based dishes. Also on offer are traditional spring onion pancakes, always stacked high at the counter, which are seriously satisfying and addictive. The prices are more than reasonable; with a *youtiao* going for €1.30 and tofu pudding costing €2.20, you can try a bit of everything for less than €10.

ADDRESS: *9 Boulevard de la Villette*

ARRONDISSEMENT: *10th*

CLOSEST MÉTRO STATION: *Belleville*

The Bouillon of Paris

RESTAURANT

Nineteenth-century France's answer to fast food, a *bouillon* is a large, traditional restaurant serving classic French dishes quickly and affordably, chiefly its namesake broth.

Occupying a small corner house in the Marché des Enfants Rouges (p 326) with big windows flung open in summer, The Bouillon of Paris has refined the tradition for a new generation of diners.

An extension of the next-door butcher's stall, The Butcher of Paris, the menu preserves the spirit of the *bouillon* with simple and comforting dishes including *planches* (boards) of charcuterie and cheese, steak tartare and roast chicken and potatoes. On weekdays, which are quieter, Parisians come here for languid aperitifs with friend, or to sit at the window counter to read a book with a supply of cheese and wine to last the afternoon.

ADDRESS: *4 Rue des Oiseaux*

ARRONDISSEMENT: *Paris Centre*

CLOSEST MÉTRO STATION: *Avron*

EAT & DRINK

Caractère de Cochon

—— SANDWICHES

Affectionately known as 'Solo', Madagascan-born Solofo Ravelson fondly remembes his father giving him a sandwich after a swimming training session. Years later, after moving to Paris, this childhood memory inspired him to open Caractère de Cochon, a sandwich shop that has resurrected the classic *jambon-beurre* (Parisian ham and butter sandwich) to mouthwatering effect. Sliced to order, your ham of choice can be anything from French black pork to Hungarian Mangalica, Sicilian Nebrodi or Spanish Ibérico.

ADDRESS: *42 Rue Charlot*

ARRONDISSEMENT: *Paris Centre*

CLOSEST MÉTRO STATION: *Filles du Calvaire*

Chalet de l'Oasis

—— BRASSERIE

Perched on top of a hill in the sprawling grounds of the vast Parc de Saint-Cloud, Chalet de l'Oasis offers a country getaway without leaving the city. Enter through a wisteria-laden pergola and emerge onto the terrace of this *guinguette* (open-air café) filled with tartan-covered tables and colourful parasols. Paired with views of Paris in the distance, the French menu is suitably laid-back with dishes including boiled eggs with mayonnaise and rib steak with homemade fries. For dessert I highly recommend the Saint Tropez tarte – a halved brioche filled with cream.

Open from March to October, Chalet de l'Oasis opens onto the estate's parklands where kids (or the young at heart) can seize the rare opportunity to run barefoot on the grass. Once a royal residence, the park contains a rose garden established by Marie Antoinette that still blooms today.

ADDRESS: *Butte aux Chèvres Parc de Saint-Cloud*

ARRONDISSEMENT: *Saint-Cloud*

CLOSEST MÉTRO STATION: *Pont de Sèvres*

Chalet de l'Oasis (opposite)

Joli

—— CAFÉ

Paris changes its face with the seasons and in summer not only do the trees transform, but also some of the city's most iconic institutions. Joli is one of Paris's outdoor restaurants that opens only for the summer season.

Taking over the usually sombre manicured garden of the Musée Carnavalet with white enamel tables, chairs and chaises lining the manicured hedges, Joli's food and cocktail menu is renewed each season with a new guest chef, but always with a focus on fresh, seasonal produce. Café fare and cocktails are served until 6 pm, with dinner service beginning at 7 pm.

ADDRESS: *16 Rue des Francs Bourgeois*

ARRONDISSEMENT: *Paris Centre*

CLOSEST MÉTRO STATION: *Saint-Paul*

Partisan Café (above and opposite, top right)

Partisan Café Artisanal

CAFÉ

This Brooklyn-inspired café is a favourite of the young creatives of the Marais, both for its lively ambience and its coffee. Take your pick between two types – Italian (a traditional dark roast) and New Wave (a lighter roast designed to bring out the coffee's aromatic profile) – with all coffee roasted on-site. Baked goods are also on offer.

Here you will see all the archetypal characters of the neighbourhood: freelancers on their laptops, a model working on her novel, a young couple debuting their new puppy to society and fashion publicists mid-meeting. Perhaps designed to encourage mingling, the café's seating features long benches where space is usually tight – awkwardly shuffling into a spot can be the conversation-starter for a new friendship.

ADDRESS: *36 Rue de Turbigo*

ARRONDISSEMENT: *Paris Centre*

CLOSEST MÉTRO STATION: *Arts et Métiers*

46 & 3rd

CAFÉ

An all-day brunch café in the Arts and Metiers district of the Marais, 46 & 3rd brings a relaxed, North American–style brunch culture to the Parisian scene. Its specialties include thick pancakes generously drizzled with chocolate sauce and caramel maple syrup, a version of eggs Benedict with bacon served on a brioche bun and 'Cali toast' with guacamole.

The interior is warm and rustic with an open kitchen, counter seating and industrial elements combined with raw wood accents that evoke an American-West-Coast-coffee-shop feel.

ADDRESS: *46 Rue de Turbigo*

ARRONDISSEMENT: *Paris Centre*

CLOSEST MÉTRO STATION: *Arts et Métiers*

CHEAT

PARIS'S BEST MUSEUMS

NAME	TYPE	ARRON-DISSEMENT	FOCUS	ABOUT
MUSÉE DE LOUVRE (p 115)	Art museum	Paris Centre	Antiquity to nineteenth century	The world's most famous art collection, covering 9000 years of art history
MUSÉE DE LA L'ORANGERIE (p 117)	Art museum	Paris Centre	Impressionism	The home of Claude Monet's *Nymphéas* (*Water Lilies*)
PALAIS DE TOKYO (p 197)	Exhibition space	Paris Centre	Modern art	Temporary exhibitions of avantgarde and innovative art
MUSÉE NATIONAL PICASSO (p 116)	Art museum	Paris Centre	Modern art	One of the world's foremost collections of Picasso's work
FONDATION AZZEDINE ALAÏA (p 286)	Fashion museum	Paris Centre	Contemporary fashion	Intimate museum celebrating fashion designer Azzedine Alaïa's legacy and his extensive personal collections
MAISON DE VICTOR HUGO	Literary museum	Paris Centre	Romanticism	A house-museum dedicated to the life and works of writer Victor Hugo
MUSÉE D'ORSAY (p 118)	Art museum	7th	Nineteenth- and twentieth-century art	Exhibits nineteenth-century Impressionist and Postimpressionist art
MUSÉE RODIN (p 195)	Sculpture museum	7th	Modern art	Former home and workshop of Auguste Rodin, housing his life's works
QUAI DE LA PHOTO (p 323)	Exhibition space	7th	Photography	Floating museum on the Seine hosting photography exhibitions

FAMOUS WORKS	ONSITE DINING PICKS	OPENING DAYS
Mona Lisa by Leonardo da Vinci, *Venus de Milo* by Alexandros of Antioch, *Liberty Leading the People* by Eugène Delacroix	Café Marly, Café Richelieu / Angelina (p 134) and Café Mollien	Wednesday–Monday
Nymphéas (*Water Lilies*) by Claude Monet	Le Café de l'Orangerie	Wednesday–Monday
N/A	Café du Palais	Wednesday–Monday
Guernica, The Weeping Woman, Les Demoiselles d'Avignon	Le Café Sur le Toit	Tuesday– Sunday
Azzedine Alaïa's fashion creations	Le A (café, restaurant and bar)	Daily
Victor Hugo's works and personal artifacts	Café Mulot	Tuesday–Sunday
Starry Night Over the Rhône by Vincent Van Gogh	Café Campana	Tuesday–Sunday
The Thinker, The Kiss, The Gates of Hell	L'Augustine	Tuesday–Sunday
N/A	Quai de la Photo Restaurant	Wednesday–Sunday

CHEAT

PARIS'S BEST MUSEUMS

continued

NAME	TYPE	ARRON-DISSEMENT	FOCUS	ABOUT
DEYROLLE (p 234)	Taxidermy shop and museum	7th	Natural history	Known for its historical collection of taxidermy and natural history exhibits
MUSÉE DE LA VIE ROMANTIQUE (p 255)	Literary museum	9th	Romanticism	Tribute to the Romantic era with works by Delacroix and others
MUSÉE NATIONAL GUSTAVE MOREAU (p 254)	Art museum	9th	Symbolism	Former home of Gustave Moreau, famous for its magnificent winding staircase
MUSÉE MARMOTTAN MONET	Art museum	13th	Impressionism	Home to the largest collection of Claude Monet's works
MUSÉE BOURDELLE (p 255)	Sculpture museum	15th	Modern art	The former studio of Antoine Bourdelle, famous for its sculpture-filled room
FONDATION LOUIS VUITTON (p 191)	Contemporary art museum	16th	Contemporary art	Contemporary art housed in an innovative Frank Gehry building
PALAIS GALLIERA (p 196)	Fashion museum	16th	Haute couture	Paris's first fashion museum
MAISON DE BALZAC (p 193)	Literary museum	16th	Realist literature	The former home of French writer Honoré de Balzac
HALLE SAINT-PIERRE (p 152)	'Outsider art' museum	18th	Modern art	A space in the centre of Montmartre housing offbeat art

FAMOUS WORKS	ONSITE DINING PICKS	OPENING DAYS
Famous taxidermy collections dating back to 1880	N/A	Monday–Saturday
Portrait of George Sand by Eugène Delacroix	Le Café de la Vie Romantique	Tuesday–Sunday
The Apparition	N/A	Wednesday–Monday
Impression, Sunrise	N/A	Tuesday–Sunday
Hercules the Archer	Le Rhodia	Tuesday–Sunday
Balloon Dog (Yellow) by Jeff Koons	Le Frank	Wednesday–Monday
Creations by Coco Chanel	Les Petites Mains	Tuesday–Sunday
Original manuscripts and personal objects	Café de la Maison de Balzac	Tuesday–Sunday
Unique temporary exhibitions	Café de la Halle Saint-Pierre	Daily

CHEAT — SHEET

PARIS RESTAURANT GUIDE

TYPE	DESCRIPTION	AMBIANCE	BOOKING REQUIRED	PRICE RANGE (€ PER PERSON)	DRESS CODE	TIPPING ETIQUETTE
CAFÉ	Serves coffee, pastries, breakfast/brunch and light lunches like sandwiches and salads.	Relaxed and social, good for people-watching	No reservation required	€5–30	Casual	No tipping required; rounding up the bill is appreciated
SALON DE THÉ	Tea rooms offering a variety of teas, pastries and light dishes like quiches, sandwiches and salads	Elegant, serene, popular for an afternoon break	Usually not required but advised for groups	€10–25	Casual	No tipping required; rounding up the bill is appreciated
BISTRO	Small, cosy eateries offering home-style French cuisine	Informal, rustic neighbourhood vibe	Recommended for peak dining hours due to limited seating	€15–40	Smart casual	Rounding up or leaving €1–5 is common
BRASSERIE	Large, lively restaurants serving classic French dishes all day	Bustling, spacious, casual yet professional	Usually not required but advised for groups and during peak dining hours	€20–50	Smart, jacket recommended, no sportswear	Optional 5–10 per cent for excellent service
TRADITIONAL RESTAURANT	Standard French dining with a structured menu (*entrée-plat-dessert*)	Comfortable, welcoming	Advised for dinner and weekends	€25–60	Smart casual	Rounding up or leaving €1–5 is common
RESTAURANT GASTRONOMIQUE	Fine dining with elaborate multi-course menus, often Michelin-starred	Formal, refined, special occasion	Reservation essential, sometimes months in advance	€100+	Smart	No tipping required; rounding up or leaving €1–5 is common

ACKNOWLEDGEMENTS

This guidebook was two years in the making, a journey that led me through every nook and cranny of Paris and deepened my love for the city in the process. It also led me to collaborate with countless people to whom I am profoundly grateful.

First, to the business owners whose restaurants, stores and other venues are featured in this book – thank you for allowing me to share your unique stories. You are the soul of Paris.

Thank you to my parents, Xin and Jim, who despite their traditional Chinese immigrant hopes for a stable, conventional career path for me, supported my impulsive move to Paris that started it all. It was their own life-changing move from China to Australia that gave me the courage to do so.

To my partner, Arthur, thank you for being right there beside me every step of the way and also for sharing local insights and secrets that enriched this guide with a true Parisian perspective.

To Pascale, my mother-in-law, thank you for seeing the beauty in this project before I fully grasped it myself.

To my publisher, Melissa, who sparked this project, and other key team members – Julie, the two Sarahs and Vanessa – thank you for having faith in my first project of this scope. Your openness, patience and expert guidance at every step shaped this book.

And to my many friends around the globe, in every walk of life: thank you for your encouragement, belief and feedback at every stage.

This guide is the product of collaboration, insatiable curiosity and love – including my unconditional love for Paris. Thank you all.

INDEX

ARCADES

ARRONDISSEMENTS

BAKERIES

BOOKS

BRIDGES

CAFÉS

DEPARTMENT STORES

FASHION & CLOTHING STORES

FOOD & DRINK STORES

HOMEWARES & GIFT STORES

HOTELS

ISLANDS

MARKETS

MISCELLANEOUS SHOPPING & SERVICES

MONUMENTS AND LANDMARKS

MUSEUMS & GALLERIES

NEIGHBOURHOODS

PARKS & GARDENS

PERFUME

RESTAURANTS

SQUARES & STREETS

Published in 2026 by Murdoch Books, an imprint of Allen & Unwin

Murdoch Books Australia
Cammeraygal Country
83 Alexander Street
Crows Nest NSW 2065
Phone: +61 (0)2 8425 0100
murdochbooks.com.au
info@murdochbooks.com.au

Murdoch Books UK
Ormond House
26–27 Boswell Street
London WC1N 3JZ
Phone: +44 (0) 20 8785 5995
murdochbooks.co.uk
info@murdochbooks.co.uk

For corporate orders and custom publishing, contact our business development team at salesenquiries@murdochbooks.com.au

Publisher: Melissa Kayser
Editorial manager: Julie Mazur Tribe
Design manager: Sarah Odgers
Designer: Vanessa Masci
Editor: Sarah Reid
Cartographer: Claire Johnston
Production manager: Natalie Crouch

Murdoch Books acknowledges the Traditional Owners of the Country on which we live and work. We pay our respects to all Aboriginal and Torres Strait Islander Elders, past and present.

EU Authorised Representative: Easy Access System Europe, Mustamäe tee 50, 10621 Tallinn, Estonia, gpsr.requests@easproject.com

ISBN 978 1 76150 081 7

NATIONAL LIBRARY OF AUSTRALIA
A catalogue record for this book is available from the National Library of Australia

A catalogue record for this book is available from the British Library

Colour reproduction by Megan Ellis
Printed in China by C&C Offset Printing Co., Ltd.

10 9 8 7 6 5 4 3 2 1

MIX
Paper | Supporting responsible forestry
FSC www.fsc.org FSC® C008047